P9-AFU-845

"Every home needs at least one Marcella Hazan Italian cookbook. Her new memoir deserves to become as classic as her recipes." —*O, The Oprah Magazine*

"This story is a real inspiration to me, how a small town girl became the empress of Italian cooking." —Isaac Mizrahi

"Marcella Hazan's memoir is as delicious as her food. Full of affection, friendships and deep connections to her roots, she ladles a grand minestrone into our bowls." —Frances Mayes, author of *Under the Tuscan Sun*

"Reading this evocative memoir will perceptibly elevate one's senses and make one appreciate Marcella Hazan's fascinating journey—from girlhood in Italy to womanhood in America, from relative obscurity to her certain fame in the food world." —Pamela Fiori, editor in chief, *Town & Country*

"Marcella Hazan has done for Italian cooking in the United States what Julia Child did for French cuisine and James Beard for traditional American cooking. I think of her as the Johnny Appleseed of real Italian cooking." —Burt Wolf, television journalist

"Marcella Hazan is an icon in the American food world, and her one-of-a-kind experience makes her own story not only compelling but truly marvelous." —Patricia Wells, author of *The Paris Cookbook* and *The Provence Cookbook*

© BARBARA BANKS

Recipient of two Lifetime Achievement Awards (from the James Beard Foundation in 2000 and the IACP in 2004), and a knighthood from her own country, **MARCELLA HAZAN** is the author of six classic cookbooks published over the past thirty-five years. She lives in Longboat Key, Florida, with her husband, Victor, her lifelong collaborator and writing partner, himself an authority on Italian food and wine.

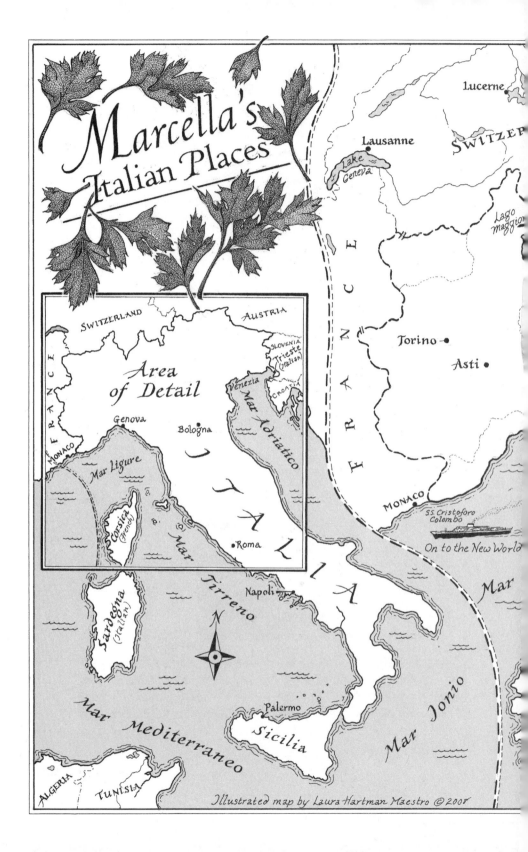

Marcella's Italian Places

Illustrated map by Laura Hartman Maestro ©2008

Lucerne
SWITZER[LAND]
Lausanne
Lake Geneva
Lago Maggiore
Torino
Asti
F R A N C E
MONACO
S.S. Cristoforo Colombo
On to the New World
I T A L I A
Napoli
Mar Tirreno
Roma
Sardegna (Italian)
Mar Mediterraneo
ALGERIA
TUNISIA
Palermo
Sicilia
Mar Jonio
Mar

Area of Detail

SWITZERLAND
AUSTRIA
SLOVENIA
Trieste (Italian)
Venezia
CROATIA
Mar Adriatico
FRANCE
Genova
Bologna
MONACO
Mar Ligure
Corsica (French)
Mar

LICHTENSTEIN

AUSTRIA

...AND

Lago di Como

• Como

• Milano

In wartime Desenzano with my bicycle

Desenzano

• Verona

Lago di Garda

Fiume Adige

At home in Venice pausing in the court-yard on our return from the Rialto market

N
W   E
S

SLOVENIA

G.H. Trieste • Trieste

Venezia

CROATIA

EMILIA –

In the Bologna produce market

• Ferrara

Fiume Po

• Modena

• Bologna

ROMAGNA

Mar Adriatico

• Genova

• Ravenna

• Cesenatico

SAN MARINO ☆

• Firenze

Ligure

• Siena

In nonno Ricardo's arms in Cesenatico, wearing my baptismal gown

Elba

Mar Tirreno

Corsica (French)

Fiume Tevere

Fiume Santo

Città del Vaticano

☆ • Roma

Scale of Miles

0   20   40   60   80   100

Scale of Kilometers

0   20   40   60   80   100

Amarcord

MARCELLA REMEMBERS

*The Remarkable Life Story
of the Woman Who
Started Out Teaching Science
in a Small Town in Italy,
but Ended Up
Teaching America
How to Cook Italian*

MARCELLA HAZAN

GOTHAM
BOOKS

GOTHAM BOOKS
Published by Penguin Group (USA) Inc.
375 Hudson Street, New York, New York 10014, U.S.A.

Penguin Group (Canada), 90 Eglinton Avenue East, Suite 700, Toronto, Ontario M4P 2Y3, Canada
(a division of Pearson Penguin Canada Inc.); Penguin Books Ltd, 80 Strand, London WC2R 0RL,
England; Penguin Ireland, 25 St Stephen's Green, Dublin 2, Ireland (a division of Penguin Books Ltd);
Penguin Group (Australia), 250 Camberwell Road, Camberwell, Victoria 3124, Australia (a division of
Pearson Australia Group Pty Ltd); Penguin Books India Pvt Ltd, 11 Community Centre, Panchsheel Park,
New Delhi–110 017, India; Penguin Group (NZ), 67 Apollo Drive, Rosedale, North Shore 0632,
New Zealand (a division of Pearson New Zealand Ltd); Penguin Books (South Africa) (Pty) Ltd,
24 Sturdee Avenue, Rosebank, Johannesburg 2196, South Africa

Penguin Books Ltd, Registered Offices: 80 Strand, London WC2R 0RL, England

Published by Gotham Books, a member of Penguin Group (USA) Inc.

Previously published as a Gotham Books hardcover edition.

First trade paperback printing, October 2009

1 3 5 7 9 10 8 6 4 2

Gotham Books and the skyscraper logo are trademarks of Penguin Group (USA) Inc.

Copyright © 2008 by Marcella Hazan and Victor Hazan
All rights reserved

Photo credits: pp. 3, 8, 12: © Foto Nanni; p. 131© The New York Times; p. 146 © Tara Heinemann;
p. 148 © Jim Lorelli; p. 231 © Gianni Berengo Gardin; p. 273 © Henry Grossman; p. 274 © Lou Manna
Studio Inc.; p. 289 © Giuliano Hazan. All remaining photographs are courtesy of the author.
Cartoon on p. 295 by David Sipress

The Library of Congress has cataloged the hardcover edition of this book as follows:

Hazan, Marcella.
Amarcord—Marcella remembers: the remarkable life story of the woman who started out teaching science in a
small town in Italy, but ended up teaching America how to cook Italian / by Marcella Hazan.
p.   cm.
ISBN 978-1-592-40388-2 (hardcover)   978-1-592-40489-6 (paperback)
1. Hazan, Marcella. 2. Hazan, Victor. 3. Cooks—Biography. 4. Cookery, Italian—History—20th century.
5. Italian American women—Biography. 6. Women immigrants—United States—Biography. 7. Italian
Americans—Biography. I. Hazan, Victor. II. Title. III. Title: Marcella remembers.
TX649.H378A3   2008
641.5092'2—dc22
[B]   2007046197

Printed in the United States of America
Set in Centaur with Buccardi • Designed by Sabrina Bowers
Illustrated map by Laura Hartman Maestro

Romagna solatia,
dolce paese . . .

Romagna, the "sunlit, sweet land" that the nineteenth-century poet Giovanni Pascoli described in his verses, is part of the northern Italian region known as Emilia-Romagna. If you travel southeast of Bologna, leaving Emilia and that hyphen behind, you come to a land of orchards, of cherries and peaches and pears, of old farm towns, of hills whose slopes are strung with vines bearing the purple clusters of the Sangiovese grape. Turn away from the hills and go due east—go until there is sand in your shoes—and you will gaze upon the Adriatic, a broad blue line stretching out to meet the sky. I ran on that beach, and swam in that sea; I ate the fruits of those orchards, and drank that purple wine. I am a daughter of that land; its heat warms my blood; all that I am started there; there I learned to play, to eat, to love. My life's story begins in Romagna, and to Romagna I dedicate it.

Contents

Preface

LITTLE IS LEFT of the world I was born into eighty-four years ago. It was a world where most of the food on our table—vegetables and fruit, wine and olive oil, chickens and rabbits—came from our farm or from that of a neighbor or a relative. The sausages we grilled and the salami we sliced were made from a pig we had raised; our house linen was woven from the hemp we had grown; we would go to the *pescheria*, the fish market, to buy fish that had been caught that night; and we did not buy pasta from a grocer because my grandmother— using a rolling pin nearly as long as she was tall—rolled it out every day using our own eggs and flour. It was a world in which the most common form of personal transportation was the bicycle. Automobiles were so rare—my father never owned one—that when Sandro, the richest man in town, roared down the road in his sports car, everyone ran out to look.

That old world of mine was in Romagna, the southeastern, sea-rimmed corner of Emilia-Romagna, a region in northern Italy. It has its own distinctive dialect, as every place in Italy does. In

Romagnolo, the dialect of Romagna, *amarcord* means "I remember," compressing the three slow-footed Italian words *"io mi ricordo"* into a single swift, emphatic one. Federico Fellini, the late great film director, who was also a native of Romagna, used *Amarcord* as the title of one of his finest films, an evocation of life as it was when he was young in Rimini, a town that my own Cesenatico closely resembles. His example came immediately to mind when I sought a title for this collection of my memories.

If you have lived as long as I have, when you open the door to the past, a vast hoard tumbles out in no particular order. The beam of memory does not necessarily sweep over life in strict chronological sequence. It may alight here on a person, there on a significant happening, without troubling to reconcile them or to plot them exactly on the graph of time. The characters and incidents that fill these pages were those caught in the random swings of memory's searchlight. If, during my tale, I digress or skip ahead or reverse course, it is not out of capriciousness. It is the way that one looks back on life.

In Nonno Riccardo's arms, wearing my baptismal robe

Alexandria and Cesenatico

1931–1937

*Y*OU COULD DESCRIBE the road my life has taken as a series of unexpected and even improbable turns. When I was seven years old, I fell on the beach and broke my right arm. It was a commonplace event, yet it set my life on the variable course that it has since traveled. *Amarcord*—I remember. Some of it, indeed, I remember too well.

The beach I fell on was in Alexandria, Egypt, where my parents were then living. My mother's side of the family, the Leonelli, were expatriate Italians long settled in the Middle East. Maria, my mother, one of six children, including two pairs of twins, was born in Beirut. Riccardo, her father, was the general manager of a cigarette manufacturer, a circumstance that may have encouraged me, when in my teens, to form an attachment to tobacco that lasts to this day.

My father, Giuseppe Polini, was an accomplished tailor whose gifts had landed him excellent positions abroad, in Zurich, in Paris, and finally in New York. After five years in New York as the head cutter of B. Altman's men's custom department, he collected his savings and came back home to Cesenatico, a quiet fishing town on the northern Adriatic Sea, a 120-mile drive south of Venice along two old Roman roads, first on the Romea, then on the Adriatica.

It is a short stretch of coast that Cesenatico lies on, but it has forever been known for the exquisite flavor of the seafood that populates its waters. Maine has its lobster, the Sacramento River its chinook salmon, Cesenatico its sole. It is a small fish, less than half the size of a Dover sole, but its firm, sweetly nutty flesh earns it first place among soles of any provenance. The same sea also produces a less glamorous fish, a type of sprat, larger than an anchovy and smaller than a sardine, but with similarly dark and unctuous flesh. It is known only locally, and even there, it is too humble to put in an appearance outside the home kitchen. There is nothing humble about its flavor, however. Its scent, rising from the grill, and its flesh, dissolving under one's teeth, travel a direct line to one's deepest gustatory emotions. The name it goes by in Cesenatico and its neighboring towns in Romagna is *saraghina*. Devotees of Fellini's films may recall a wild, sensual woman by that same name, based on a character out of real life who used to roam the beach during Fellini's youth.

When Cesenatico's fishermen sail back home in the afternoon, having fished all night, they dock their boats along a canal designed by Leonardo da Vinci, which bisects the town and winds its way through it toward the sea. I remember waiting for the men to return and unload their catch. They were grizzled and hungry from the night spent working the sea. They set up grills over wood charcoal on the pavement of the quay where their boat was tied up, and on the hot embers, they grilled a mess of *saraghine*. That is the moment I waited for, because the men always shared some of their *saraghine* with me. I had quickly learned to eat them as they do. Holding the small fish by the tail and the head, I brought it to my mouth, pulled back my lips, and used my teeth to lift the entire tiny fillet off the

Back from a night of fishing, the crew snacks on grilled *saraghine*, eating them *col bacio*.

bone and suck it into my mouth. Then I turned the fish around and sucked away the fillet from the other side. Oh, the succulence of it! *"Si mangiano col bacio,"* the fishermen say; you eat them with a kiss.

After the Second World War, Cesenatico grew to become one of Italy's most popular beach resorts, but in the 1920s and '30s it was a sweet, simple village. There were two main parts to it. Well-to-do burghers from Bologna and other cities of the north summered in the pretty, art nouveau villas that, before they were eventually replaced by hotels, congregated in the shade of umbrella pines on the boulevards that run parallel to the beach. The fishermen and their families lived then, as many of them do now, in the center of town, in a huddle of modest one-story houses that face both sides of Leonardo's canal.

When my mother and her sister Margherita were young women, their mother, my grandmother-to-be Adele, took them to Italy for a summer holiday. On the advice of acquaintances, they stopped in Cesenatico, taking rooms in a *pensione*, a boarding house. The three women were tall, straight-backed, and exotically handsome, and like their friends back in Egypt, they wore broad-brimmed straw hats with blue veils that screened their faces from the strong summer light, and the inquisitive gaze of strangers. Into their curiously ac-cented Italian, they dropped words from the other languages they spoke, Arabic and French. For most of my life I would continue to hear about the effect their appearance had produced. If three naked tribesmen from New Guinea had padded through town, they would certainly have been gawked at, but, once gone, forgotten. Whereas, when my widowed mother had turned ninety—she lived to a hun-dred and one—a man fifteen years her junior came forward to pro-pose marriage, saying he had been dazzled by her sixty years earlier and had longed for her ever since.

At the holiday's end, my mother did not return to Egypt. The proprietress of the house where they were staying had introduced her to a personable man, a tailor, who was more worldly than the other townspeople; he had lived abroad and spoke several languages, including French. A brief courtship led to marriage, and Maria Leonelli and Giuseppe Polini set up house in Cesenatico, where, the following year, I was born. When I was two, my mother longed to rejoin her family in Egypt; my father was happy to please her, and so they moved to Alexandria, where Papi, as I called my father, opened a tailor and fabric shop.

My mother and papi
on my baptismal day

My broken arm was set in Alexandria's Italian hospital, named after Benito Mussolini. They put it in a full cast that extended from my shoulder to my knuckles. The doctor told my mother to return for a checkup in a week. By the second day, however, I had so much pain that my mother took me back to the hospital. The doctor dismissed her, saying, "Of course her arm hurts, it's broken. Go back home and be patient for a few more days." Before the end of the week, my hand had become swollen and had turned blue. I cried constantly. Back at the hospital, the doctor took one look and called for the cast to be removed immediately. What they saw made my mother ill. There was a purulent sore at my elbow. Gangrene had set in. I was put to bed with my arm raised high, hitched to the rod of the mosquito net in the hope that the swelling would go down. But the sore grew larger and the doctor told my parents that to save my life they would have to cut off the arm, a recommendation that my mother refused to accept. She had heard that in Bologna there was a world-famous orthopedic surgeon, Professor Putti, who had performed miracles. She booked passage on the first boat for Italy, and soon we were in the professor's study, which—aside from a small examining table in a corner and a sterile-looking white cabinet—looked as though it should have been in a mansion rather than in a hospital. The professor's walnut desk was enormous; there were Turkish carpets on the floor and ample leather armchairs where patients and visitors sat. After he had examined me, Putti told my mother, "This needs a miracle. You pray and I'll try to do the rest."

Putti operated several times. He saved my arm and succeeded even in straightening my hand. One last operation held the hope that

At six years old, the year before I broke my arm

I would be able to flex both the elbow and my wrist. Putti was not available just then, so the operation was performed by his assistant, who was later to become a renowned surgeon as well. It wasn't on my arm, however, that he made his reputation. After that final operation, I could not open my arm out at more than a ninety-degree angle, and my hand curled inward, assuming the clawlike shape that has endured to this day.

I was in and out of the Istituto Rizzoli—as the hospital was, and still is, known—for several years. When it became evident that my right hand would be useless for writing, I started learning how to write with my left. It was more difficult than you might imagine, and at first, I did better holding the pencil in my mouth. I had become the nurses' mascot, with freedom to roam around and, as I grew older, to help with small tasks. What I had the most fun doing was pushing around some of the younger patients in wheelchairs, although, because I had just one working arm, I had been forbidden to do so. One day I had built up too much momentum and the wheelchair escaped the grasp of my good hand. The boy sitting on it had a leg in a cast stiffly stretched out. It collided with a wall, bringing the swiftly rolling chair to an abrupt stop. His screams brought the nurses running, and I began to wail so loudly and uncontrollably that it was not clear at first which of the two of us had been hurt.

For a great many years after I had left the hospital for good, not a day passed that I was not conscious of my arm. When I was in grade school I cringed every day that I went to class, fearing that my classmates would make fun of me as children are cruelly wont to do. As a teenager, I did everything my friends did and more: I bicycled with them all day long, I swam out farther, took dives as high as any of theirs, ran as fast. From my youth and forever after in my life, I strove to spare others any embarrassment over my handicap by doing everything that was required of me as nonchalantly as possible. The embarrassment became mine, however, when I became old enough to be interested in boys. I adopted a style of dress that masked my arm. I had a collection of shawls that matched or contrasted prettily with my dresses, and I folded them over my arm. Had someone told me then that one day I would cook on television, exposing that arm to millions of people, I would have said *"Ma sei matto!"*—"You're out of your mind!" I can go for long periods now without a thought for my lame arm, but I avoid looking at tapes of my television appearances. To see my twisted hand so publicly exposed still makes me cringe, as it did when I was a small schoolchild.

Shortly after I had left Egypt with my mother, my father, who had been devastated by my pain and by the prospect of my losing an arm, closed his business in Alexandria and moved back to Cesenatico, where we could live close to the medical attention I needed. Right then is when my life took its first large, unscripted turn. I had left Egypt behind me, never to return. Instead of growing up in Africa, I grew up in Italy, where I would know war at first hand and where I would meet the man who became my husband, who led me into yet another unforeseen turn, leaving my country to come to America. Nor was that the last great turn my road would take. That one came at middle age, when, at forty-five, I suddenly found myself plunged into a career wholly unrelated to the one I had expected would be mine forever, propelled again into a world new to me, the world of food.

Fishing boats tied up in the harbor of Cesenatico before the Second World War, when many boats were still under sail

Cesenatico, *La Comitiva*

1940

I AM LUCKY to have spent so many years when I was young in a small, provincial Italian town with a stupendous beach. The sunlit days of that last summer in Cesenatico before the war darkened our sky still shine brightly in my mind. In our *comitiva*—our "gang"—there were a dozen or more of us, all in our late teens. A few, like me, were natives of the town; others, from Bologna, Milan, and Rome, were there with their parents, who had come for the summer. No one had much pocket money to speak of, or if they did, no one else knew about it. It didn't interfere with our good times, because there was very little that we needed or wanted to spend money on. We didn't even have to do very much. I remember long afternoons when we spent the entire time talking about what we could do next. We sat in someone's garden, or on the rocks by the harbor, or, if we had the money, in the chairs of a gelato parlor, examining and discussing the alternatives, but we rarely felt pressed to reach a consensus. Talking about it was good enough for us, and after a couple of idle hours, we gave up talking and returned separately home. We were happy with life, too happy even to pay any mind to the black cloud of war that was approaching from over the border.

The most potent draw for us was the glorious beach that sloped into the unruffled Adriatic. It was broad enough to accommodate twelve parallel rows of umbrellas and deck chairs, and it seemed endless as it ran toward infinity along the Romagna coast. We crossed it nearly every morning to run into a transparent sea that was so shallow, one could walk for almost a hundred yards before the water came up to one's chin.

The father of one of the members of our gang was a *bagnino*, the concessionaire of a beach establishment. Public beaches in Italy are parceled out to concessions that put up umbrellas and deck chairs. On the landward side of the beach, the bathers patronizing a concession have access to changing rooms, restrooms, and a bar. On the opposite side, at the water's edge, there are rudimentary crafts that one can rent for short excursions. In my day, the basic model consisted of two benchlike slatted seats facing each other that were bolted perpendicular to a pair of wooden pontoons. They could accommodate up to four persons, including those manning the oars, which were the sole means of propulsion. Curiously, the boat was called a *moscone*, Italian for "bluebottle fly." We had no money to rent one, but our friend's father, the *bagnino*, would let us have one or two of them for brief periods during those times when there were few customers on the beach. The sea was not polluted then; it was clear and clean even close to the shore, and we often ran into it for a swim straight from the beach, but it was so much better to take a *moscone* out at large and splash down from it into water that was exhilaratingly cool and deep.

At lunchtime, the beach emptied as people headed for home. Only a few returned in the afternoon. Whenever I could get excused from going home for lunch—I used to plead with my mother to

With some of my "gang" in Cesenatico in 1940, the year that Italy went to war.
I am on the left on the lowest step.

let me take a *panino* and some fruit with me to the beach—it was a
beautiful time, the time I loved the best, because my friends and I all
but owned the beach, and after the din of the morning crowds, any
loud voices we might hear were only our own.

Replacing the midday meal with a *panino* was not as natural
a thing to do as one might think. It was, in fact, exceedingly unorthodox. The sacramental quality of the noontime dinner in Italy,
il pranzo, when factories, stores, and offices close to allow everyone to
gather at the family table for the longest and most important meal
of the day, has been for generations a dominant feature of Italian
life. It is the central act around which an Italian day turns. It has
proved to be the solid foundation of my own marriage. In the years
that we spent in New York, Milan, and Rome, the place where we

lived had to be within my husband's easy reach at lunchtime. Even now, in Florida, while our neighbors are playing golf or bridge, or going shopping, or making appointments with their hairdresser or trainer or doctor in the middle of the day, we set those hours aside for our *pranzo*. I have a confession to make, however. Although I cook a full hot meal every day that we are at home, I still love sandwiches as much as I did on those sunny days of my sixteenth year. If I can fit something from my plate in between two slices of bread or spread it on a single slice, I will do it. One of the nicknames that my husband has laid on me is *mangia panini*, and I have earned it.

At some distance from the shore, there was a diving platform—*il trampolino*, we called it—that we liked to swim out to. It didn't matter that we could not dive well, because we weren't really there to dive, but to lounge around and talk while cultivating a devastating tan.

Our diving platform in Cesenatico. I was not alone in doing belly flops.

We had a fellow from Rome in our company who was older than the rest of us. Most of the company was, like me, sixteen or close to it. He was eighteen, a small, but at that age significant, difference. He stood out both physically and in his manner. He was more than six feet tall, which was an exceptional height in Italy then and is not that common even now. He had strong, austere good looks that were complemented by, or perhaps responsible for, an imperious manner. His name was Vittorio Gassman. He had already achieved a certain celebrity as a star basketball player, but he would become even more famous in later years as one of Italy's great actors, both in the theater and in films. In the middle of his career he was called to Hollywood, where he stayed for only a brief period, yet long enough for him to marry Shelley Winters.

Vittorio was always ready to prove that whatever someone else could do, he could do as well, if not better. We once got to the *trampolino* on a day when a group of local boys had gone there to practice their diving form. They were really quite good, entering the water headfirst, arms extended forward, making hardly a ripple. *"Ma che bravi, vero Vittorio?"* ("They are really good, aren't they?") I said to Gassman, knowing that would get a rise out of him. *"Mah!"* he said, making a wry mouth. *"Non mi sembra nulla di particolare"* ("It's nothing special"). *"Vorrei vedere te, farlo"* ("I'd like to see you do it"), I said. His ego wouldn't let him ignore the challenge. He jumped but never managed to stretch his body forward, and he landed in the water feet first. Along with everyone else, I was laughing and clapping my hands when he climbed back up. Because of the speckles in my light brown eyes, Vittorio used to call me *la gatta dagl'occhi a pallini*, the cat with polka-dot eyes. Glaring at me, he said, *"Va bene, gatta dagl'occhi a pallini, provaci tu!"* ("All right, you try it!") I did, performing a perfect belly flop. That evening, at home, my legs, tummy, and chest looked as though they had been spread with strawberry jam. As soon as he got to Rome, Gassman sent me a little book of his poems that he'd had printed and bound, inscribing it to *"Alla gatta dagl'occhi a pallini."* I had it with me when we left Cesenatico to pass the war years at a farmhouse on Lake Garda, where it must have remained.

After the war, when I was in Milan visiting a girl who had been in our *comitiva*, Vittorio had the lead in a play. My friend and I saw the play and went backstage afterward to say hello. Gassman dismissed us brusquely, unable, he said, to recognize us or to remember anything about the *comitiva* in Cesenatico.

Sometimes in the afternoon we went bicycling. It is still the most popular way to move around in my town, and if you visit Cesenatico today, you will find the streets busy with bicycles rather than with cars. At that time, the bicycling was more adventurous because the town had not yet been enlarged by the development that took place after the war, and we were quickly able to leave it behind us. We traveled in rough country, where the ride was spine-jarringly bumpy, provoking shrieks, squeals, and laughs, one of our many occasions to make cheerful pandemonium. There were never enough bicycles to go around, so some of the girls rode on the handlebars or the top tube while the boys pedaled. The position was not kind to our buttocks and thighs. Our stiff-legged walk, whenever we got off, was regarded as uproariously funny by those who had been spared the martyrdom to which our aching muscles had been subjected. Occasionally, we came upon an abandoned shack that would become our clubhouse of the moment, where we puffed on our clandestine cigarettes, played cards, replayed the funny dialogue of a movie we had just seen, or relieved ourselves of profound observations on the nature of things.

We were a prankish lot, and no one was exempt from our stunts, not even my father. Some of my companions had noticed that the door to the cellar where Papi stored some wine could easily be unlocked. One day he called me to show, with exaggerated indignation, what he had found hanging on the garden gate. It was an empty fiasco—a two-liter flask of his excellent Sangiovese—and a note attached with the following verse:

Alla salute di Marcella,
così cara e così bella,
questo fiasco benvenuto,
i suoi amici han bevuto.

In toasting the health of Marcella,
so dear and so lovely,
this welcome flask
her friends have drained.

Everyone in our *comitiva* had signed it.

Maria Carla was a Cesenatico native like me and a friend since childhood. Her family's house was near ours, but they lived most of the year in Rome, where her father, a concert musician, taught bass at the Conservatorio di Santa Cecilia. She did not run with our "pack," but moved in a small circle of her own. Maria Carla had allure and sophistication beyond her years and ours. Soon after the war ended, she met and married an older man, a distinguished Neapolitan lawyer who practiced in Rome. It was an achievement that none of us, at the time, could have pulled off, and we all felt painfully callow by comparison. We gloated briefly a few years later when Maria Carla found that her husband was sleeping with their maid and divorced him. But she one-upped us soon enough again by marrying a handsome and prominent architect.

Her Cesenatico house lay at an angle to a large lot that had been transformed into an open-air movie theater for the summer. It was not a drive-in, but a sit-in, with as many rows of rickety wooden seats as the lot could accommodate. Even though Maria Carla did not frequent our *comitiva*, we were friendly enough that from time to time, when she and her own friends or her parents did not choose to have the place to themselves, she let us into her house to watch the movie being projected on the open-air screen next door. A strategic placement of chairs by the rear windows of the house enabled us to watch and hear a movie very comfortably without having to buy a ticket.

We followed movie nights at Maria Carla's with a cone of gelato or a *piadina*. If it was a really steamy summer night, the choice would be gelato; otherwise we preferred to go down the street where, in a shack by the harbor canal, Tonina made her incomparable *piadina*. This ancient specialty of farmhouses in Romagna is a yeastless flat bread, made to order, like pizza, for immediate consumption. One may cover it with a soft cheese, or prosciutto, or fold it over a clump of wild greens sautéed in garlic and olive oil. In the latter instance, it is called a *consùm*. Tonina rolled out an eight-inch disk of dough by hand with a rolling pin, then cooked it over a searingly hot terra-cotta griddle. It came off that griddle charred, crisp, mingling the tangy tastes of smoke and hot terra-cotta with the nutty sweet one of freshly grilled wheat dough. There are scores of roadside stands in Romagna today that make *piadina*, but none makes it like Tonina's. They roll out the dough between steel rollers and cook it on a steel griddle. It is limp and tastes bland. Today, in Cesenatico, if I were looking for an after-the-movie, late-night snack, I would settle for a pizza, which was unknown in northern Italy before the war.

All the girls in the *comitiva* loved to dance, and so did some of the boys. This was the age before discos, however; before cassettes, not to speak of CDs; before transistors and boom boxes. There were elegant establishments with live orchestras and waiters in dinner jackets, but we were too poor and too young to dream of admittance. When we did dance, and it was not very often, we were hemmed in by dark furniture in the parlor of someone's house where we played music on a wind-up gramophone. The most glamorous place where people then danced in Cesenatico was on the terrace of the Grand Hotel, a white, lacy art nouveau structure on the beach, the only hotel on the beach in those years. It looked to us like something out of a romantic Hollywood movie. The terrace was a few steps above the level of the street, from which it was separated by a balustrade of curvaceous marble posts. There was just enough room for our heads in the gaps at the bottom of the posts, allowing us to observe the dancers above, on whose skill, or lack of it, on whose attire, on the nature of a couple's relationship, we would maliciously comment and elaborately speculate. From time to time, we danced in the street to the music floating down from the terrace. In Fellini's *Amarcord*, his evocation on film of a comparable period in Romagna, there is a similar scene, on a similar summer evening, that takes place in a similar hotel, so true to life that when I saw it in a Manhattan theater my cheeks were suddenly overrun by tears of overpowering nostalgia.

By the end of August, everyone left for home, and soon after, we packed and moved north to Lake Garda, where we thought we would find refuge from the war. There were other good summers in Cesenatico after the war, but none filled with such simple-hearted joy. Neither we nor the world would ever again be so young.

The War

1940–1945

*I*T WAS THE WINTER of 1939. Germany was at war with Britain and France, and Italy was waiting for an advantageous moment to join her. Zio Tonino, a well-connected uncle by marriage who lived north of us, on Lake Garda, in the town of Desenzano, had formed a syndicate with a few prominent members of the government, a cabinet member, a senator, and some others. Their purpose was to acquire agricultural land as a sound investment for money, whose value was likely to collapse in the coming war. Someone had to manage the large farm they had assembled by the lake, but when Tonino found that the draft was taking all the capable local men, he turned to Papi. Papi had shown, by the skillful management of our own small farm, that he could handle the job, and moreover, the chronic emphysema that he lived with and would not kill him until decades later exempted him from the call to arms. Garda was, and is, a famously beautiful lake, but its appeal to our family at that portentous moment lay in what was optimistically presumed to be its remoteness from military targets. That optimism would eventually prove to have been gravely misplaced.

Papi left for Desenzano ahead of us to take charge of the farm and to prepare for our arrival. War was approaching, but its rumble was still too distant to intrude greatly on my parents' thoughts. Their foremost concern was my education. In the Italian educational system of the time, schooling began with five years at the elementary level, followed by five years in middle school, known as *ginnasio*, that in turn led to three years at the *liceo*, the rigorous upper school whose diploma qualified you to study for a doctoral degree at a university. I had half a year left at the *ginnasio*, which my mother decided I should complete before moving to the lake. At the end of school, the summer season began in Cesenatico, the happiest time of the year for a beach town, so when my mother proposed to postpone our departure until September, I threw my arms around her with joy. There were no further postponements after that. We had left Papi alone for almost a year; I had to enroll in the *liceo* at Desenzano, so my mother, my grandfather, my two grandmothers, and I packed up, said arrivederci to Cesenatico, and set off for Lake Garda. I went gaily, looking forward to the new world on the lake that I had started dreaming about.

The farmhouse Zio Tonino had allotted us resembled nothing I had seen in my daydreams. There was no heat, and the sole bathroom, at the top of the stairs that led to the upper floor, had only a toilet and a sink. We sponge-bathed for the duration of our stay. The bedrooms were bare of all furnishings save for rickety iron beds with squeaky, sagging springs and lumpy wool mattresses. We hung our clothes on tautly strung metal wire and stowed other items in packing boxes. Papi had bought an ancient wood-burning stove for the kitchen and a long, rough wooden table to work on. For the other room on the ground floor he had found two large, dark cupboards, a battered and immensely heavy walnut dining table, and a miscellany of chairs. Twenty years later, when my husband and I were living in Milan, we restored that table, converting its top into a large coffee table and recycling the massive base as sturdy support for a handsome writing desk.

I remember the cold of that winter, the first I had ever experienced without heat indoors. We spent as much of the day as we could in the kitchen, where we kept feeding the stove. An hour before retiring, we warmed the beds with a contraption that we irreverently called *il prete e la suora,* "the priest and the nun." The "priest" was an open wooden frame placed between the top and bottom sheets; embraced within it was the "nun," a terra-cotta brazier filled with hot embers from the stove. We had brought only our personal effects to Desenzano because my mother expected it would not be long before we could return to Cesenatico, and in the farmhouse, we had found only one thin blanket for each bed. For more warmth, as we took off our clothes we spread them over the top sheet and then covered them with the blanket, tucking it firmly under the mattress.

While I was still in Cesenatico, completing my fifth year at the *ginnasio,* Italy sent its troops into France, entering the war at Germany's side. Many years later, living in America, I remember hearing a recording of Roosevelt's speech when he declared, "The hand that held the dagger has plunged it into its neighbor's back," a description of the event quite at odds with the one our leaders had given us. At the beginning, the war did not seem to affect our life too much. On the lake, it was so quiet that we felt justified in expecting that the war would pass us by. Then the Allies' planes began to fly over us, dropping bombs or diving to strafe anything moving on the road or the railroad tracks, the supply lines that connected the Axis forces in Italy with Austria, our neighbor north of the border. When the Allies landed in southern Italy and the Fifth Army began slowly to push the front northward, the German High Command for Italy moved north too, establishing its headquarters little more than a mile from our farm. Hoping to take Italy out of the war, the king had had Mussolini arrested, but the Germans liberated him and brought him north. Where? To Lake Garda! There, in the neighboring town of Salò, he formed a fascist republic that kept his followers fighting on the Nazi side. Not only was the war not passing us by, it had made us one of its prime targets. Every day there were more planes and more bombs.

Air raid sirens usually gave us advance warning of the bombers' approach, but one attack from the air, designed primarily to demolish our morale, always came unannounced. It came at night, a single plane with two bombs. We named it Pippo. Shortly after its arrival overhead, Pippo dropped one of its bombs. It circled buzzard-like above, sometimes appearing to be very close, then pulling away. Shaken out of our sleep, we waited, waited for Pippo to drop the second bomb, after which, if we were still alive and unharmed and had not lost our minds, we would try to piece together a little more sleep out of the broken night.

Surviving the raids and getting enough to eat were what we thought about, virtually to the exclusion of everything else. There *was* nothing else. The country was desperately short of food. Nearly all the men able to work the fields were in uniform, and a large part of the food that was produced was requisitioned to feed the German army and its fascist allies. We were among the lucky ones, because even though the Germans kept an eye on what we produced and confiscated most of it, Papi was able to conceal enough corn to make polenta and wheat to grind into flour for our bread. We also roasted some of the wheat kernels to make coffee, which had vanished along with sugar. We called our coffee *granato*, from *grano*, the word for wheat, and sweetened it with honey.

Our most precious possession was salt, which had become a nearly unobtainable commodity. My mother's sister, Margherita—Margò, we called her—was married to Tonino's brother, an electrical engineer in charge of production for the company that supplied electricity to the northeastern regions of Italy. In the kitchen of the house in Venice where they lived, Zia Margò kept an electric burner going constantly to boil down seawater from the lagoon—unpolluted then—until only salt was left. From time to time, she sent us a little bag of it, more valuable to us than diamonds. Some of the salt we used for ourselves, some we bartered. The local pharmacist had beehives, and for a little salt he let us have honey for our coffee. For a few spoonfuls of salt, we were able to get fresh milk from a neighbor who kept a cow. This exchange led to one of my first culinary tasks. My mother poured the milk into a broad pan that she kept overnight in a cold place, with which that house was well supplied. In the morning, she skimmed off the cream that had floated to the top and ladled it into a fiasco, an empty Chianti flask. My job was to shake the flask until the cream clotted into butter, another priceless ingredient for our kitchen. Not that there was much of it. It takes more cream than one might think to make a spoonful of butter.

We fenced in a small part of a yard for the few chickens that we were able to raise. They were astonishingly agile in evading capture, and if we wanted one for the kitchen, it often took three of us to corner it. One morning my mother, Papi, and I had maneuvered our quarry toward a corner when we heard an ear-splitting whine, a powerful whoosh, and an explosion close to us. The chicken we were after lay on the ground, blood pouring from its truncated neck. Shrapnel from an errant bomb had decapitated it. For a moment, we were unable to move or breathe, but when we realized that none of us was harmed, that it wasn't one of our heads lying on the ground, we ran into each other's arms, laughing hysterically. My mother lifted up the headless fowl, and we marched giddily into the house, raucously singing a patriotic song while triumphantly holding up our war trophy and dinner. We kept the piece of shrapnel, which had the shape of a shallow bowl, and used it for many years as an ashtray, reminding us of the miracle that killed a chicken and spared us.

In exchange for a little packet of salt, we acquired a piglet. To raise it, we were instructed to feed it a pulpy mixture of mulberry leaves boiled with polenta. "You will have to see to feeding the pig," my mother said to me. "I have enough to do feeding the family." It was the first dish I had ever been asked to prepare, and it was not until after my marriage that I prepared any others. The ancient Roman custom of training grapevines from one mulberry tree to another was still being followed at that time, and it was in our vineyard that I found fresh mulberry leaves for my little customer's dinner. The dust raised by the bombings lay thickly on the leaves, so I had to wash them thoroughly at home. I quickly learned how to chop them very fine, a skill that came back to me many years later when I had to chop onion for the dinners I cooked for my husband. I boiled the chopped leaves in a pot with water and polenta flour until I had a dense mush.

When it was time to serve my pig its dinner, my mother came along to help. When we opened the gate of its enclosure, we had to be very careful that it did not escape. Once, however, it did get away, slipping right through our legs. Its speed was dazzling, but to lose it was inadmissible, so we chased it through the fields, shouting after it as loudly as we could. Our shouts brought people from the adjacent farm who eventually helped us recapture our freedom-bound pig.

My mulberry mash must have been very nourishing, because the piglet grew to be a nice stout hog. By winter, it was time to slaughter it. In Italy we describe the traditional cold-weather slaughtering of a pig as *fare il maiale*, "doing the pig." The actual killing is only a preliminary to the elaborate craft of dressing the carcass into cuts and products to eat fresh or cure, wasting not a single ounce of flesh or fat or blood.

In canvassing the territory, Papi had found three women and two older men who had the necessary experience. The crew arrived early one cool December morning, bringing their equipment: a coil of strong rope, trussing string, scissors, a meat grinder, stockpots, formidable-looking knives. The men deftly immobilized the hog; firmly bound the hind legs, then the front ones; and hung it by its hindquarters from a beam, the head facing down over a large basin. One of the men slashed the hog's throat, letting its valuable blood collect in the basin. When it was dead, the two men scraped the skin, or rind, clean of its bristles, being careful not to rub away any part of the precious rind itself. Called *coteca* in Italian, the rind is gelatinous and sweet-tasting when cooked, and it has many uses: in soups or stews, or ground up and combined with the stuffing for large boiling sausages, such as *cotechino* and *zampone*. The men softened the skin with warm, but not scalding, water, and then scraped the bristles away with the edge of a large, shallow, copper ladle. They then lifted the carcass and carried it inside, laying it on top of the massive dining table, which had been covered with a double layer of heavy oilcloth. They slit the belly open and began removing the organs. The women cleaned out the intestines, washing them out many times so that they could be used as casings for the sausages and salami. The men dressed the meat into different cuts, boning some of it so that the women could run it through the grinder. It would subsequently be seasoned in different ways, depending on whether it would be used for sausages, salami, or *cotechino*. I had intended to watch their work through to the end because I had not seen it done before, but the flashing of knives cutting up a dead body; the fetid smell of the cleaning of the intestines, reminiscent of the incontinence that was associated with the panic in the air raid shelters; and the pooling blood on raw flesh provoked in me both nausea and terror. I took a long walk in the fields, letting the wintry air clear my head and cool down my thumping heart.

It was almost dark when I saw the workers leave, and I came home to find a cornucopia of salami, sausages, a prosciutto, several neatly dressed cuts of meat, and one of my favorites, a *cotechino*, a large sausage that becomes lusciously creamy when boiled. It is made with a large percentage of the rind—*coteca*—from the pig's snout, hence the name *cotechino*. In Venice and its region, they call it *musetto*, an Italian diminutive for "snout." In Venice's wine bars, a warm, tender, slice of *musetto* on a round of grilled bread is one of the city's most effective remedies for the rawness of a winter day on the lagoon. My mother pointed to a small tub filled with solid white fat saying, "There is a job waiting for you," without any other explanation just then. That night we didn't eat any pork; we had only cooked vegetables and a salad of raw greens.

The first thing my mother decided to cook the following day was the pig's blood. I had never had it, but although I felt queasy, I was curious to see how my mother would go about it. She sliced a huge mound of onions, which she put into a large skillet with some of the pork fat. She let it cook slowly for a long time, until the onion had been greatly reduced in bulk and became a dark nut brown. The blood had turned a reddish brown and jelled enough that she could cut it into pieces, which she put in the skillet, together with a parsimonious pinch of our precious salt and chopped, dried chili pepper. We used chili because peppercorns were agonizingly hard to find and the few we had, we had used for curing the salami and sausages. It was during the war that I developed a fondness for chili pepper, which readers of my recipes will no doubt have noticed. The smell of onions caramelizing had boosted an appetite that didn't really need much spurring; the dish looked like fried liver and onions, and when Mother put it on the table I fell to it without hesitation. In fact, it tasted somewhat like liver, only sweeter and more tender.

We also had the pig's liver in what I believe to be, without exception, the tastiest of all liver preparations. The pig's butchers had carefully set aside the animal's caul, a fatty abdominal membrane that looks a little like a fishnet. When it was Papi's turn to cook, he cut the liver into chunks, then stuck a fresh bay leaf to each chunk and wrapped it in a length of caul. He grilled the liver over red-hot embers taken from the kitchen stove, just long enough for most of the caul to melt and the rest to turn brown.

It became time for me to render the pork fat in the tub. Following my mother's instructions, I cut up the solid fat into pieces no larger than a walnut and put them into a large saucepan, over a section of the stove where the heat was low. "Stir every ten or fifteen minutes," my mother said. I had homework to do, so I opened my texts and my workbooks on the kitchen table with a large clock in front of me. Each time I stirred the pot I noticed that the fat had melted a little more. "Don't ever let it boil," my mother had warned me. After a few hours, I saw that the pot was full of liquid, but there was also a pulpy, pale gray substance in it. I called over my mother who said, "Take the pot off the stove; the fat is fully liquefied. Get some of our crocks"—of which we had previously collected a goodly number—"and ladle only the liquid into them." Once done, I was instructed to set the pasta colander into a bowl, empty the pulpy matter from the saucepan into the colander, and then take a smaller bowl and press it hard into the colander, squeezing through it all the remaining liquefied fat. I poured the last drops of fat into the crocks, now brimming with yet another invaluable ingredient for our larder, *strutto*, rendered pork fat. Whenever I cook with fat now,

I long for that *strutto,* so much lighter and tastier than oil or butter; it made anything you fried in it so crisp and fragrant.

My mother stopped me just as I was about to empty the mashed pulpy stuff from the colander into the trash. "Wait," she said, "with that we are going to make *ciccioli*—cracklings." She spread the pulp into an iron pan, sprinkled two or three grains of salt over it, and put it into the hot oven, where it eventually formed crisp, brown, headily scented nuggets, more delicious and satisfying than any kind of chip.

We were better off than most Italians during the war because we could produce most of our food and barter for many of the things we lacked. My mother, moreover, who had never cooked in her life before coming to Desenzano, was, to our happy surprise, brilliantly resourceful in the kitchen. She baked some of the best bread I have ever had and produced each day dishes so varied and so savory that they lifted our spirits, letting us almost forget while we ate that at any moment our lives could be blown away. We would have been so well-nourished during the war, had we always been able to finish what my mother put on the table.

It was uncanny how often the bombers showed up just as we were getting ready, or even had begun, to eat. We had learned to sit sideways, turned toward the door so that, when necessary, we could make a dash for the shelter. The house had no basement, but a covered shelter had been dug out of a nearby field. If the air raid sirens went off while we were eating, we grabbed our plates and ran with them to the shelter. If the bombs started to fall before the alarm sounded, we crouched under the table, taking our plates with us. We tried never to leave food exposed during a raid because when the bombs fell, even though we never took a hit, the vibrations shook enough plaster and dust from the ceiling to cover the food and make it inedible. There were some times when we were taken by surprise, our meal was ruined, and then we had to go without.

During the final and most cruel years of the war, acquaintances, friends, and relatives would disappear. Sometimes they were not heard from again; sometimes we were told that they'd been found hanged or shot to death, either by the Germans or by the partisans, depending on whose side they had been associated. Many persons were on the move, looking for a place safer than the one they had left behind. One day, we opened our door to find standing on the step a remotely connected, and heretofore rarely heard from, aunt Albina, with her two daughters, Elena and Matilde. The girls were untying a startling number of bundles from the bicycles on which they had traveled, and one fairly large suitcase, which would subsequently cause my mother to lose her usually unassailable composure. Wherever it was that Albina and the girls had come from, it was apparently an exceedingly dangerous place, and they begged us to extend to them the presumed safety of our farmhouse. The same week, Zio Tonino had unloaded on us a distant relative of his own, a former musician who had been a bassoon player. We promptly named him Zio Fagotto, *fagotto* being the Italian for "bassoon."

Within a few days, our family had grown from six to ten, for whom mother not only had to cook more food, but also find beds and linens. We had no extra sheets and blankets, so some of them had to be split in two. The blankets were already so skimpy that when they were cut we had to supplement them with our overcoats. Albina had put her suitcase away unopened, which caused my mother to ask what she was keeping in it. "The sheets and blankets for my daughters' trousseau," replied Albina. "Well then," said Mother, "take them out and use them for your own beds." "Absolutely not," Albina said, "my daughters' trousseau is not to be touched!" My mother was known for her inexhaustible powers of conciliation, but they abandoned her then. I watched with fascination and suspense as the two women argued with steadily increasing volume and heat. When Albina finally conceded the match I wanted to applaud, but I refrained, fearful that it might rekindle the argument.

Zio Fagotto was a different problem. He constantly complained that my mother's cooking had lamentable shortcomings; nothing she set before him was ever done to his satisfaction, yet he ate more of it than anyone else. He demanded a flask of wine for himself and never let go of it. If there was a raid, he would take the wine into the shelter, and at night, he took it upstairs with him, stowing the flask under his bed.

During this last period of the war, I saw the different ways that danger acted upon people, sometimes paralyzing them with fear, sometimes evoking what seemed to be complete indifference. The two persons most terrified of the bombs were Albina's daughter Elena and my own papi. Elena was obsessed with the thought that the bombs could come down while she was using the toilet and she might not get out because the bathroom door would be stuck. She therefore left the door of the bathroom, which was in plain view at the head of the stairs, wide open. As for her sister, Matilde, on the other hand, not even a war could upstage her need to be impeccably groomed. Her hair and makeup were always in perfect order; her clothes were clean, sharply pressed, and appropriately accessorized. When the air raid siren sounded, everyone scampered to the shelter, but Matilde tiptoed gingerly over the farm field, trying not to scuff her shoes.

My father was fairly calm in the daytime, but night terrorized him. He feared that if he slept upstairs, he would not have enough time, in case of a raid, to get down and reach the shelter. He therefore brought his little bed downstairs, but he was not satisfied to sleep alone because he slept so soundly—and was slightly deaf besides—that he feared he would not hear the air raid alarm until it was too late. He insisted on my mother sleeping next to him so that she could wake him in case they had to make a run for it to the shelter. The bed was so small that when one of them turned over in the night, the other one too had to turn.

My mother did not let peril or discomfort interfere with what she had decided needed to be done. When an air raid came while she was preparing dinner, she would not leave the kitchen until whatever she had been cooking was done or could safely be set aside to be finished later. When we ran out of olive oil one day, that evening, as everyone was getting ready for bed, she went out, walking across the fields to Tonino's house on the edge of town to pick up two large bottles of olive oil he had been holding for us. That was marvelous oil, incidentally, oil from the groves on the western shore of Lake Garda. Of all the excellent oils that Italy produces, it is still my favorite for its harmonious and elegant flavors.

The curfew was on, but mother didn't trouble to consider that if she had been seen by a German patrol she could have been shot on the spot. She had almost made it back home when she fell into a ditch, holding the oil securely aloft. In that position, she was unable to climb out, and Papi had fallen asleep so deeply, he didn't even realize she hadn't come back. She was rescued at dawn, when the early-rising neighboring farmer saw her and helped her out, the oil still intact.

In the third year of the war I completed my studies at the *liceo* and looked to enroll in a university. The closest one was in Milan, the most heavily bombed Italian city. There was round-trip train service to Milan, little more than eighty miles away, but there was no schedule to go by. The train stopped so often and unpredictably that one could never be sure when it departed and when it arrived. Moreover, it was often bombed or strafed by Allied planes. My parents' desire to see me going to the university was great, but not great enough to risk train travel. There was a truck that left for Milan in the morning and returned in the evening. The driver lived on property that was part of the farm Papi managed, inspiring enough confidence in my parents that they overcame fear and reluctance to allow me to travel with him for at least the first few times.

I had decided to work toward a degree in natural sciences. Bombs had fallen on the university, and amid the rubble and smoke from recently extinguished fires, I found the office of the professor whom I was told to consult about my course of study. He informed me that lectures were given sporadically and never scheduled sufficiently in advance to allow me, who had so far to travel, to plan to attend them. My best option was to study at home, following a curriculum that he would give me, and to show up for the exams, which would be given orally. I chose to make human anatomy my first course. He generously supplied me with the texts I needed to study, but he also pointed out that the osteological part of the exam would be conducted with actual bones and that I would have to prepare for it using a full skeleton. The very kind truck driver with whom I had traveled to Milan came for me as we had arranged. I rode back home with him that evening, giving no thought to the dangers of the road or to how I would procure a human skeleton for my studies. I had enrolled in the university, I had signed up for my first course, and after the confining years on the farm, life was about to open up for me.

Reality broke into that life the following morning. How was I to find a skeleton? There seemed to be no hope of finding one in the town we lived in, but then I remembered seeing one in the study of my former science teacher from the *liceo*. I asked him very sweetly if I could borrow it, and he very sweetly said, "Of course, my dear, you can have all of it, except for the skull. It is very delicate and some of its parts are extremely fragile." I was devastated: "No skull? How can I prepare for my exam without it? It's the most complicated part of the whole skeleton!" "Don't be so negative," he replied. "You can easily get one at the cemetery." I was stunned. "Really? At the cemetery? Are you serious?" "Of course," he said, "it won't be a problem; go ask, and you'll see."

When I got back home with my bag of bones, I thought about my old teacher's suggestion. I had no other solution, so I followed his advice and went to the cemetery. It was an active place in those days. I was directed to the chief gravedigger, who was doing just that. I explained why I needed a skull and asked him if he had one to spare. I was overcome with misgivings, but he responded as nonchalantly as though I had asked him the time of day. "Sure, I can give you one if you bring an authorization from the medical examiner at the hospital." Feeling more confident of success now, I found the medical examiner at the hospital and asked him if I could please have an authorization to obtain a skull at the cemetery. "Why do you need a skull and who told you I could give you such an authorization?" I once more gave my reasons and explained that the gravedigger had assured me that with the doctor's authorization he could give me as many skulls as I needed. He hesitated briefly, but I was so young and guileless that he couldn't think of any objection, and he wrote out an authorization on his official stationery. It emerged later that he had assumed that post only two days earlier and had no clue as to what was or was not permissible. I returned to the cemetery waving the splendid document I had been given, feeling unimpeachably authoritative. The gravedigger pocketed the letter, saying, *"Hai avuto fortuna.* ("You are lucky.") There is a fine skull here for you, which I have just dug up."

I grabbed the eagerly sought object of my pursuit, but, never having held a newly dug-up skull before, I was dismayed to find that every opening was packed solid with dirt. It certainly did not look like the polished skull in my teacher's study, and I had no idea what I could do with it. I queried the gravedigger, who said, "Try boiling it and then brushing all the dirt away." I brought my skull home to my mother, who, I had hoped, would help me. To my surprise, she was horrified, crying, *"Portalo via subito!"* ("Get that thing out of the house immediately!")

I hunted around the various farmyards for a large enough container, and finally I came across a large tin. I rinsed it out, put in the skull, set it over some broken bricks, and filled it with water. I gathered branches, kindling, and newspapers, stuffed them under the tin, and lit them. I was unable to get much of a fire going, and after a couple of hours the water had not even begun to simmer and the skull was caked as hard with dirt as ever. Once again, I felt I would never be able to prepare for my exam, when one of the neighbors, a retired doctor who had from time to time given my mother helpful advice, passed by and rescued me. Informed of my predicament, he said, "Why don't you launder it the old-fashioned way?" "Which is?" I asked. "It's how our folks used to launder and bleach sheets and other linen in the old days. Bring me a pot of boiling water and ashes from your kitchen stove and I'll show you how it is done." When I came back with what he had asked for, I found he had dug a hole in the ground for the skull. He spread some of the ashes on the bottom of the hole, placed the skull over them, covered it with the remaining ashes, and then poured the hot water over it. "We'll wait a few minutes," he said. When he decided that sufficient time had passed, he pulled out the skull and rinsed it under the water that ran into the trough where cows and other farm animals came to drink. The skull came out a clean bone-white, except for a shadow under where the nose used to be. "Look, Doctor, he has a gray mustache!" I cried. *"Sciocchina"* ("Silly girl"), he said, laughing. "Those are his capillaries. Go back into the house and bring me an old toothbrush." With it he brushed away the "mustache" and a few remaining specks. My skull was magnificent, and even though some of its teeth were missing, I thought it smiled at me.

I had been corresponding with one of my former *liceo* class-mates who had been drafted and assigned to an antiaircraft brigade in Verona, a city close to Lake Garda. He knew about the bones I needed to prepare for my human anatomy exam, and I followed up with a letter in a humorous vein, describing the skull I had acquired and how I had managed to clean it and even erase its "mustache." I called it by the name I had given it, Giobatta, a character from a comic strip we both read. One morning, ten days later, two police-men came looking for me, asking me to go with them immediately to the police station. My fear was that someone had died and I was going to be asked to identify a body. I had the sick feeling that something had happened to Papi.

At the station, the chief gave me a very black look. He showed me a letter, asking me if I recognized it. It was the letter I had written to my classmate in Verona. There were the censor's yellow lines all over it. I was so relieved that I laughed as I answered, "*Certamente!*" ("Certainly!") It was not a well-chosen moment to laugh. He looked at me even more menacingly, saying, "You stand accused of profaning a tomb and of boiling a human skull, for which you may get a sentence of forty years. But that is not all. Whose skull was it you took? Was its real name Giobatta? Did it in fact have a mustache?" His look and his words reawakened my fear, except that now I was afraid for myself. I tried to explain about the course in human anatomy I was studying for, but he wasn't listening. He kept shouting questions at me: "Who instructed you to boil the skull of a German colonel? What did they give you for doing it?" With barely the breath to get the words out, I said that I didn't know anything about a German colonel, that I had gotten the skull with proper authorization from the medical examiner. At that, one of the officers standing by said, "Let us check the girl's story and find out if she really did have an authorization." He escorted me to the hospital, where the medical examiner acknowledged having issued such a permit. "And what did you do with it?" the officer asked me. "I gave it to a gravedigger at the cemetery." "Let us go to the cemetery, then," he said. There, the gravedigger produced the document that I had given him, and with that, the questions about a German colonel stopped. It turned out that a colonel with a mustache and a name sounding vaguely like Giobatta had indeed disappeared, probably killed by partisans. In the interim, my mother had taken the bicycle and gone to the police station to find out what had happened to me. There they told her that I had gone to the hospital. When she got to the hospital, they told her I was at the cemetery, where, after pedaling furiously, she found me. We thought it was very funny, but not just then; later, much, much later.

I was still in trouble, however, charged with profanation of a tomb and the boiling of a skull. I had my hearing before a judge, an aristocratic old gentleman with a mane of beautiful, thick, white hair and the slurred, guttural "R" that you often hear in the speech of the Italian upper class. He had before him the police report, my letter, and the skull. He looked at me with a shadow of a smile that helped me stop the trembling of my legs. "*Signorina,*" he asked, "do you know you could go to jail for forty years for what you have done?" "Yes, your honor." "And do you know," he continued, "that in my lifetime as a judge I have never before had to judge someone accused of boiling a skull? We have much more serious work to attend to here. Do us a favor, take the *corpus delicti*"—the evidence—"and go home."

I**T WAS FINALLY OVER**; Germany had surrendered, and Allied tanks were in the town square. But it wasn't quite over for everyone. The partisans came down from their hideouts in the mountains to round up those they knew or suspected to be fascists or sympathizers. Some they shot immediately. Others they locked up. There was hardly any food for those in prison, and some of them began to starve to death. We had friends among them, and my mother baked bread that I loaded on my bicycle and brought to the prison.

That didn't sit well with the partisans. One evening, three armed, bearded young men stormed into the house. One of them was holding a pot of pitch, which he put on our stove's hot top. Another had shears and a straight razor. We understood immediately what they intended because we had seen newspaper photos of women whose heads had been shaved and covered with hot pitch to keep them bald forever. There was nowhere to run. I jumped up on the dining table and my mother and father threw themselves screaming against the men, desperate to keep them from grabbing me.

Walking my bicycle in Desenzano, 1944, the worst year of the war

When the son of our neighboring farmer had earlier seen the partisans approaching our compound, he bicycled at top speed to get Zio Tonino, who, breathing hard, came instantly. He ordered the men to leave the house immediately, and to our amazement, they obeyed. Our amazement increased when we learned that during the war, Tonino had been a double agent. With his German wife, Zia Ernie, he entertained German officers, but he would pass information about German troop movements to the partisans. We never discovered whether Ernie knew it. At a later date, when he was decorated for it, we also learned that he had harbored two American secret agents in his attic who radioed intelligence back to their base.

I was safe. Those who wanted to disfigure and humiliate me had gone, and we owed it to a Tonino we never suspected existed. The panic and bewilderment that I experienced that evening left a deeply buried trace in my consciousness—a trace, however, that can still surface and briefly throb whenever I see a woman who covers an implicitly bald head with a turban or skullcap.

My son has asked—and so has my husband; neither one of them experienced it—how it felt to be in the war. It was a life that I now remember as having felt truncated at both ends. The past seemed too remote to have really existed, and the future had no face; there was only the present.

During the war years, it had been almost impossible to summon a steady image of the past. What had peacetime been like, when there were no bombs falling, no machine guns cutting people down from the air, when the possible loss of those close to us did not enter our thoughts, when we slept a whole night through, when eating was prompted by the pleasure of it rather than by the fierce, competitive struggle to survive, when the shops were filled with goods that we could buy, when we lived without fear? When I tried to recall my life before the war, the image wavered, and went out of focus.

And the future? What future? I had nothing to compare it with. It was like thinking about Paradise; it was beyond imagination. Only the present was real. Death was close to me and around me, but I was a young girl, and I wanted to feel alive. I sang, which I was unfit to do, I danced, I was noisy, I laughed, I played pranks. The present was unnaturally cruel, uncomfortable, mortifying, dangerous, but it was life, and I threw myself around it because I could not think past it.

Home Again

1945

MAY 1945: The German army in Italy had surrendered; our lodgers, Zio Fagotto, Albina, and Albina's daughters, had gone; and my mother, my grandmothers, and I prepared to quit the Lake Garda farmhouse. We collected the few belongings that we could carry with us on the bus that would take us home, while the rest, along with what little furniture was worth keeping, was made ready for shipment to Cesenatico. Papi went ahead to get the house ready for us, as he had done when we moved north at the beginning of the war. It is a good thing that he did. He found our house nearly uninhabitable, damaged equally by the retreat of the German army and by the advance of those who replaced it. The Wehrmacht had dynamited the bridge over the canal on whose banks our house stood. When the bridge blew up, part of the house went with it. In the interval between the Germans' retreat and the arrival of Allied forces, looters moved in, carting away furniture and ripping out the boilers, the radiators, and all the piping that could come loose to sell for scrap. They were followed by a unit of General Mark Clark's

Fifth Army that bivouacked in the house, where they broke up what had remained of its furniture into firewood for the campfires they lit on our tiled floors.

During the following two decades, the final ones of his life, Papi would steadily lose momentum until, in his last years, he spent his days sitting by the window observing the passage of people, or perhaps simply of time. At that moment, however, his energy was still at full strength, and in a few weeks, moving sure-footedly on his native sod, he performed miracles. He found bricklayer friends to rebuild what had crumbled, and he went from farm to farm looking for furniture and household necessities to supplement what would be coming down from the Lake Garda house. He bought, for as little as he could because his pockets were bare, what the *contadini*—peasant farmers—were willing to dispose of or planning to discard. He could not afford to replace the vanished central heating system, which he supplanted with a terra-cotta stove in the dining-living room and a *cucina economica*—a wood-fired stove—in the kitchen. Living without central heating no longer seemed too great a hardship; we had grown used to it, and moreover, we even had something of a luxury, a little *scaldabagno*—a small and parsimonious electric heater that doled out hot water in the bathroom.

On Christmas week, we waited for Bajòn, the faithful *contadino* who worked Papi's small farm. "Bajòn" was a nickname that, through constant usage, had erased everyone's recollection of his real name. In Romagnolo, the dialect spoken in Cesenatico, the word means "easygoing," "good-natured," and it fit him perfectly. Bajòn would be bringing the traditional year-end presents that were part of the ancient crop-sharing covenant governing the relationship between a *contadino* and the farm's owner.

The mule that, with no discernible enthusiasm, drew Bajòn's cart also had a nickname: Moto Guzzi. It had been named, mockingly, after the Italian racing motorcycle because of the animal's disinclination toward any form of guided locomotion, although sometimes, in sporadic and misguided attempts to live up to its sobriquet, it would tear off in brief, untimely, and aberrant trots. We heard Bajòn's whoops, urging Moto Guzzi on, coming up the path to the house, and presently the mule's forlorn shuffle brought him into view.

When Bajòn pulled up in the yard with the two-wheeled cart that Moto Guzzi had so reluctantly drawn, it seemed to me that our own gift-bearing magus had come. He unloaded a sack of flour milled from our own wheat, the soft variety known as *doppio zero*— 00—that is used throughout Emilia-Romagna for handmade pasta; two dozen freshly laid eggs with wisps of straw from the chicken coop still stuck to their shells; a long, knobby salami; a couple of yards of sausages, and my favorite, two thick *cotechini*, the boiling sausages made largely with *coteca*, the sweet, tender rind from a pig's snout; and an earthenware crock of *strutto*, the rendered pork fat that is unequaled for making pastry crust and for producing crisp, light, fragrant fried foods.

There was a basket of sauce tomatoes, small, round, slightly puckered, and still attached to part of their vine. Bajòn had been keeping them hanging in the farmhouse, and we strung them up from beams in the kitchen ceiling, alongside bunches of golden Albana grapes. In a cold room, they can last an entire winter, with flavor more concentrated than fresh tomatoes and a lot fresher than that of canned tomatoes. He handed over several cardoons of the variety grown in Romagna called *gobbi*, "hunchbacks." As they grow, earth is piled over them to keep them white, and in the struggle to push through the mound of soil toward the light, their stalks hunch over, even to the point of cracking. They look deceptively like large celeries, but they are in the thistle family, like artichokes. Conventional cardoons can be bitter, but Romagna's *gobbi* can be as sweet as artichoke bottoms. The stalks have to be thoroughly stripped of tough strings, my papi's job. *Gobbi* can be braised or baked, but our favorite way to have them was to boil them in milk and water until tender—it could take more than an hour—and eat them while still warm, sprinkled with salt and bathed in the dense, fruity olive oil of our hills. Bajòn also had a bushel of apples for us, a small type known as *renetta*, their skin a dull rose-red, the flesh juicy and sweet. Lastly, we had a couple of shallow baskets lined with orange-red persimmons, the fall fruit that in Italy we call by its Japanese name, *kaki*. The persimmons grown in Romagna are plumper and more globelike in shape than other varieties, their taut, thin skin marked by a web of fine, dark lines. Half a lifetime later, I would hear them touted in Venice's Rialto market, the stall-keepers calling out, *"Gavemo kaki co' ragno!"*—"We have persimmons with the spider [web]." When ripe, the silken, honeyed flesh is succulent like that of no other fruit.

Last of all, Bajòn reached into a corner of his cart for two heaving clumps of feathers, a stout capon and a young rooster live and tied by their legs. He dropped them on our kitchen floor, where they desperately flapped their wings in a futile try for freedom. After upending a glass of sweet Albana with Papi, and a ritual exchange of *buon natale* ("happy Christmas") wishes with all of us, Bajòn climbed onto his cart and turned back. Moto Guzzi must have been thinking of the supper that waited for him at the farm, because he set off at a sprightlier pace than we had thought him capable of.

My grandfather, Nonno Riccardo, had died during the war, so there were five of us left that Christmas: Papi, Mother, Nonna Adele, Nonna Polini, and myself. The two *nonne* could not have been more dissimilar. My papi's mother, Nonna Polini—which is what everyone but her son called her—was born and raised on a farm, had never been as much as twenty miles away from her birthplace, except for Lake Garda during the war, and spoke only Romagnolo, our local dialect. Ninety and going blind, she did not quite reach five feet, but she was quick-witted, impish, and earthy. Her customary dinner was a bowl of wine that she sopped up with bread. She never drank water. Water, she said, *"fa infradicire i pali"* ("will rot a fence post"). Like all the farm women, she wore only ankle-length dark dresses, preferably solid black. Her underpants were open at the crotch so that she could relieve herself without having to remove them.

Nonna Adele, my mother's mother, was fifteen years younger, a straitlaced patrician standing five feet ten. She had been brought up in Damascus and spoke not a dialect, but standard Italian, with the warmly accented, sonorous vowels common to the speech of Italians raised in the Middle East or in North Africa. Her eyes were large and kind but museful, as though fixed on matters at some remove from

Papi's mother, Nonna Polini, at ninety

immediate circumstances. Nonna Polini and Nonna Adele's zany exchanges, entirely in dialect on the part of the former and in Italian spiced with Arabic and French on the part of the latter, would tentatively embark on what appeared to be the same course, only to tack in separate directions before returning for a brief excursion along parallel lines.

With Bajòn's departure, the topic for discussion became the Christmas menu. We quickly came to an agreement on the first course, *cappelletti in brodo,* stuffed pasta dumplings in capon broth.

Nonna Polini proposed we follow that with *cotechino,* a suggestion to which I gave my immediate support. There was nothing I loved more, and in all the years of the war we had had it only once. Nonna Adele, picking up the word *cotechino,* observed that when her husband was alive, that was what they had for New Year's Day, together with lentils. "Lentils?" countered Nonna Polini. "We are going to have *cotechino* with mashed potatoes." "Mashed potatoes on New Year's Day? I have never heard of such a thing!" said Nonna Adele. Nonna Polini was nonplussed: "New Year's Day? What has New Year's Day got to do with it? We are talking about Christmas dinner."

Slipping into his head-of-the-house role, Papi settled it. Christmas dinner in Romagna meant *cappelletti* in capon broth for the first course, and the boiled capon itself for the second. Moreover, because a holiday meal allowed one to indulge in an additional second course, we would have *pollo alla cacciatora,* using the rooster and some of the preserved tomatoes that Bajòn had brought us. As for the *cotechino,* we would have that on New Year's Day, together with lentils because they brought luck.

We started the preparations on the twenty-fourth. Papi twisted the capon's neck, and Nonna Polini, working deftly, if mostly by touch, plucked and singed it. To make the stuffing for the *cappelletti,* Mother sliced off a piece of the breast from the capon and sautéed it in a mixture of olive oil and *strutto.* Then she chopped it very fine, together with a fragrant piece of mortadella from Bologna that she struggled to keep me from pecking away at, and mixed it with fresh ricotta, eggs, grated Parmigiano, and nutmeg. According to the classic recipe, she should have included some veal, but we had none. Papi dipped his pinkie into the mixture and pronounced it perfect, save for an additional pinch of salt.

There was no question that Nonna Polini would roll out the pasta, as she had been doing for all but the first twelve of her ninety years. The slender pasta pin was nearly as long as she was tall, and she had to stand on a crate in order to reach the table. In minutes, her hands, moving as fluidly as the arms of a prima ballerina, had rolled out a transparent sheet of pasta nearly as large as a bedspread. She cut the sheet into squares, Mother dotted the squares with a thimbleful of stuffing, and Nonna Adele, Papi, and I folded and twisted the squares into *cappelletti*—dumplings in the shape of soft, peaked caps—working quickly before the pasta became dry and brittle. We spread kitchen towels on the mattress of a spare cot and lined up the dozens of *cappelletti* on them in neat rows to dry, making sure none of them touched; otherwise, by the following day, they would have been stuck together and the pasta would have torn when pulled apart.

The last thing to be prepared that day was dessert, Mother's wonderful bread pudding, with raisins and rum. Actually, there was no rum to be had then, so she put in some of Papi's homemade grappa.

Christmas morning was a morning such as we had doubted, during the last dark years on the lake, we could ever know again. Everyone was up early to complete preparations for the meal that was to be the only present any one of us would get. Mother had a surprise for Papi, however. She rose earlier than anyone else to bake a *ciambella*, the ring-shaped breakfast cake Nonna Polini had once taught her to make. It was Papi's, as it later became my husband's, favorite thing to have with a large morning coffee. To complete the gift, Mother also made custard cream, which Papi enthusiastically slathered over his slice of *ciambella*.

The capon was boiled with carrots, celery, onions, a potato, and two or three of the little tomatoes to produce the fragrant, ruddy broth for the *cappelletti*. Papi dispatched the rooster and Nonna Polini plucked and singed it as flawlessly as she had the capon. It went early into the pot so that it would have time to cook slowly through and through, until the meat came easily off the bone.

We sat down at noon, a full hour before our customary midday mealtime, because the tempting thoughts of what we were about to eat could not be resisted longer. After dinner, it was Papi who had gifts for us. He brought out little packets of hazelnuts and almonds, dried apricots, dates, and figs. They were rarities then, and they must have cost him a notable part of his ready cash, but he knew that without them, Christmas dinner at home would have been incomplete. He poured tumblers full of his own still very young and slightly fizzy Albana, a lusciously sweet, golden wine.

I listened to the elders reminisce about remarkable Christmases they had had. I listened wide-eyed and open-mouthed, it not having completely sunk in yet—and it took some years before I was capable of taking in the full sense of it—that I had just had the greatest Christmas I would ever know, the Christmas that had given me, through the recaptured flavors of our cooking, through the carefree sounds that had returned to my mother's and Papi's voices, through the comforting familiarity of the rooms I had grown up in, the one incomparable gift, the gift of life once imperiled and now regained.

Out of the University,
into Love and Marriage

1949-1955

"*Bocciata!*" ("Failed!") said Professor D'Ancona. I was at the University of Padua, trying for the third time to pass the two-year oral exam in zoology. If I didn't pass it, I could not submit the thesis for the *laurea*—a doctor's degree—in natural sciences on which I had already begun to work. I had studied diligently, I felt prepared, and I had finished giving a commandingly thorough exposition of the characteristics of sea anemones, jellyfish, and other members of a group of marine animals known as coelenterates. The examining professor had listened quietly—and approvingly, I had assumed— for the more than thirty minutes that I had spoken. "Failed! Why?" I exclaimed. "You have told me all there is to say about coelenterates," said D'Ancona. "Unfortunately, I had asked you to talk about ctenophorans." I had succumbed, overcome by nervousness, to a tendency to get names mixed up, a failing with which my husband, my friends, and my own students are well acquainted. "You bastard!" I wanted to cry. "Why didn't you stop me? Why didn't you ask if I had understood the question?" Ctenophora is a simpler group of marine animals, and I could even have tossed it off backward, had I been given the chance. In Italy, however, it is safer to doubt the ancestry of the head of the government than to question your professor's judgment. Had I remonstrated, it might have meant good-bye to any chance of getting a degree. So I rose; I said, *"Grazie, professore, buongiorno"*; and I held back the tears until I had left the room.

Padua was my third and next-to-last stop in my travels through the university system. I had started at the University of Milan, when we were living in the farmhouse on Lake Garda, but once we had left the lake, it was too far for me to commute, and staying in Milan would have been too expensive. I had briefly attended the University of Bologna, in my native Emilia-Romagna, when Zia Margò, Mother's sister, proposed that I go to stay with her in Venice and enroll in the University of Padua, a short train ride away. Her daughter Didi had just enrolled there and Margò was uneasy about her traveling alone. My parents urged me to accept, because had I stayed in Bologna, I would have had to find permanent lodgings in the city, which would have been a heavy load for their frail finances.

For reasons that I found difficult to fathom, I was not blessed with my aunt's esteem, and the welcome that I had expected to enjoy at her house became with time ever more reluctant. After my third disastrous attempt to pass the zoology exam, Margò opined that I might not be intellectually equal to the demands of university study, and that it might not be worth my while, or anyone else's, for me to continue. I don't back away from hard choices, and I have never been a quitter, but she got to me when my self-confidence had gone through the bottom. When I told my mother that I might abandon my studies, she dissuaded me, saying, "You know you have a good head, Marcella; ignore anyone who says otherwise. Put zoology out of your mind for a while, calm down, continue working on your thesis, prepare for some of the other exams you need to take, accumulate some good grades on your record, *then* get ready for zoology. You will do well, believe me."

The subject of my doctoral thesis had been suggested to me by a stimulating teacher, Professor Leonardi, whose course in paleontology I had taken and completed with an excellent grade. The purpose of the thesis was to determine whether a particular family of marine animals had existed on the slopes of a specific area in the Alps of Cadore, in the mountainous north of the Veneto, when, in an early geological age, those slopes had lain deep under the sea. To conduct my research, I had to climb nearly perpendicular rock walls and, wherever I found traces of fossils, knock off pieces of rock with a mallet and scalpel. I let the pieces drop to level ground, where, when I was finished, I would examine them, label them, and stow them in my knapsack. I was elated when I was able to collect enough suitable samples to make my sack bulge, but by the time I had walked with a sackful of rocks the three kilometers to the bus that would take me back where I was staying, elation had been replaced by aches in my legs and back. It is hard for me today, when a fifteen-minute stint on the treadmill leaves me gasping, to believe that once I could have been so agile and so strong.

I was well along on my thesis when Professor Leonardi informed me that he was joining the faculty at the University of Ferrara. He proposed that I follow him and complete the thesis there. The alternative was to get my degree in Padua, where I would have to start over on a different thesis with a different professor. I didn't waste even a minute thinking about doing that, but to transfer my credits to Ferrara I had to have the permission of Padua's dean of the faculty of natural sciences. The dean happened to be the same ogre who had failed me three times in zoology, and he made the permission to transfer conditional upon my passing the zoology exam with him. At my fourth and final appearance for the exam, I was so careful and so well-prepared, and the grades in all my other courses were high enough, that even that spiteful man could not flunk me. It was his prerogative, however, to give me as low a passing grade as he deemed appropriate, and he gave me the lowest one possible. As I thanked him and got up to leave he said, "Um, I see that Leonardi has given you top marks in paleontology. He must have a crush on you."

I was happy at last in Ferrara. I turned my back on Padua and Venice, on the trauma of three failed zoology exams and on Zia Margò, to live alone and unvexed in a town of my native Emilia-Romagna. The sound of Emilian speech, with its broad vowels; the

In Venice while I was living with
Zia Margò, June 1948

warm color of a familiar building material, brick; the homemade pasta; the incomparable salami: I was at home again, even though I had never before been to Ferrara. It is one of Italy's handsomest towns, strung out on splendid streets and circled in part by miles of ancient walls where I could take long walks. Serenity is palpable in Ferrara. Five hundred years ago, it even brought some peace into the turbulent life of Lucrezia Borgia when she came there to be its duchess. I was loath to leave it. I had no sooner taken the *laurea*—the doctor's degree in natural sciences—than I found I could apply most of those credits toward a degree in biology, which gave me a reason to continue working there. I produced a suitable thesis, and in 1954, with respect to Zia Margò, I was a *dottore* not once but twice.

I lived in a rented room in Ferrara while I was working toward my first degree, but as soon as I had passed the final exam and my thesis had been accepted, I returned to Cesenatico to look for work. As a new graduate with no previous experience, there wasn't very much available to me. I grabbed the first job I was offered, a position teaching mathematics and science at the *magistrali,* colleges that train students to become teachers at the elementary and high school levels. The school that had the opening was in Rimini, twelve miles south of Cesenatico. I had to take a train at seven thirty in the morning, which I boarded always at the last minute—more likely the last second—after a furious bicycle ride from home. There were mornings when I did not even stop to park and lock my bike. I just dropped it on the curb and flew to the train, knowing that my friend the stationmaster would pick it up and put it aside for me. It was so old and battered that there was little risk of anyone stealing it. My mother was convinced nearly every time that I couldn't possibly make it, and she stood for a little while at the top of the steps of our house expecting me to round the corner on the way back home. I never once missed that train, although I was breathless as I collapsed into my seat at nearly the identical moment that the locomotive was pulling away from the station.

Classes in Rimini broke at midday. I ate a *panino* on the train that took me to Ferrara, where I still had some laboratory work-shops to take and where I was working on the thesis for my degree in biology. In the evening, I caught another train, wolfed down an-other *panino,* and returned to Cesenatico, bicycling home from the station. My mother often waited for me with something warm to eat. I was rarely in bed before midnight. It felt good to be taking the first steps toward the career for which I had been studying since my teens, but the days were long and overfull. I was relieved when summer brought a pause. Into this routine and into my life, one summer evening, all the way from America, came Victor, the man who in less than two years would be my husband.

Victor was born in Cesena, a prosperous town eight miles inland from Cesenatico. The war had not yet started when his parents, who were Jewish, disposed of all their property and left for New York. It was the spring of 1939 and Victor was ten and a half. He had come back to Italy after fourteen years because, he said, he wanted to repair the torn connection to the places of his Italian childhood and stay in Italy to write.

A cousin of his, with whom I was slightly acquainted, brought Victor over one evening after dinner. It was the briefest of introductions on the steps of the house, because I was on my way to join some friends. He was very slight, with a mass of black, wavy hair, and in the dim light, he looked to me no older than fourteen. The following day, when, as we had arranged, we met in front of the hotel where he was staying, I was startled to find him wearing blue jeans and going barefoot. No one I knew wore jeans then, and no one went barefoot except on the beach. I took a closer look at him and added four more years to my earlier estimate of his age, but I was still seven years short.

We went on the first of many long walks and had the first of many long talks. I spoke of my studies and of my plans for a teaching career in the sciences. He was not impressed. To my dismay, he was brusquely dismissive of anyone wasting time on science when they could be spending it on literature and art. Literature was what he had hoped to major in, but a long illness had interrupted a college career that he never returned to. He had gone to work for his father, who had a fur business in New York, but it was not what he wanted to do; he wanted to write, and he wanted to live in Italy. I had never known anyone who talked the way he did. Italians take an emphatic yet circuitous approach to conversation, spilling words in torrents, frequently changing direction, compensating for likely moments of inattention on the part of their listener by repeating everything three times, avoiding anything resembling a conclusion because it might bring the discourse to a premature end. Victor spoke quietly, deliberately, in spare but complete sentences that were often discomfiting in their directness.

As friendship grew and affection developed, I was bewildered to find that what Victor most wanted to talk about was food. Aside from our obsessive concern with food during the war, or perhaps because of it, I never gave it any thought. I accepted the pleasure that mealtimes at home always brought as a naturally recurring part of daily life. And if circumstances obliged me to have a *panino* stuffed with mortadella or prosciutto as my lunch or dinner, I didn't feel the least bit deprived. Victor, on the other hand, would add to an appreciative description of everything he'd just had for lunch anticipations of what might be available at dinner and declarations on what he'd like to have for lunch the following day. He was powerfully drawn to the seafood of the Romagna coast, whose flavors, during the years he was growing up in America, had survived as a haunting taste memory of his childhood in Italy. He loved the lobsterlike scampi; he adored the small, nutty soles; he smacked his lips over the magnificent flesh of our *rombo*, turbot; he doted on *coda di rospo*, monkfish; he learned to eat the spratlike *saraghine col bacio*, pursing his lips as with a kiss; but what he really lost his head over were the sweet and tender *calamaretti fritti*, fried whole fresh squid, no bigger than a child's pinkie from the end of the tentacles to the tip of the sac.

It was through *calamaretti* that Victor revealed an aspect of his

Summer 1952. In Cesenatico with Victor shortly after we had met

My first evening out with Victor, at Cesenatico's Grand Hotel, 1952

singular style. One afternoon, we had been sitting on the rocks of the pier at the mouth of Cesenatico's harbor canal, watching the fishing boats coming in after their night at sea. The sight of the men pulling up fish from the hold to load it into crates for the market, and the spiced scent of the freshly caught fish, stirred in Victor an irresistible longing, notwithstanding it hadn't been more than two hours since he'd had a substantial lunch. "I have to have a plate of fried *calamaretti*," he said. "Now?" "Yes, now, *adesso*, right away," he answered. "But," I pointed out, "it's the middle of the afternoon, the restaurant isn't even open, this is Italy, they don't start serving until eight." "Oh, there is always someone in the kitchen," he said. We walked back to his hotel and sat in the empty dining room until a shirt-sleeved waiter, who was setting up tables for that evening's dinner, came over to ask what we wanted. "Some *calamaretti fritti*, please," said Victor sweetly. The man had just enough self-possession not to let his mouth drop open, but his eyebrows rose and his eyes widened. He said that he would find out what could be done and shuffled off to the kitchen. In not too long, a steaming platter of freshly fried *calamaretti* was on the table.

Many similar exploits, not necessarily limited to restaurants, have taken place throughout our lives, wherever we have been throughout the world. It is not through pushiness, or flattery, or cajolery, or guile that Victor is so successful at pursuing the seemingly unobtainable. What works the spell is that open, candid, direct gaze of his, a disarming smile, and the solid conviction that what he is asking for cannot possibly be a problem for others to give. I passed on to him one of my grandfather Riccardo's favorite sayings, which Victor has since made his own: "Do you know why frogs don't have a tail? Because they didn't ask for it."

Victor imagines himself to be an innocent, but he is not above a little slyness. He was leaving to go to Venice as the guest of someone he had met on the *Andrea Doria,* the ill-fated Italian liner on which he had sailed to Europe. On its return across the Atlantic, the beautiful new ship would collide with a freighter and sink off the Long Island coast. "I am going to my room to pack," Victor said. "Would you like to come and help me?" I went, expecting indeed to be helpful. When I saw how neatly he was folding his shirts, so immaculately that they could have just come out of the shop, and packing a miscellaneous assortment of personal articles, both small and big, thin and bulky, long and short, soft and hard, transforming them into deftly organized flat layers, leaving no hollows, no gaping spaces, I understood that what he wanted me there for was not help, but admiration. It was a seemingly insignificant episode, but one that opened a window into the character of a man who had begun to fascinate me. I learned how important it was for him to be appreciated, although, as I kept learning, he never called attention to his work or his skills, never advertised his accomplishments, never indulged in the slightest bit of self-praise. It was, moreover, my first opportunity to discover how agile his hands were, as agile as his mind.

When Victor left Venice he came back to Cesenatico, returning to me, I was happy to feel. The problem of his finances had since grown large. He had not yet negotiated an allowance from his parents, who were distressed that he hadn't returned. Fortunately, Italy was astonishingly cheap at the time, and Victor still had some of the money he had saved for the trip, as well as the money he had gotten by cashing in his return trip ticket to the States. There wasn't enough, however, for him to continue staying at Pino, the restaurant-hotel where he had been boarding. Our house had three small apartments that we rented out for the summer. Summer was over, the apartments were empty, and my mother suggested that Victor could stay there at no cost until he found a solution that allowed him to live in Italy. He would, in any event, have to leave as soon as it grew colder, because the apartment had no heat.

It became a very pleasant, however temporary, arrangement. Victor was extraordinarily kind and thoughtful toward my parents. He loved my mother's cooking. One of his favorites was a veal dish of hers that she called *messicani*. They were little veal roll-ups, stuffed with pancetta and grated Parmigiano, sautéed and served with a fresh, light tomato sauce. He also loved Papi's wines, his Sangiovese and particularly his Albana. Albana is a delicately sweet wine, which anyone reading this might think is not appropriate to drink with food. Yet, not so far back in history, all wine was sweet, and discriminating palates found it quite congenial with all manner of food. So did Victor. He found it so congenial, in fact, that one time, having drunk a pitcherful of it, he rose abruptly from the table after lunch and said he had to take a walk to clear his head. When he didn't return after a few hours, I went to look for him. I was walking along the pier of the main canal where the fishing boats dock when one of the fishermen called to me. "*Signorina?* If you are looking for the American, he is sleeping right there." He had climbed onto the deck of one of the anchored boats and was sleeping off the Albana, curled over a pile of nets.

Victor's parents had been hoping he would change his mind and come back to New York, but he persuaded them that he was serious about staying in Italy to write. He obtained a small allowance from them and began to look for a cheap place to live. Old friends of his parents from before the war, the Lippas, who lived in Bologna, had a wine farm on a beautiful hill called Bertinoro. It was near enough to Cesenatico that from its peak, looking east on a very clear day, you could detect a deep blue line at the horizon's edge, a slice of the Adriatic sea. Mrs. Lippa told Victor that there was an extra room at her farm in the caretaker's house, and he could stay there indefinitely. She cautioned him, however, that the facilities were primitive. There was no electricity, only kerosene lamps; no running water—it had to be pumped up ice-cold from the well; and no heat, just wood-burning terra-cotta stoves. Victor was delighted. "I always wanted to live in the eighteenth century," he said.

He never did get to do any writing in Bertinoro. He slipped immediately into the leisurely life of the country squire, walking in the woods, reading, observing the winemaking operation that was taking place that fall, and consuming the excellent meals that the caretaker's wife cooked. He was also moved to try his own hand at cooking. He bought a copy of Ada Boni's *Il Talismano della Felicità*, the cookbook that became my first reference when, shortly after we were married, we moved to New York and I began to cook. Like many novices, he was drawn to intricate productions, which he invited me up to Bertinoro to try.

Having seen large snails in the vineyard, he was inspired to try an Ada Boni recipe for them, Snails Roman Style with Anchovies and Tomatoes. The first step, once you have collected the snails, requires you to starve the poor animals; in the second, you must persuade them to abandon the protection of their shells by heating them up in a pan of water; several other elaborate rinsing and cooking procedures fol-low. They may well have been delicious, but I can't really remember the taste and I have never had them that way again.

Another of Victor's elaborate productions out of his Ada Boni was Sweetbreads with Fresh Wild Mushrooms. Following instruc-tions, he first soaked the sweetbreads in several changes of lukewarm water to bleed them white; he then blanched them for a few minutes in simmering water so that he could subsequently more easily peel away the membrane that enclosed them; he sautéed them with but-ter, chopped onions, and prosciutto, and simmered them in broth that he had made with veal bones and meat scraps the butcher had given him; when they were done, he removed and sliced the sweetbreads, boiled down the remaining broth, deglazed the pan with Marsala, and poured the pan juices over the meat. The fresh porcini mushrooms he made separately, cooked in olive oil with garlic and parsley. It took longer than he had surmised, turning into something between a very late lunch and an early dinner, but it was worth waiting for, a delectable concoction that I would love to make myself today, if only I could find fresh sweetbreads in my Florida markets.

Victor came frequently down the hill to Cesenatico. Once he climbed out of a taxi that overflowed with dahlias. He explained that he had found a woman selling them by the roadside and he had bought all she had. We took lovely walks in the boulevards of Cesenatico, which in the off-season we had all to ourselves. He held me close to him and would frequently stop to kiss me, a very unconventional thing to do then in a provincial Italian town, and illegal to boot. The newspapers would publish reports of kissing couples being stopped and fined. But it felt wonderful, and I didn't care.

A letter came from New York. "Your father is sick," his mother wrote. "Please come home." His father had pneumonia. Victor packed and left, promising he would be back. I had hoped we would have our first Christmas together that year, but I spent it instead pushing ahead on the work for my second degree, the one in biology. In the spring, when Victor returned, he went to Florence. He had visited there the previous year and thought it would be the most promising place to settle down and write. He traveled by train from Paris, carrying with him in the compartment six boxes of books and a tall painting, a nude self-portrait that a woman friend had brought to the boat for him when he sailed from New York. When the train crossed the border into Italy, the customs inspector asked Victor what he was carrying in those boxes. "Books," he said. "Books? Please let me see them." The inspector pulled some out at random and began carefully riffling the pages, finding it hard to believe that they were not concealing contra-

band. Why else would someone travel in a crowded railway compartment with six heavy boxes of books?

He had found an unfurnished apartment in a villa that had once
been part of a princely estate. Most of the land had been sold off
and several apartments had been carved out of the villa. The glory
of its position, however, remained undimmed; it was ensconced on
a hill bristling with olive trees from whose height Victor enjoyed an
unobstructed, if distant, view of Florence and its silvery river, the
Arno. Victor settled in, hoping for an indefinite stay. This was the first
place of his own, the first time he could indulge his penchant for interior design. Prophetically, he focused most of his attention on the
kitchen. It was a large and handsome but naked space, equipped only
with a raised fireplace for cooking and heating. Victor created a pantry by closing off a corner of the room with an L-shaped wooden
partition, the upper half of it mostly glass. He had had the raw
wood stained a deep chestnut color, to match the old wooden beams
overhead. Happily for Victor, labor and materials were inexpensive
then in Italy. Inside the pantry he put an icebox he had bought, and
he had craggy-looking wooden shelves made for open storage. He
hung his pots, battered secondhand copper that he'd had retinned,
on one wall. In the summer he had bought a couple of bushels of
small, round tomatoes on the vine for making sauce, and he had
hung them from the beams, giving the pantry an immensely cheerful look and providing, moreover, a ready supply of tomatoes well
into the winter. For the dining table, Victor took a thick, old door
he had found and had his accommodating, if startled, carpenter
make legs from four narrow tree trunks that Victor left gnarled and
unfinished. They were set at diverging angles in the center, forming
a pedestal that went right through four holes made in the tabletop.
Wood putty and glue filled in the gaps, and the ends of the trunks
were planed flush with the top. At that time in Florence, one could

buy unfinished, rustic wood chairs with straw seats that looked as though they had been lifted out of a van Gogh painting. Victor made the similarity even more striking by painting them yellow.

The villa's impoverished owners had a housekeeper, Assunta, a tall, hungry-looking, perpetually black-frocked woman with glowing, dark eyes and the largest feet I have ever seen on man or woman. When Victor asked her if she had time to look after the apartment for him, her face shone as though she had just been awakened from a long bad dream by the handsome young prince. It turned out she was rarely paid and infrequently fed. In exchange for a small regular monthly stipend and an occasional shirt she stole for her husband, Pasquale, Assunta did everything for Victor: cook, wash, iron, gather firewood for the kitchen fireplace and the terra-cotta stoves that heated the apartment, and in season, bring in for breakfast every morning fresh, ripe figs from the few trees remaining in the orchard. And she made wonderful beans.

Unlike many Tuscan cooks, Assunta didn't cook the beans in a fiasco, the traditional glass. She had an old cast-iron pot into which she dropped several handfuls of fresh cannellini beans, which she covered with olive oil and water, adding salt, pepper, garlic, and sage. She laid a thick, damp cloth over the pot, put a lid on it, and cooked the beans for two hours or more over hot embers from a wood fire.

Victor didn't get to do any writing in Florence either. He slipped into the country squire mode again, hiking the woods with Assunta's husband, Pasquale, a small, hard-muscled, sun-blackened man, the skin of whose hands looked like bruised and twisted cowhide. Together they foraged for mushrooms and thin, wild asparagus. In the fall, Pasquale introduced Victor to the ancient practice of crushing grapes with the feet, the softest of all grape-crushing methods. It was the Sangiovese grape that Pasquale made into a wine that, if commercially bottled today, might be labeled Chianti, but it had a fresher wine taste than any Chianti that you are likely to buy. It was the only wine that Victor had on the table then. When he and I speak of our meals at the villa, and recall that pure purple wine, our palates stir to the memory of its bracing quickness, of its sweet scent of iris, of its ripe taste of plums and cherries.

It was no longer so simple to see each other as it had been when Victor was staying in Bertinoro. It was a laborious journey from that Florentine hilltop to Cesenatico. To reach Vicchio, the nearest hamlet, where he could hop on a tram for Florence, Victor had to walk a mile down a very steep road, so steep that taxis refused to drive up to the villa. In Florence, he took a bus that crossed the mountains separating Tuscany from Romagna and that stopped, after a four-hour journey, in Cesenatico. On weekdays, I was still teaching in Rimini in the morning and taking the train to Ferrara in the afternoon. Occasionally, Victor joined me in Rimini on a Friday, keeping me company on the train to Ferrara and then back to Cesenatico, where he stayed with us for the weekend before returning to Florence. The distance to Ferrara could not have been more than fifty or sixty miles, but the only train that negotiated that route was a local one that stopped at every little station, so we spent at least three hours traveling each way.

My mother allowed me to visit Victor, a rather broad-minded concession for those times. He would come to meet me in Florence, where we sometimes stopped for dinner, and then we'd share the tram ride and the steep walk up to the villa. It was there that we had our first Christmas together. It was also the first Christmas tree for either of us, the first of the fifty-three consecutive ones that followed. Victor's parents were observant Jews who did not celebrate Christmas. My Catholic family did, but in Italy then, the tree was not a traditional part of the holiday. Nor did children expect gifts from that Protestant gentleman, Santa Claus. If they had been good, they got theirs on Epiphany, the gift-bearing day of the three wise men, the sixth of January. With Pasquale's help, Victor brought in a tree that he had cut down in the woods. He could get the ornaments for it in Florence because there were customers for them among English and American residents. It was on Christmas Eve that, for the first time in my life, I drank enough wine to get pickled. I remember how hilarious we thought it was that the coffee pot we had forgotten on the fire overheated and flew across the room with a resounding clap.

Shortly before the Christmas break, I was in Ferrara to present the thesis for my biology degree. There were printed copies, of course, but I had to present it orally, discussing it with a panel of professors who looked as glum as that dull December morning. When I had finished my presentation and had replied to all the questions they had posed to me, they asked me to step out into the hall and wait to be called back into the room after they had come to a decision. I left the exam room, but I didn't wander too far from the door, because I didn't want to miss the call when it came. Other students, who were there waiting for their turn, crowded around me to ask what the examining panel was like. If all went well, this was to be my last day at the university, and my heart was pounding from the excitement. Down at the end of the hall I spied Victor standing still with a huge bouquet of roses in his hand, which gave my heart an additional flutter. I was about to wave to him when I was called into the examination room. The head of the panel addressed me as *"Dottore in Scienze Biologiche,"* which meant they had accepted my thesis, to which they awarded an excellent grade.

Overjoyed, I rushed out into the hall to look for Victor. He was no longer there. I ran down the steps hoping to find him at the building's entrance, but he wasn't there either. What I did find was the bouquet of roses, all mashed up in a trash bin. I sat down on the steps sobbing, unable to understand what might have happened. When I felt calm enough to face him, I went to the hotel where he was staying. I found him sitting at the café; his eyes, which I was used to seeing sparkling like sunlight, were ice-cold with anger. I approached him with more terror in my heart than I had felt when standing before the panel examining my thesis. "What have I done wrong?" I asked. "If you don't know there is no point my explaining," he said, a phrase I was to hear many times during the fifty-three years that followed.

Quietly I began to tell him about my freshly awarded degree, about my presentation and the panel's questions, about having to step outside to wait for their call, about my return into the examination room, about my rushing out to give him the news but finding in his place the battered roses. I saw the brightness returning to his eyes as he once again began to look at me with tenderness.

He explained that when I had stepped out of the room the first time, he thought I was finished and that, even though I had seen him, I had preferred to stop and chat with the other students. Every time I think back to the day on which I obtained my second degree and left the university, I remember how, in a short time, I experienced great joy, followed by despair, followed by relief and contentment.

After New Year's, we were at table in Cesenatico when Victor announced that he was going to marry me and that he wished we could have the wedding later that week, if possible. He was very matter-of-fact, as though he were calling off the time of day. Papi choked on something he had been about to swallow and started to cough violently. I couldn't speak, but as Victor put his arm around me, I thought I might be dreaming. As soon as Papi collected himself, he said, "You can't do that so quickly in Italy. You must publish the banns, and only three weeks after that you can marry." With a twinkle in his eyes, Victor looked at me and said, "We can wait, can't we?"

His parents were violently opposed. They were Sephardic Jews whose ancestors had lived in Spain until, in 1492, Queen Isabella expelled all the Jews whom the Inquisition had failed to convert to Catholicism. The Sephardim, as they were called, settled in the countries of the Mediterranean basin, in the Balkans, in Greece and Turkey, in North Africa. They were an extremely clannish group, speaking and writing, as Victor's parents still did, the fifteenth-century Spanish of their ancestors, mingled with a few words borrowed from the languages of the countries to which they had repaired. Not only did they not marry outside their group—to them the Yiddish-speaking central European Jews were another race— they often didn't even marry outside the family. Victor's maternal grandmother was the sister of his paternal grandfather, which made his mother and father first cousins.

Victor's father flew to Italy to persuade Victor to change his plans. Unsuccessful at that, he tried to convince my parents that it was an ill-considered match, that Victor would be incapable of supporting himself and his wife, and that in their daughter's best interest, they should withhold their consent. Having failed at that too, he flew back to New York and broke off with his son. We were married the following month, on the twenty-fourth of February.

We had a civil wedding at City Hall, with two old friends of mine, Gianni and Marcello, as witnesses. They were also the only guests at the simple wedding lunch Mother had prepared: tortellini in capon broth, followed by both the capon, which Victor skipped because he doesn't like fowl of any kind, and a platter of *messicani*, Victor's favorite veal roll-ups. A local baker provided the pastries.

Immediately after the wedding, we went to Tuscany, spending our last night in the place where we had taken large draughts of love and beauty. In the morning, we packed Victor's things, the antique furniture and lamps he had collected, his copper pots, his books, his nude painting, and a *damigiana*—a twelve-gallon straw-covered glass container—of Pasquale's wine, and shipped them to Cesenatico. Victor no longer had an allowance and had little immediate hope of getting a work permit and a job; I had been earning just enough in Rimini for my train fare and *panini*; and Papi, long since retired, was eking out a scanty income from the small farm and the summer rentals. Our financial outlook at that moment was, if not ominous, at least unpromising.

We used a small gift of cash from Papi for the briefest of honeymoons. We spent a single winter night in Sirmione, a narrow peninsula at the southern end of Lake Garda, a tonguelike extension of land impudently stuck into the underbelly of the huge lake. Sirmione has long since been devastated by tourism and the cheap shops and souvenir stalls that thrive on it, but it was deserted that February, a beautiful and romantic place. In the morning, we clambered over the ruins of a Roman bath, past a grove of olive trees planted before the birth of Christ, to reach the lake's icy edge, our exhalations dissolving in the wintry mist as we gaily chucked stones to see who could send them bouncing farthest over the water.

On the evening of our arrival, we had leek and potato soup, which I have made many times since, partly for the nostalgia, partly for the invariably comforting taste. On that cold February night, in the poorly heated dining room of a modest hotel, when we were exhausted from the long trip to Tuscany, when our hearts and backs ached from the dismantling of a place we loved and the melancholy labor of packing, when we were astonished at what we had done and baffled by what might befall us, that steaming soup, so earthy yet so gentle, seemed to us miraculously reassuring. To this day, Victor recalls it with almost more warmth than anything else that took place during our stay.

On to the New World

1955–1962

Six and a half months after my wedding day, I was on the S.S. *Cristoforo Colombo*, traveling to America by myself. It was a warm and hazy September day when the great ship sailed up the Hudson, and I remember thinking, "What if Victor isn't there when I disembark?" I was about to land, for the first time, in an immense country of whose language I neither spoke nor understood a single word, and of whose millions of inhabitants I knew only one, my young husband. Ten days earlier, in Genoa, I had been leaning against the railing of the liner, waving good-bye to my mother. She was smiling bravely as she waved back from the pier, although the previous evening she had wept as she wondered whether she would ever see me again. Papi had stayed in Cesenatico. He could not face seeing me off on the boat that was taking me to America, presumably for good.

Victor's parents had broken off all contact with him when we married, but after a few weeks they began to correspond, and by early summer Victor had flown back to New York to work again in his father's fur business on Fifty-seventh Street, in Manhattan. I had

My mother, in the white blouse, standing at the rear, waving good-bye to me on the S.S. *Cristoforo Colombo*, about to sail for New York, September 1955

stayed behind in Cesenatico until summer's end, drawing close to my parents, who were bewildered by the changes in my life and fearful that the ocean that would soon separate us would forever thereafter keep us apart. It was not yet the age of jet travel, of cheap flights, of direct dialing, of global television. I was going to New York, but in their hearts, it could just as well have been to another planet.

Victor was on the pier, alone. It would be quite a while before his parents could overcome some of the hostility that my marrying their son had generated and bring themselves to see me. When I had gone through immigration, collected my bags, and cleared customs, we climbed into a taxi that took us to an address in Forest Hills. All I knew about Forest Hills was that we were going to live in an apart-

ment that my in-laws had taken when they came to America shortly
before the Second World War, the same apartment that Victor had
grown up in and lived in until he left for college. His parents had
moved to Manhattan while he was in Italy, but the prewar, rent-
controlled place in Forest Hills cost so little that they continued to
hold on to it.

The taxi drove across Manhattan, going east on Fifty-seventh
Street, as Victor had asked, so that I could get a quick look at the
windows of his family's store. By the time we were on the Fifty-ninth
Street Bridge, I was in awe of the huge city, of the two majestic riv-
ers that embraced it, of the height of its buildings, of the waves of
cars that flowed down the boulevards, of the crowds thronging the
vast sidewalks. I had never seen anything like it. "Could I be dreaming?" I thought. When the driver came off the bridge, he took a road
with several lanes of cars that Victor said was called Queens Boule-

With some of the other passengers on the boat for New York. I am the second
from the right in the second row.

vard. "Have we come to another city?" I asked. "Oh, no, we have left Manhattan, but we are still in New York. This is called Queens."

The apartment was on the fifth floor of a six-story brick box of a building that was completely innocent of any architectural aspirations. When I stepped into the elevator, I felt seized for the first time by the suffocating grip of claustrophobia, which I have since experienced every time an elevator's doors close in before me. My in-laws had left very little furniture in the apartment. There was a large bed and Victor's old bookcase, painted green. There were two items that were new to me: a television set, and in the kitchen, a large refrigerator. We had never had a refrigerator at home. We had an icebox that, in warm months, we kept cold with the blocks of ice we bought from the iceman who came around once a week. In the winter, we kept a box made of wire netting outside a north window. The television was to become my private tutor, tuning my ear to the sound of English.

More than fifty years after that time, I can feel the anxiety in my breast stirring again as I recall how I found myself cut off from everyone who had inhabited my world up to then, my parents, my friends, my colleagues and students at school, our neighbors, the shopkeepers of our town, our chatty mailman. Except for my husband, who was away at work the whole day, every day but Sunday, in this new world of mine I knew no one and could speak to no one. If I had taken a vow of silence, my lips could not have been

With Victor, shortly after arriving in New York

more buttoned up. It was a world whose newspapers I couldn't read, a world where the look of the streets, of the buildings, and of the people was different from any I had known, a world of an unending procession of cars and not one person on a bicycle!

Victor would dream up errands for me so that I could become used to going out alone. He had shown me where the newsstand was, and on a Sunday morning, he suggested I go there and buy a copy of the *Times*. On the way over, I saw a man holding what seemed to me to be a large bundle of newspapers. "What luck," I thought. "I no longer have to go all the way to the newsstand." I approached the man, pointing to the papers he was holding, offering him money, and saying, as clearly and confidently as I could, "Please, *New York Times*?" He looked at me, dumbfounded at first, and then irritated. I didn't understand what he said, but he held on to his papers and pointed in the general direction of the newsstand that I had originally been headed for. How was I to know that the *Times* needed scores of pages to print the news? The Sunday edition of our local paper, *Il Resto del Carlino*, was just twelve pages, doubled on Monday with the addition of the sports section.

The paramount problem quickly became that of satisfactorily feeding my husband and myself. We could not afford to eat out, and those first occasions when we tried it were not successful. Victor had taken me to a coffee shop where he ordered what he called the national dish, hamburger. He poured some red sauce from a bottle over it and encouraged me to try it. "It's called ketchup," he said, "and it's tasty." I was not prepared for its cloying flavor and I found it inedible. (That sweet taste over meat was an experience that I would be subjected to again, bringing me grief at my first Thanksgiving dinner.) The coffee tasted as though I had been served the water used to clean out the pot. I thought to console myself with dessert. I was able to figure out what the words "coffee cake" on the board meant, and that was what I ordered. It was stupefyingly sweet and loaded with cinnamon, which I loathe, yet with not the slightest trace of coffee flavor. "This must be a mistake," I said to Victor, "there isn't any coffee in here." "Oh, it's only called a coffee cake because it is served with coffee." To this day, I am mystified. A chocolate cake has chocolate, an almond tart has almonds, an apple pie has apples; why doesn't a coffee cake have coffee?

I had never cooked anything, save for the mush I made for our pig during the war, and I couldn't negotiate the purchase of ingredients from the greengrocer and the butcher and the other food shops in Forest Hills, because I didn't speak English. To overcome my lack of kitchen experience, Victor pulled out for me his old copy of Ada Boni. To mitigate my language handicap, he introduced me to the Grand Union, a supermarket that was just around the corner from our building. I had heard descriptions of American supermarkets, but I had never seen one. At home, we bought our fruit and vegetables from the *verduraio*, the greengrocer—or the *frutarol*, as he is known in Venice—and the fish from a *pescivendolo*, a fishmonger. Their place of business may not have been anything more permanent than a market stall, and sometimes something even more mobile, as when a woman would pedal past the houses hawking, out of the baskets on her bicycle, the produce and fresh cheese from her farm or the fish her husband had caught. For meat, we went to the *macellaio*, for milk and cheese to the *lattaio*, for dry goods to the *droghiere*. We didn't just buy something; we had a conversation about it. At the Grand Union, it was all replaced by display shelves and refrigerated counters, with produce and meats already measured out in plastic-wrapped portions. Fortunately for me then, no conversation was necessary or expected. I had not been acquainted with frozen foods, and these left a disquieting impression that stayed with me when, nearly twenty years later, in my first cookbook, I described deep-freeze lockers that looked to me like "cemeteries of food, whose contents are sealed up in waxed boxes marked, like some tombstones, with photographs of the departed."

Not only did I not know how to cook, I had no idea what to cook. To look for ideas, I began to turn the pages of my Ada Boni. As I did so, I was awakened by sensations from another time and other places. I saw, I smelled, I tasted dishes that, until recently, had been commonplace in my life. When I read some of the instructions I said, "I understand that. Yes, sure, I remember, that is the way my mother used to do it, or Nonna Adele, or Nonna Polini, or Papi, or Anna, Lucia, Marta, Bruna, Giovanna, any one of the succession of farm girls who, from time to time, used to clean and cook for us. I think I can do it too!" You do talk to yourself when you have no one else to talk to. It was true, though; I knew that I could do it. My taste memories were being released, and attached to them, mysteriously, was an intuitive understanding of how to produce those tastes. Cooking came to me as though it had been there all along, waiting to be expressed; it came as words come to a child when it is time for her to speak.

Soup was one of the first things I started to cook, and remembering the one that we had so enjoyed on our honeymoon, my first soup was potatoes and leeks. I also made cannellini-and-parsley soup, one of the two irresistible soups that Papi used to make. The other was his masterly fish soup. Both are now in *Essentials of Classic Italian Cooking*. And I produced many a minestrone. Our dining table was an old bridge table whose top sagged precipitously in the middle so that I could never fill more than a portion of the soup bowl at a time. We had to have multiple servings of soup, which I chose to attribute to the merits of my cooking rather than to the shortcomings of the furniture.

I soon discovered a natural inclination for frying. I learned to make *pastella,* a light flour-and-water batter that produces the crispest and freshest-tasting of crusts on virtually any vegetable. Sliced zucchini fried in that batter has forever been one of our favorites, and our son once got a job as chef at an Italian restaurant in Portland, Oregon, on the strength of a platter of those zucchini. I tried frying soles because we did that often in Cesenatico, using our incomparable, small local soles. I wasn't too successful because the flesh of the sole from Long Island was too flaky. I also made Milanese-style breaded veal cutlets. I once served them with a side of peas sautéed in butter with diced ham. I used peas from a can because they were tiny and beautiful. At that time, canned vegetables were already salted, but not having read the label, I didn't know it, and I added lots more salt. The peas were inedible, my first failure. Victor doesn't eat chicken, or I would have cooked it often. I sometimes made it for myself, when I was alone, because I adore it, but I had to wait for our son to come along before I could put it on the family table.

Whenever I produced a dish for the first time, Victor and I lifted a bite to our mouths circumspectly, even apprehensively, but with ever more rare exceptions, the taste was satisfying, and apprehension gave way to celebration. Our conversation was largely about what we were eating. I described how I made each dish; my husband complimented me on the ones that were successful and consoled me when they were not. When my efforts proved to be especially triumphant, he would leap out of his chair and throw his arms around me.

After Victor left in the morning, the days were long and lonely, and often I felt desperate, but when he returned and it was time for dinner, my culinary achievements were greeted with encouragement so tender, and the food I had cooked brought us so much joy, that as I think back on that time, daunting though it had been, I am nonetheless filled with happiness.

I had never before taken any interest in professional sports, but that first autumn in New York, I became a baseball fan. To be specific, I became a Brooklyn Dodgers fan, and there could not have been a better year to be one than 1955, when they became the champions, beating the Yankees in seven World Series games. Victor was distressed over the long hours I was spending at home by myself and kept looking for anything that would keep me occupied and make me feel less lonely. "Have you ever seen a baseball game?" he asked. "No." "There are some very exciting games going on right now, with a team from Brooklyn that may win the championship. If I explain how baseball works, will you watch it?" "Sure," I said. He drew a baseball diamond on the top of a white shoebox to help me understand the different positions while he explained the structure of the game. Soon, I had learned the meaning of "pitcher," "batter," "ball," "strike," "hit," "walk," "out," "home run," and many other terms. The vocabulary of baseball instantly became the largest part of my English vocabulary. I even learned the names of the Dodger players, a startling accomplishment for someone who never remembers names. Duke Snider, Gil Hodges, Pee Wee Reese, Jackie Robinson, Roy Campanella—I loved them all, but my favorite was Carl Furillo, in part, no doubt, because he was Italian, but also because he made such beautiful, timely hits and such amazing throws from the outfield.

On the *Cristoforo Colombo*, I had shared a cabin with a svelte, black-haired young woman from Rome who had taken a doctor's degree in chemistry. Luli was on her way to Charlottesville, Virginia, with a grant from one of the tobacco companies to work at the University of Virginia on a research project involving nicotine. Unlike me, she spoke English fluently. She was spirited, straightforward, outgoing, well read, altogether *molto simpatica*, very likeable, and we quickly became friends. Before parting, I gave her our address in Forest Hills and our phone number, and we agreed that as soon as she could come up to New York she would visit us. To prepare for her coming, Victor bought an army cot that we put into what had been his room when he had lived there with his parents.

Luli stayed with us for a long weekend in October, and she and I probably talked the entire time that we were awake. She described Charlottesville as a charming town and the people she had met there as warm and hospitable. She had spoken about me to a couple she had met at the university, saying she was hoping she could get me to come down to stay with her for a few days. They suggested that I come down for Thanksgiving so that I could experience my first Thanksgiving dinner; they would invite both of us, and on that same morning, we could witness a foxhunt that they were hosting.

Victor laid out all the reasons why I should go: Thanksgiving was a unique American family celebration, and this would be a fine opportunity for me to become acquainted with it; I would again be enjoying Luli's company, escaping for a while the silence and loneliness of Forest Hills; I would get to see a beautiful part of America; and perhaps I would begin to make some headway in my effort to learn English. "But how will you manage so many days by yourself?" I asked. "I do not mind at all to be by myself, but when my parents find out that you are going away, they will take advantage of the opportunity to have me over for dinner." "Well," I thought to myself, "perhaps that will begin to make a few cracks in the wall of ice between us."

On the Wednesday before Thanksgiving, Victor put me on a bus for Charlottesville. He was smiling and relaxed, trying to make me feel at ease. "You have nothing to worry about," he said. "Luli will be at the bus stop when you arrive, and you'll find me here when you get back." I could hardly believe that I was doing this, but Victor was so reassuring that I just let it happen. It didn't take too long, however, after the bus pulled away, for my usual apprehensions to break to the surface. What if I didn't find Luli at the bus stop? What if the bus was seriously delayed? How would I get word to her? What if, during the long trip to Virginia, I felt ill or needed some help? How would I make myself understood? In any undertaking, my thoughts always turn to what could go wrong. I try to check that inclination by reminding myself of another of the sayings that Victor picked up in Italy and is wont to use: *"Non ti fasciare la testa prima di essertela rotta"*—don't bandage up your head before you break it.

My dire expectations to the contrary, everything went smoothly. I stepped off the bus into a warm embrace from Luli. The following morning we went to see the hunters off after the fox. It was so beautiful. The horse is my favorite animal, and they were magnificent, as were their riders in scarlet jackets and black caps. Everything shone in the sharp light of a cool November morning. The vast lawns were a deep green. I had never seen such lawns. To the country eyes of an Italian girl, it seemed incredible that there could be so much good land without anything edible growing on it. Someone blew a horn. The dogs were irrepressible in their excitement, and mine, although manifested differently, was no feebler than theirs. I felt that I was living in a fable.

Thanksgiving dinner was at two, and we showed up punctually at that time. I had had nothing since early morning but a few sips of terrible instant coffee in Luli's apartment, and I was achingly hungry. I was eagerly anticipating the arrival of the huge turkey that Luli had explained would be the centerpiece of the dinner. The house was festive: There was a fire going, a beautifully decorated table at one side, and many people standing, milling around. I was offered a drink, which I declined. It's no secret that I enjoy a whiskey or two after dinner, but never on an empty stomach. Mine was worse than empty, it was cavernous. From time to time, little nibbles were passed around, but they made no impression on that ever-larger hollow in my middle.

So much time was going by that I was becoming light-headed. No one was sitting down. People would kindly come up to me and try to make conversation, but all I could do was smile. I never smiled so much as I did in the two bewildering hours it took before a monumental turkey was brought out and set on the table. The host, who must have become aware of my befuddlement, and probably of my lame arm, picked up a plate, came over to me, and offered to serve me. I understood the gesture, if not the words; I flashed a smile once more, and I think I said thank you, although it may have been *"grazie."* He cut two magnificent, steaming slices for me and spooned a bright red sauce over them. I thought it was a kind of *peperonata,* the sauce made from red peppers and caramelized onions that we sometimes dollop onto meat. He also put on the plate a long potato, whose orange flesh startled me when I cut it later, and some other vegetables. I took a place at one of the small tables that were scattered around the room and lost no time in propelling a piece of sauce-laden turkey into my mouth. I had to draw deeply from my diminishing reserves of self-control to refrain from spitting it out. There it was again, that cloying, sweet taste laid over meat, jarring and alien. I have since learned to use a touch of ketchup on hamburger, but I have never been able to make my peace with cranberry sauce. I ate the vegetables and the potato, which, although sweet, did not taste altogether strange to me. It strongly reminded me of *zucca barucca,* a pumpkin we use in Italy. Many years later in New York, when I made *cappellacci,* the ravioli-like pasta from Ferrara whose stuffing is made with *zucca barucca,* I substituted red sweet potato for the *zucca* and called them *Cappellacci del Nuovo Mondo,* New World Cappellacci.

At the end of that winter, Victor saw an announcement from

Columbia University offering an intensive course in English for for-
eigners. It was a six-week course, with classes every day from ten
A.M. to five P.M. I had not added many new words to my baseball
vocabulary, and he thought the course might help me break through
the language barrier. Predictably, my thoughts went immediately to
the terror of the long subway ride from Forest Hills to Columbia,
which involved a complicated transfer of trains. What if I got lost?
How would I ever get back home?

Victor insisted. I couldn't have a life in America without understanding and speaking English, and this seemed to be the most
promising way to start. He enrolled me in the course, and the first
two or three days he escorted me, showing me the trains to take, at
which station to get off, and how to reach the school building. The
first few afternoons he was there to pick me up and show me the
way back home. The first week on my own, I was very careful and
successfully negotiated the itinerary both to and from class. I probably became complacent, and one morning during the second week,
I got on the wrong line. When I reached the street from the station,
I found myself someplace that I had never seen before, where nearly
everyone was black. I stood paralyzed, and I must have looked out
of place and desperate, because after a while, a woman came up to
me and spoke to me in Spanish, seemingly wanting to help. I showed
her the card with the traveling instructions that Victor had written
out. I couldn't understand very much of what she said, but she was
kind and friendly, and motioned for me to follow her back down to
the subway. Evidently, and fortunately, she must have been going
in the same direction that I had to go, because eventually she led
me to the right stop on upper Broadway. When I related my adventure to Victor that evening, he said, "That's wonderful! You got your
first look at Harlem."

There were about twenty students in the class, most of them

young, of different nationalities. There were several Russians, but not one Italian. All of them, except for me, already knew a little English. I completed the course, but it is evidence of my hopeless lack of an ear for languages that I left Columbia with only slightly more English than I had before I started. I still could understand only very little of what people said to me, let alone carry on a conversation. It was not a total loss of time, however: Whereas at the beginning of the course I had been hearing the language as one continuous, unvaried sound, at the end I was learning to detect the presence of separate words, each with a beginning and an end.

Even when he was much younger, Victor had yearned to live in Manhattan. He wanted, moreover, to live closer to his work, where he was spending long hours. He was directing his creative energies to bringing greater notoriety to his father's business, having done away with his dreams of living and writing in Italy. He had persuaded his father to produce an exclusive couture line of furs, and he had found in Italy an immensely gifted young couturier, Roberto Capucci, to design it. We found a place and a location we liked, the third floor of a brownstone on Sixty-fifth Street, between Madison and Park avenues, and late in the spring, we moved in. It was a walk-up, but we were used to stairs in Italy, we were young, and besides, I was glad to dispense with elevators. Many years later, when we lived in Venice and visited New York, we sometimes stayed on the same block, at the Mayfair Hotel, whose manager was then a Venetian, Dario Mariotti. We stood at the window of our room and looked at the street where we had passed what seemed like another life. The memories came flooding back, great joys and indelible pain riding upon them.

One of the immediate benefits of our move was felt in the kitchen. There were so many ingredients I couldn't get in Forest Hills: olive oil, real Parmigiano, pancetta, and such fresh vegetables

In the kitchen of our brownstone flat on Sixty-fifth
Street, in 1957

as artichokes and fava beans. While we still lived in Forest Hills,
Victor had shown me the way to Ninth Avenue, where the Italian
food stores were, but that involved subways and buses and the carrying of heavy packages up and down many steps and through crowds.
In Sixty-fifth Street, I kept a special piggy bank for taxi fare, and
periodically I rode over to Ninth Avenue in comfort. Not that my
expeditions were always a success. For one thing, the olive oil was a
coarse imitation of what we used to call olive oil back home. And
the grocers and vegetable men did not respond with the warmth
I had expected when addressed in Italian. Not infrequently, they
slipped into a dialect corrupted by dialecticized English that was
incomprehensible to me. One of the men was so irritated by my
failure to understand him that he ended by insulting me: *"Ma vai, non
sei mica italiana, tu"* ("Go on, you are not Italian"), he said, offensively
using the familiar *"tu"* form of address. If there was another good

reason to improve my English, it was to speak to those oafish men in a language they could understand. I also made blunders of my own. I once thought I had found Jerusalem artichokes, which Victor adores, and I asked the man to give me two pounds of them. "Two pounds? What are you going to do with them?" he asked. "Let me worry about it," I said. "I know how to cook." When I got it home, I found I had bought two pounds of ginger. It would take me another decade, and a course in Chinese cooking, to learn what I could have done with it.

Aside from cooking, which I enjoyed, the role of housewife did not fit me well. I decided it was time for me to look for work. I would have liked to go back to teaching, but my English, although improved, was not yet equal to it. I thought about working in a laboratory. I was strong in scientific theory, but gravely lacking in

In the lab of the Guggenheim Institute for Dental Research, Bellevue Hospital, New York

practice. When I was going to university, the labs had so little equipment that we had to take brief turns at using it, and some instruments we saw only in books. I took a course in histology at New
York University that gave me the opportunity to practice on many
different instruments, while at the same time, I was acquiring the
English terminology related to their functions. As soon as I finished the course, I started going to interviews. My first two were
at Jamaica Hospital and at Helena Rubinstein. I had to walk away
from them because I couldn't understand what the interviewers were
asking me. I then had an appointment at the Guggenheim Institute
for Dental Research, at Bellevue. The doctor in charge carefully read
the curriculum vitae that Victor had prepared for me, and after a
brief conversation that I was barely able to follow, he said, "Well, do
you want to work here?" That much I managed to understand and
I promptly said yes. "Now I have a job," I thought to myself, "but
how long can it be before they find that they have made a mistake
and fire me?"

I was very lucky. The technician who worked at a table next to
mine, a young woman from Argentina, immediately took a liking to
me and, with inexhaustible patience, helped me get started. We were
doing research on pyorrhea by provoking it in the gums of laboratory rats. Here again, I benefited from generous help, that of the
man in charge of the animals, who taught me how to hold them and
anesthetize them before injecting them. The director of the laboratory, Dr. Sigmund Stahl, was also very kind, and very patient as I
struggled with my English. The long hours I spent there, where only
English was heard and spoken, were the decisive ones that opened a
way for me into the language.

We used the pauses in our work to exchange looks into each
other's lives. Dr. Stahl called me Marcella and wanted me to call
him Siggy. For someone coming from a hierarchical Italian back-

ground where no title could be ignored, that was impossible. He was always, and in my memories continues to be, Dr. Stahl. We talked about food, which had already become a load-bearing pillar of my happiness. My colleagues were surprised that every evening at home we had a freshly cooked dinner and that when I left the lab at the end of the day, I rushed back to my kitchen to prepare it. Dr. Stahl had never heard of the dishes I was making. He had never tasted such things as eggplant, or artichokes, or *finocchio*, nor had he any acquaintance with olive oil or Parmigiano. And when he learned that we usually drank a bottle of wine at table, he was stunned and troubled.

I was busy and happy, at work and at home. Victor too, for the first time in his life, found satisfaction in his work. The high-fashion line of furs he had introduced into his father's business was getting attention from *Vogue* and *Harper's Bazaar*. He was working with Richard Avedon and other prominent photographers; important private customers such as Doris Duke, Marjorie Merriweather Post, and Patricia Lopez-Willshaw placed orders; and he traveled with the collection, showing it in some of the greatest specialty stores in the country. It appeared that we had got off to a good start and that our lives would continue to roll on a smooth track. Not too long after came the derailment.

In the spring of 1958, I became pregnant. We decided to take our two-week vacation that summer in Woodstock, where we enrolled in a drawing and painting class. Coming down fast, one afternoon after class, on a steep, unpaved Catskill road, Victor lost control of our car and we crashed into a tree. My face was covered in blood when they took me to a hospital in Kingston, but it was only from a superficial cut to my forehead. Victor, who was otherwise unscathed, had smashed his kneecap. He was transferred by ambulance to a hospital in Manhattan not too far from the lab, where I continued to work. He would not touch the hospital food, so I cooked his meals at home in the evening and brought them in large thermos containers to the hospital, where I spent my lunch hour with him. Warmed-over pasta was not for Victor, no matter how desperately hungry he might have been, but he loved my zucchini stuffed with meat and cheese, and my meatballs. Fifty years later, I am still making them, and they have lost none of their power to satisfy him.

I am expecting Giuliano

A stubborn infection established itself in Victor's knee, and it was many discouraging weeks before they could operate to repair the crumbled kneecap. The operation touched nerves that, to a degree, are sensitive even now. At that time, the pain was agonizing, and they kept him in the hospital another month, giving him morphine so that he could sleep. I put off the decision as long as I could, but it was obvious that I couldn't continue working in the lab. My belly was getting between me and the microscope, Victor would be coming home to our third-floor walk-up needing a lot of attention, and I would have to stay home with the child, once it was born. Sadly, I quit my job.

1958, Victor recovering from his knee operation

There was no more morphine for Victor at home, even though the pain was extreme. I had to bathe him and dress him, because his leg was still in a full cast. The sedatives and sleeping medicine that had been allowed him had little effect; he ate almost nothing; and for long periods, he was delirious. Fortunately, by the time my labor pains arrived, the first of December, he had regained his mental equilibrium. I called my doctor, who said, "Have Victor help you dress and collect your things. I'll meet you at the hospital." I can chuckle now when I recall those words. It was I who had to help Victor dress, because his leg was still stiff and he could not pull on his pants. And it was I who had to help him down the three flights of stairs on his crutches, stopping every few steps to wait for a pause in my contractions. When we got out of the taxi at the emergency room, Victor looked cadaveric, and a nurse came running over to him with a wheelchair. "Not for him," I yelled. "For me!"

When we brought our infant home, Victor felt strong enough to return to work. I was left alone at home with Giuliano, our baby boy. It was he now, instead of Victor, who interrupted my sleep. We bought a convertible double bed and took up sleeping in the living room, leaving our bedroom to Giuliano. We had the one really jolly moment of that terrible year when Mark Pratt, who had been Victor's best friend since college, came to visit from Japan, where the foreign service had posted him. He brought us two beautiful eighteenth-century paintings of the Kano school and good-naturedly accepted sharing the bedroom with Giuliano. Mark needed a place to entertain some of the people he hadn't seen since his last trip to the States, and we gladly let him have ours. He was an excellent cook and baked a delicious ham in our oven. An American baked ham is, in my opinion, one of the most wonderful dishes of any cuisine. He had bought too much ice for the refreshments, and there was a large bag of it left after the party. We discussed how to dispose of it. "Easy," said Mark. "I'll flush it down the toilet." We flushed and flushed, but the cubes massed together and we found ourselves with a small iceberg in the bowl. It was a long while before we could use the only toilet of our only bathroom. It seemed an eternity had passed since we had been able to laugh as we did that night.

Giuliano was born on December first. We put up a small Christmas tree that I carried up the stairs, but Christmas Eve came before I had had time, or a calm enough head, to think of presents. "But I do have a great present for Victor," I thought. After dinner, while he was in the bathroom, I took my baby out of the crib, wrapped a big red bow around him, and put him under the tree.

With Giuliano's arrival, our apartment became too small. We left our cozy walk-up on Sixty-fifth Street for a large two-bedroom at 65 Central Park West. We left the first apartment that, in our married life, we could call our own, a bright apartment from which, on its sunny side, we observed the traffic of pedestrians and cars just below, and from the rear windows, the gardens of the brownstones on the block behind us. In our new place on the tenth floor, every window faced a dark, grimy, lifeless courtyard. We almost always had the lights on.

When, earlier in my life, I thought that someday I might have a baby, I worried that because of my lame arm, I might hurt it when holding it or bathing it, or scratch it with the sharp, talon-like fingers of my crooked hand, or even drop it. Nothing like that ever happened. When he began to crawl, Giuliano once managed to open one of the lower cupboards of the kitchen where I kept a gallon can of olive oil. How he did it I cannot understand, but he upended the can, pouring oil all over himself and the floor. When I found him, he looked at me with the sly expression of someone having

Giuliano at eleven months

a wickedly good time. I managed to lift him, wriggling and slippery as he was; bathe him without letting him slide under and drown; dry him; dress him; and put him safely away in his crib before attending to the kitchen floor. Rare is the challenge a mother cannot rise to.

Victor returned to a different fur business than the one he had left. While he was incapacitated, his father felt he could not continue alone to produce a separate couture line, and he cancelled the contract with Capucci. Victor once again began to chafe at doing work he described as *insopportabile*, insufferable. For my part, I found myself trapped in a dull apartment with my child. The spirit had gone out of our lives. One fall evening, three years after his accident, as we were having dinner, Victor said, "We have got to leave, we are going to go back to Italy." My heart jumped, first with joy, then with terror. Of course I longed to be in Italy, to be close to my parents and friends again, to be able to speak my language, but then I gave way to dread. How were we to support ourselves? Victor was thirty-three and had had no other job but at his father's, and he had no experience of working in Italy. Where would we live? Even if we could adapt to staying with my parents, in a house with no central heating, with only one bathroom and precious little hot water for it, where in Cesenatico would Victor find work, on the fishing boats?

Unlike me, Victor seems to have no fears, and when he comes to a decision, he won't be dissuaded, whatever the risks. He told his father that he would stay through the winter, to the end of the season, and that in the spring we would move to Italy. Early in June 1962, Victor, Giuliano, and I were on a plane to Milan.

Back to the Old World

1962-1967

PAPi SENT A DRIVER to Malpensa, Milan's international airport, to meet us and take us to Cesenatico. My parents moved into the room that had been Nonna Adele's—she had died while I was in New York—and let us have the big bedroom. For Giuliano there was a small spare room next to ours. Cesenatico was both familiar and disquieting. What could have been more familiar than the house in which I had grown up and been married, than my parents' voices and faces, than riding my old bicycle, than the friends I ran into on the street, than the foods in the market stalls, than the language everyone spoke? It was familiar, but it wasn't reassuring. For the first time in my life, it troubled me to be there. We had almost no cash left. We have always lived to the full extent of our resources, and our modest savings account had vanished after we paid for packing and storing our furniture and books for their eventual shipment to an Italian port, and for our airfare. I inquired about a teaching position in the public school system, but I had lost seniority during the years I was in New York, and there was a long line of recent university graduates waiting for an opening. How would we ever manage? It would take a miracle. But lo, the miracle didn't keep us waiting long.

Every day I bought the *Corriere della Sera*, Italy's most respected newspaper, published in Milan, and the big city editions of our regional paper, *Il Resto del Carlino*. I read the classified ads, hoping to find something that could be suitable for Victor. He would get very upset. "Why are you trying to stick me in some job?" he asked. Whenever I tried to read to him one of the help-wanted ads that sounded vaguely possible, he brushed me off. I was puzzled that he seemed to show no interest in finding a way out of our predicament. On the other hand, all of the plausible offers of employment that I came across were from Italian companies that would have asked Victor for Italian work papers, which he did not have.

While in New York, Victor had taken over and expanded his father's advertising program. He collaborated with a small but well-thought-of agency, whose owner, Clarence Herrick, became a friend. Together they wrote and produced gorgeous brochures and ads for *The New York Times, Vogue,* and *Harper's Bazaar*. Before leaving for Italy, Victor asked Clarence to give him a letter testifying to the years they had worked together and commending his creative skills, without specifying the narrow range of that experience. "How do you expect to use it?" I asked him. "I don't know yet," he said. "Outside of furs, advertising is the only thing I understand a little bit about, and I am certainly not going to look again for work in the fur business."

The summer had gone by and not a single job worth considering had yet turned up, when I saw an ad in the *Corriere della Sera* by an American advertising agency, BBD&O, which was seeking the services of an experienced copywriter for the position of copy chief in their Milan office. To my surprise and discouragement, Victor could think only of objections. "BBD&O is a major agency with major industrial clients, and I don't know a thing about industry," he said. "Copy chief is a big position. My only experience is in writing fashion ads for one furrier. I don't even know most of the technical vocabulary they will expect me to use. I would have to learn it on the job, if they let me get away with it." "That doesn't sound like you," I said. "You have never before been afraid of trying something. When can we ever expect to come across another opportunity like this? It seems made-to-order for you." I felt desperate and I began to cry. "All right, all right, I'll answer the ad," said Victor. My mother's twin brother, Zio Alberto, had a small travel agency in town, and that is where Victor went to type his letter to BBD&O. He wrote a very persuasive letter, which is something he knows how to do. At the end of it, he stated his salary requirements, which the ad had asked applicants to specify. When I saw it, I thought to myself, "Why bother wasting money on the stamps to mail it?" The salary Victor had asked for was American-scale. The cost of living was still very modest in Italy then, and no Italian would have dreamed of asking such a figure. "You don't understand," he said. "I am applying as an American who claims to have solid American advertising experience. The salary I am asking for is in line with the job they are offering. The claims I am making wouldn't be credible if I asked for any less. Besides, I wouldn't work for less."

I put BBD&O out of my mind. Victor and I needed a change of scenery, a release of tension, so we accepted an invitation from Zia Margò to spend a few days with them in Venice. Victor didn't need to be cajoled. He had formed a passion for Venice even as a small boy when he had first visited it with his parents. We had spent only one night at Zia Margò's when my mother called to say that she had just opened a telegram from BBD&O asking Victor to come to their offices the following morning at ten thirty for an interview. We caught the bus back to Cesenatico, where we had to solve a problem of logistics. There was no direct train connection between

Cesenatico and Milan. There was bus service, but there was no *autostrada* then, no fast highway from the seashore to the north, and it took six hours, with many stops along the way. Whether by train or by bus, Victor would have had to travel into the night and present himself at the interview in less than mint condition. My dear old papi came to the rescue, digging deep into his pockets once again: Victor would leave early in the morning with a driver, who would wait for him and bring him back. "Don't keep me in suspense," I begged Victor as he got into the car. "Call me the moment you have news." The telephone rang at half past twelve. "Where are you?" I asked. "On Via Montenapoleone." (Montenapo, as the Milanese call it, is the city's most famous street of smart shops.) "What are you doing on Via Montenapoleone?" "I have just bought you a silk shawl at Biki's." (Biki was the Prada of that time.) "A shawl? But what about the interview?" "Oh, the interview. It didn't last too long. But it went well, I got the job."

BBD&O wanted their new copy chief to get started right away. They had a critical presentation to make to a major client. Their main source of billing at the time, a French gasoline company called Total, was taking over a chain of filling stations in Italy. We left Giuliano with my parents and went up to Milan, Victor to start work and I to look for an apartment. We had no idea where to stay while I was apartment-hunting. Victor remembered the name of a hotel where he had stayed with his father, when his father had come to Italy to dissuade us from getting married. It was called the Duomo, in the center of town and within a short walk to the BBD&O offices. It has since lost its luster, but it was then Milan's most modern hotel and, as I soon discovered, extremely expensive. It is not considered good form in Italy, when you check in, for reception to announce the room rate unless you ask. And Victor has never asked the price of anything. Upstairs in the room, when I opened the closet door, I saw the figure on the rate card posted on its back. If we had continued staying there, all the money we had come to Milan with would have been gone in less than a week. The following morning, I put off apartment-hunting to look for a cheap hotel.

Just one block down from the Duomo, I caught sight of a modest hotel sign down a narrow side street. I asked inside whether they had a double room with a bath available, and the man at the desk said yes, looking rather quizzical. I asked the price. It was a small fraction of the Duomo's. "May I see the room?" I asked. It was one flight up, no elevator, very bare but reasonably clean. Its one window looked on the alley below. "*Va benissimo*, I'll take it," I said. "I'll be right over with our bags." Back at the Duomo, I packed and checked out. The doorman got me a cab and loaded the bags. "*Dove deve andare, signora?*" ("Where are you going?") asked the driver. I pretended to check the address on a piece of paper, reading it to him. He gave me a look and drove the block and a half to the other hotel. "*Eccoci qui!*" ("Here we are!") he said. "Oh, already?" said I. It's not customary to tip taxi drivers in Italy, but I did so nonetheless. After carrying my own bags up to the room, I telephoned Victor to give him our new address. Back from dinner that evening, he was looking out the window when he turned to me and said, "*Vieni, vieni a vedere*" ("Come, come to see what goes on here"). From the window, I saw some flashy-looking women lounging near the hotel. From time to time, a man would approach, look them over, have a brief conversation with one of them, and enter our hotel with her. We couldn't afford to go to the movies, but for a few evenings, we didn't need entertainment. It was entertaining enough to observe the ladies and their clients, to try to anticipate, whenever a man appeared, whom he would choose, and speculate, according to the length or brevity of the couple's stay, how they might have amused themselves.

I went all over Milan looking to rent a furnished apartment

that we could afford until Victor was settled in his new career and we had paid back all the money we had been borrowing. It had to be furnished because our things were still in storage in New York. There seemed to be none available, until one turned up in a new development very far from the center of town, a good walk past the last stop of the tram. It was so far from downtown Milan that when we opened the windows we could hear frogs croaking in the fields near us. The furnishings, of which the landlady was exceedingly proud, were exceedingly awful: rococoesque sofas and chairs upholstered in metallic brocades, with gold leaf—or was it paint?—laid on everywhere. Victor found one china vitrine and its contents so offensive that for the entire time we stayed there he kept it covered with a sheet.

The furniture issues aside, it was a happy time for both of us. Giuliano was in Cesenatico with his grandparents, and I enjoyed cooking just for Victor and myself, as I did when we were first married. It was a working-class neighborhood and the markets were scaled to its means, yet I had vegetables that for variety and freshness outmatched anything that I had been able to buy in New York. There was a woman who sold at her stall red beets such as I have never tasted, before or since. They were as large as a large orange and had been baked in the embers of a slow-dying wood fire. We peeled them, sliced them, and had them with salt, wine vinegar, and olive oil, abandoning ourselves to their amazing sweetness. I had an artisan butcher who cut the meat himself from a carcass hanging in his shop. He would be shocked if he could see the butchers in my Florida supermarket use their knives mainly for slitting open the plastic bags their precut meats arrive in. There was a fishmonger's stall offering inexpensive varieties of seafood so fresh they glistened.

The distance from his office notwithstanding, Victor managed to come home when they closed for lunch. He couldn't call me because we didn't have a telephone. It took weeks and a well-stuffed unmarked envelope to get one, but I knew his office hours, and I had everything ready to go to the table when he walked in. My cooking was very simple, usually guided by the vegetables that looked best to me that day. We might have pasta with zucchini or fresh tomatoes or cauliflower, or a frittata with asparagus or green beans or peppers and onion, sausages with fresh borlotti beans, veal stew with foraged mushrooms, or my mother's veal roll-ups, of which Victor was so fond. From a trip to the fish market, I might have brought back *sgombero*, small mackerel that I cooked over the stove like a pan roast, in olive oil, garlic, and rosemary. Or a kilo or more of our tiny Adriatic clams, peppery and soft like butter, a small mountain of them, sautéed with lots of olive oil, garlic, and parsley, which we would eat with nearly their weight in marvelous crusty bread, sopping up their juices. Those noontimes together at home gave us such strength and encouragement. Ever since, except when we have traveled or had to defer to professional engagements, lunch for two at home has been the steady center of our lives.

When my parents came to visit, I was feeling so confident of my culinary accomplishments that I wanted to cook something that I knew they had never tasted. In New York, I had learned to cook pompano fillets in a very un-Italian way, in butter. There is no pompano in Italy, but there is a highly prized and costly fish, *orata*—the French name is *daurade*—that I was sure would be delicious done that way. Buying and cooking fish had always been my father's specialty, and when he saw me put butter in the pan, he stopped me. "You are going to cook that beautiful *orata* in butter? Please, go talk to your mother. I'll take care of the fish." And he did. He boiled it and served it lukewarm, pouring over it a little sauce of olive oil beaten with a clove of garlic chopped very fine and parsley. In time, my mother and father would look forward to having me cook for them, but that time had not come yet.

In the early 1960s, there were only a few international advertising agencies in Milan. Perhaps just four or five, I don't remember exactly. The creative people working there hung out together. Victor has always been a solitary man, and this was his first, and remains his only, experience of participating in a *comitiva*, a peer group. We formed a boisterous eating club—wives were automatically admitted—that met one or two evenings a week to sit at a long table at the Torre di Pisa, one of the Tuscan trattorias that were popular in Milan. Torre di Pisa, which is in the elegant Brera museum and art gallery district, eventually became fashionable and very expensive, but we were there before Italy's explosive rise in cost of living. In those years, the restaurant was easygoing and so absurdly cheap that it could have cost us more to eat at home. It was also very, very good. Nostalgia may be softening the memory, but it seems to me that at the Torre we ate some of the best food we have ever had. It was simple and sincere, real food produced by cooks who had not yet learned to call themselves chefs, who wouldn't have known the meaning of "creative cuisine." Unlike Milanese cooking, which can be ponderous and laborious to prepare, the Tuscan dishes at Torre di Pisa were fresh and light-handed: *fagioli sgranati*, boiled, fresh cannellini beans, served lukewarm with olive oil and cracked black pepper; magnificent soups, such as a black cabbage and bean *ribollita*; vegetable frittatas, of which the most memorable, with artichokes, started Victor on eating eggs for the first time; juicy veal roasts; chicken fricassees that Victor passed on; steaks and pork sausages from a charcoal grill; crisp fried vegetables; terrific salads that we dressed ourselves with beautiful, dense olive oil and fragrant, bracing, genuine red wine vinegar—that phony, sticky balsamic stuff that has replaced good vinegar on many tables was fortunately not yet widely known. Uncounted fiaschi of Chianti kept coming to the table throughout the evening, followed at the end by *cantucci*—homemade almond cookies—and *vin santo*. What good times those were, bibulous, gluttonous, funny, young, comradely, and delicious times.

Victor had not been working a year when Total, BBD&O's gasoline client, asked the agency to remove him from their account. The people at Total did not believe him qualified to handle gasoline advertising. He didn't have a car; he never drove; he was then, and still is, mechanically ignorant; he was not at home with, as they put it, "Italian car culture." They may have been right. A year or two later, Victor would have the satisfaction of handling a hugely successful print and television campaign for Esso, as Exxon is called internationally. He would also be introduced to the mysteries of Italian car culture through a little Lancia sports car of his own. But all that was yet to come. The here and now of it was that he had been fired. It was a stunning blow for Victor. For a day or two, he was comatose. One of our pals at the eating club was the copy chief at Lintas, the in-house agency for Unilever, the giant soap and food conglomerate. When he heard the news, he asked Victor to come to Lintas, where there was an opening for a writer to assume creative responsibility for the company's dishwashing detergent, one of their key brands. In less than a week, Victor was working again.

Shortly after Victor started at Lintas, two fellows from J. Walter Thompson rang our doorbell. "We know that Victor has just started at Lintas, but we badly need an experienced copywriter at the agency, and we could make him very happy at Thompson. Please have him call us," they said. It happened that Victor was not enthusiastic about working for Unilever. The atmosphere was industrial and cold, and he was bored by the product to which he had been assigned. He hadn't been at Lintas a week when he accepted an offer from Thompson. At Thompson, Victor found an American art director who became his chum and with whom he had an immensely satisfactory working relationship. It did not compensate, however, for the contentious discussions he had with the general manager of the agency, a foppish, patronizing Englishman given to wearing his handkerchief tucked inside the end of his shirtsleeve. They argued over Victor's creative proposals, which the manager would praise effusively at first, but then recast to his own satisfaction. After a few weeks, the American art director left to take a job at McCann-Erickson. Victor lost no time in joining him, his fourth job in not as many months.

With every move, Victor's salary had improved. His last move, to McCann, which gave every sign of being the final one, allowed us to take a very good apartment to which we had our furniture sent. It was a large, modern flat in one of the well-made postwar buildings that replaced older structures bombed during the war. It was exceptionally well-finished, with marble floors and bathrooms, fine woodwork, and real plaster walls. It had an air-conditioning system I have not seen elsewhere. During the summer, cold water ran through pipes laid under the floors. It didn't produce the nipping briskness of the conditioned air we are used to in the States, and there was no thermostat with which we could control it, but the temperature was pleasant and felt natural. The kitchen was large and bright but, except for the sink, completely bare, as is the custom in Italy. We had beautiful teak cabinets made and put in German appliances. Our cooktop and oven were Gaggenau, which, more than thirty years later, is what I put into my Florida kitchen. There was also a room for a housekeeper, whom I would later bring up from one of the small farm towns near Cesenatico. The last one to work for me in Italy, Lucia, would join us in New York when, a few years later, we returned to the States, and she eventually became my first assistant in the cooking class I taught at home.

After a year and a half with his grandparents, our son could join us at last to stay in a room of his own. There was even a vast terrace that we kept unencumbered so that he could freely run his bicycle on it. It was wonderful having Giuliano with me. His reactions to being in Italy were sometimes so unexpected. When we had first arrived, I had taken him to a toy shop to let him choose some replacements for the ones that we had left behind in New York. I presently became aware that he was paying more attention to the conversations of the people in the store than to the toys. *"Mamma,"* he said after a little while, *"tutti parlano italiano!"* ("Everyone is speaking Italian!") To him, Italian was the language we used at home, whereas English was what others spoke outside. A year after coming up to Milan, I enrolled him in our neighborhood's public elementary school, and I lost no time getting him the mandatory uniform of Italian grammar school children, a black smock with a huge blue bow. He looked so adorable!

Our building took all of one side of a small, hidden street close to Piazza del Duomo, Milan's main square. It was within walking distance of McCann-Erickson, and two of the blocks that Victor walked every day on his way to work, Via Spadari and Via Speronari, I walked every day, too. It would be closer to the truth to say that I camped there. Those two blocks may be responsible for the tight focus on cooking that my life has had since. Italy's celebrated food shop, Peck, was the most prominent presence on Via Spadari, a blazing, stellar presence, and huddling close to it, across from it, and over on the next block were several other smaller shops, each purveying a single category of food: La Pescheria, the fish market, displayed the country's freshest and most varied selection of fish and crustaceans. It was not unusual for one of the clerks to have to retrieve some of the *moleche,* the soft-shell crabs, that had crawled out of their baskets, hoping to escape their fate. At La Bottega del Formaggio, the cheese shop, large wheels of cheese were stacked to the ceiling, and dozens of small ones were piled on marble tables and counters: little round, soft *tume* from Piedmont; the gamut of pecorini from Tuscany and Sardinia, young and milky to aged and straw yellow or chalky white; *squacquarone*, the day-old farmer's cheese spreading out in a bowl; a snowy mountain peak of mascarpone; mysterious cheeses cloaking their identities within layers of leaves. The scents in the cheese shop made my head spin, and my heart ached when I eventually left with the choices I had made, because of all the others I had to leave behind. La Bottega del Maiale, the pork butcher, sold fresh cuts of Emilia-Romagna's savory hogs and extraordinary salami, sausages, prosciutti, *cotechini, zamponi,* all the cured or smoked specialties of Italy's unparalleled charcuterie. L'Ortolano, the greengrocer, sold produce of incomparable freshness and flavor.

In the 1960s, the Peck store was a food lover's fantasy brought to life. Every day it produced a vast array of prepared dishes: *i ripieni,* the aromatically stuffed vegetables of the Riviera; *vitello tonnato,* cold sliced poached veal marinated with tuna sauce; roasted meats; *insalata russa,* the shrimp and diced vegetables salad known as "Russian" because it has beets; various seafood salads; whole steamed, baked, grilled, or fried fishes; suckling pig. No jam or condiment was too obscure to be on its shelves. It housed a fully stocked wine shop. Peck had a butcher from Tuscany, Vasco, who could do what I think only he was capable of. If you have ever made *fegato alla veneziana,* Venetian sautéed liver and onions, you know how hard it is to find the perfectly even, thin slices you should be using. Cutting thin and even slices from liver is only slightly less difficult than cutting them from a block of Jell-O. Vasco, however, could put a whole calf's liver on his block and cut slice after flawless slice of unvarying thinness, with the fluid and unhesitating motion with which you or I might peel Post-it notes from a pad.

When I first started to cook after arriving in New York, not even a year into married life, it was as though I were telling a story I had heard as a little girl in another land. To judge how closely my tale corresponded to the original, I had nothing but my memory and my cookbook. I was not acquainted with any other recently arrived Italians who might have been able to corroborate some of my culinary recollections. The so-called Italian food I found in New York at that time—spaghetti and meatballs; machine-made ravioli with pungent, dark tomato sauce; manicotti; lobster fra diavolo; veal parmesan or *alla francese*—resembled only occasionally in name, but never in appearance, taste, or intentions, what I had known at home.

On returning to Italy, eating at simple trattorias, shopping the markets, bringing home ingredients whose flavors, in 1950-ish New York, had existed largely in my imagination, I had the confirmation I had longed for: My story was not a fairy tale I had invented; its characters, the components of my cooking, were real. An unleashed enthusiasm for cooking took over my thoughts. I wanted to look at every single ingredient I saw on market stalls and in stores, I wanted to talk cooking with the woman selling vegetables, with the fishmonger, with the butcher, with the grocer. I wanted to go to restaurants and taste everything. I would run home, having bought more food than any small family could eat, and I cooked for the happiness of it, for my husband, for my son, for myself.

Victor's career at McCann-Erickson was moving fast. As the chief of a small staff of copywriters, he was involved in preparing proposals and campaigns for all the agency's clients, a roster that contained some of America's iconic companies: Exxon, Coca-Cola, Gillette. When McCann's T.V. producer left, Victor took his place. The agency sent him to workshops in Munich and London for a rapid immersion in creative commercial television.

At that time, Italy had just three television channels, owned by the state. Mr. Berlusconi and his private channels were still several years away. The government was sensitive to ideological pressures from the left, and while it sought the profits that selling space for commercials would bring, it wasn't ready yet for unrestricted commercial exploitation of public airtime. They compromised by devising a one-minute-thirty-second format called *carosello*, thirty seconds of which could be used for a commercial at the end of one minute of pure entertainment. Victor devised his *caroselli* so that there was a smooth and memorable connection between the two parts, even though the product was, perforce, kept out of the noncommercial section. Some of Italy's gifted movie directors made *caroselli*, turning the entertainment portion into fast-moving, tightly cut miniature films. Several *caroselli* were shown together in a program broadcast early in the evening, before children went to bed. In those early days of Italian television, it was the most popular thing on the air.

Most of McCann's filming took place in Rome, under Victor's supervision. He fell in love with Rome, with its relaxed life, with the soft radiance of its golden light, its sunny winters, the umbrella pines, the fountains, the antiquities, the beautiful streets, the magnificent river, and by no means least, the delicious food that, in those years, you could have in almost any restaurant that you dropped into. He was happy with what he had achieved in Milan, but he had never felt tenderness for the city. It was hard-driving, homely, grim, treeless, and still encumbered by some of the rubble from the war. Rome had the Tiber. Milan had the Naviglio, a canal that had become a squalid ditch, partially paved over and driven underground. Rome was Italian, warm, and Mediterranean; Milan was Teutonic, cold, and gray. Nor was he deeply attached to our apartment. He appreciated its comforts and its location, but it was too new for Victor. "It has no history," he would say. It was a wasted opportunity, he thought, to live in Italy, the country with more history per square foot than any other, and live in a place with no past.

At the end of a season of filming, the director on one of the sets took Victor aside and asked, "How would you like to live in Rome?" "What do you have in mind?" Victor replied. "A friend of mine is planning to open a studio equipped to produce the best commercials in Italy, and he has asked me to find out whether you would be interested in becoming its creative director." That is how, exactly four years after arriving in Milan, we happened to leave the apartment and the neighborhood where I thought I could be settling down for life, to move to the Eternal City, which soon proved to be anything but that for us.

"IF NERO HAD lived here," I was saying to the real estate agent, "he would have had a terrific view of Rome burning." We were on the *altana*—the roof terrace—of a Roman palazzo, open to the four points of the compass and high enough above the city to let one's eye wander over the cupolas, the rooftop gardens, the parks, the Spanish Steps, the pattern of streets emptying into squares like so many streams spilling into ponds, which form the most brilliant of urban tapestries. Stacked directly below the *altana* were the other two tiers of the apartment that became our Roman aerie.

Our new domicile had been carved out of the uppermost corner of Palazzo Ruspoli, a massive pile in the Florentine style erected in the sixteenth century on the most central street corner in Rome, one block down from Piazza di Spagna. The Ruspolis, a large and princely Roman family, moved into it more than four hundred years ago and have been living in it ever since. The palazzo's celebrated architectural feature is a broad staircase of one hundred steps, each one hewn from a single magnificent block of marble. You breathe grandeur with every step you take. Victor liked to climb it to the first landing and then take the candy box of an elevator the rest of the way up to our apartment. He also enjoyed swinging open the enormous wooden front doors and driving his little Lancia into the old columned courtyard, where he had a reserved space alongside those of the princes.

We ate out often when we lived in Rome. The food was deeply satisfying; so was the check, and so was the social rhythm. It was not unusual for friends to organize a midnight *spaghettata*, straddling the end of one day and the beginning of another with bowls of *spaghetti alla puttanesca* or *alla carrettiera*, or more often perhaps, *bucatini all'Amatriciana*. The food I ate in Rome threw light on an inbred regional cooking style that was new to me. The difference from Milan was startling. Milan had opened its arms, or more precisely its workplaces, to immigrants from Italy's less industrious regions, as well as to professional people from over the border. Its own professional and entrepreneurial class traveled more than any other in the country. The city's approach to food was consequently cosmopolitan, easily drawn to traditions other than its own. Few were the restaurants where, aside from the ubiquitous risotto, osso buco, and breaded veal cutlet, you would be offered an excursion through the byways of domestic Milanese cuisine. The most popular establishments were Tuscan, while immigrants from the south were to open trattorias that featured the specialties of Apulia, Naples, and Sicily.

Even though Rome was the capital of the nation and the beneficiary of millennia of history, at the time we lived there it was essentially a glorious provincial town where the dishes of the restaurants—as well as the ingredients sold in its markets—were not radically different from those you might have found in the home

Rome, 1966. Some of the one hundred marble steps of the staircase at Palazzo Ruspoli

kitchens of their patrons. We did have a few Tuscan trattorias—one of them, Fontanella Borghese, was down the street from the palazzo—but they did not rise to the level of those in Milan. And we had a few Bolognese restaurants, of which one, in Piazza del Popolo, was famous. But none of these stole the hearts, or rather the palates, of Roman eaters who knew that what they really wanted was the cooking on which they had been raised.

Once we had safely moved in, my first thought was to see what was in the food shops and the markets. Around the corner from the palazzo there was the kind of greengrocer we call a *primizaro*. *Primizie* in Italian are the earliest, and by extension, the finest and sweetest-tasting fruits and vegetables. L'Ortolano, our Milanese greengrocer, had splendid produce, but that of the Roman *primizaro* surpassed it in appearance, in flavor, and by a vast margin, in price. It was worth it, however, and I regret that ill-placed frugality prevented me from getting more of my produce there.

We are hugely fond of good green beans. If they are at their best, I don't bother making a sauce. I just boil them until done, neither crunchy nor mushy, usually less than seven minutes, and toss them, while still warm, with red wine vinegar, then with salt and olive oil. I remember a time my mother had come to visit and I had bought a kilo of the *primizaro*'s green beans. They were so fresh that they glistened and so firm, they snapped as sharply as dry twigs. They were perfectly formed and slender; a kilo of them made a daunting-looking mound on the kitchen table. "I have never seen such beautiful beans," said my mother. "Shall I trim them for you?" *"Grazie,"* I said, wondering whether she realized what she was letting herself in for. My mother was many endearing things, but long-suffering was not one of them. By the time she finished snapping off both ends of the last bean in that formidable heap, the drain on her patience had been such that her hands were shaking as though palsied, and so was her voice as she cried, *"Mai più!"* ("Never again!") "The next time you buy a kilo of such beans, get someone else to trim their little ends off!"

At my local Publix or Whole Foods now, when I feel the rock-hard peaches and pears, or I try to pick up a scent from the unforthcoming melons, when I bring home green beans or zucchini that have little more taste than the water with which they have been abundantly irrigated, not to mention the times that the musty smell of long storage forces me to discard what I have just bought, I think of the fragrance and juicy, sugary flesh of the *primizaro*'s fruits, of the concentrated flavor of his vegetables, and I wonder why we in America can't have better-tasting produce. Why aren't we showing the people who raise our produce how to be better farmers? Not necessarily organic farmers, or more efficient farmers, just plain old cultivators of good food. If our vegetables had taste and cooks were shown what they need to do with them, which is very little, everyone would eat more vegetables. Italians don't eat as many as they do because a government agency or the press tells them how healthy it is for them. They eat them because they taste so good. It is through irresistibly good taste—never mind "organic" or other fashionable categories—that food makes people happy and healthy.

There was a small open-air market close to the river that I could easily walk to, and it filled most of my needs, but the market I remember most fondly was the one at Campo dei Fiori. Its name, until I first went there, led me to think it was a flower market. It was much too far for me to walk to, but I sometimes had a friend drive me, and when she couldn't, it was worth my taking a taxi. They were very cheap then, and no tipping was expected.

I have never received better or more desirable instruction about any subject than what I was taught about the Roman way of cooking vegetables at the Campo dei Fiori market. It was there that I became acquainted with *mammole*, the large, round-faced artichoke essential to two Roman preparations, *carciofi alla romana*, artichokes Roman style, and *carciofi alla giudia*, artichokes Jewish style. The woman selling them patiently showed me how to prepare both, and both techniques made themselves at home in my kitchen, eventually landing in my cookbook. For Roman style, the artichokes are trimmed of the tough part of the leaves, but the thick, long, meaty, virile-looking stem is left on. Only its leathery rind is peeled away. The whole artichoke, its stem thrusting upward, is braised in a tall saucepan in very little olive oil and water. "Cover the pan with a moist towel, to hold the moisture in, and put the lid over the towel," she told me. For *carciofi alla giudia*, Jewish style, the stem is sliced off, but it is not thrown away, because it is so good. It is reserved for use in a soup or a meat stew after the rind has been stripped from it. The head of the artichoke is here again trimmed of the tough, inedible portion of its leaves (Italians find it mystifying that others will cook something that they won't be able to eat), and it is fried in two successive batches of hot oil. A drizzle of water causes the second batch of oil to sizzle, and the leaves open, curl, and turn a golden brown. The finished artichoke resembles a chrysanthemum and is deliciously crisp.

Late in the fall, I had picked up a head of chicory to add to my purchases, intending to blanch it and sauté it, but the woman selling it, realizing that I didn't know what I had, took it from my hands and spread open the head to disclose a plump mass of twisting shoots. "*Sono le puntarelle*," she said ("They are the chicory's shoots"). She cut them away and showed me that when she dropped them into a bowl of cold water they curled up. From her I learned to make what became our favorite salad that winter, *puntarelle* tossed with salt, vinegar, olive oil, garlic, black pepper, and anchovies. It is so good that I wanted it in one of my books, even though *puntarelle* rarely appear in a stateside market. I chose Belgian endive as an alternative. It doesn't curl up in ice water, but that aside, when it is treated to the *puntarelle* seasoning formula, it provides a reasonably tasty reminder of the original.

In the spring at Campo dei Fiori, I was introduced to what I believe to be the most ravishing of all vegetable dishes, *la vignarola*. I would even be prepared to omit the qualification "vegetable" as an unnecessary limitation. You must be there at just the one moment in the spring when baby fava beans, small rosebud artichokes, and very small peas, all at the same early stage of development, appear in the market at the identical time. If it should last more than two weeks, it is a lucky year; a month, a prodigy. You also need some *cipollotti*, young onions, and a small head of romaine lettuce. The onion is sliced and cooked in olive oil until it is very soft. You add the lettuce, the trimmed artichokes, the shelled beans and peas, and cook. The vegetables are so young that it doesn't take very long. When done, it doesn't look very presentable. It is a dark, mushy mass that you might think a careless cook had produced. But when you take a mouthful, it is as though spring itself in all its tenderness has been delivered in edible form.

Often after shopping, I would drag my packages over to one of the tables of a café in the Campo, where I would have an espresso or, if it was closer to lunch, a Campari soda. Other women would do the same and I would eavesdrop. They always talked about cooking. It is from such a group that I first heard about *coda alla vaccinara*, the iconic Roman dish. A tail butcher's style? What kind of a tail and what was butcher's style? I asked and they mentioned a restaurant whose specialty it was, which Victor and I promptly visited. Thereafter, I cooked oxtail several times in Rome, with the requisite jowl and celery, but less frequently later in New York, where celery was plentiful, but neither tail nor jowl was an everyday commodity at my butcher. What I most regretted having to give up in New York was *abbacchio,* milk-fed lamb, the whole lamb weighing just fourteen to fifteen pounds from its tail to its muzzle. The best parts were the tiny offal: the kidneys encased in fat, the sweetbreads, the delicate brains, the heart. Nor can one forget the *scottadito,* the miniature rib chops, cooked just long enough to "scald the fingers."

By the New Year, Victor could take me to Campo dei Fiori on any morning I wanted to go. The studio that had brought him to Rome had folded. Once again, Victor had no job, but it neither shocked nor worried him this time. Word spreads fast in the small world of advertising, and soon there were offers from Milan as well as from London and Munich. Munich was out of the question. Most of Victor's relatives had died in concentration camps. He could not bear to live in Germany. Nor was he willing to return to Milan. London we both loved, but the problem was that he didn't want to go back to advertising. That was a surprise for me.

"What is the matter with advertising?" I asked.

"It has come to a dead end for me. It makes me think of one of those slow emulsions photographers use to pull up and print the images they have shot, when inexplicably it stops short, and nothing comes up but a blur. If I go back, there will be no definition to my life; it too will be a blur."

"What are you—*we*—going to do?"

"I don't know yet."

It was the same phrase he had used when we had just come back to Italy.

"What would you *like* to do?"

"Ideally?"

"Yes, ideally."

I could guess what was coming.

"I would like to have time to study art, more exactly crafts, and in particular, pottery. I would like to learn Japanese so that I could live in Japan and work in a pottery."

I wasn't as startled as one might think. Japanese art had been a passionate interest for him ever since college. I could not prod him toward any direction he wasn't ready to take. In his irresolution, he was resolute, but I knew he would never allow us to flounder. All I could do was wait.

We felt no pressure to decide anything immediately. We were free from work and, in the short term, from financial pressures. We were living in Rome, one of civilization's crowning treasures, which we could now leisurely explore. We chose not to budge from Palazzo Ruspoli for a while. In the morning, Victor would drive Giuliano to St. George's, a private English school on the Via Salaria. We have never spoken anything but Italian at home, and when we thought that we were going to be in Italy indefinitely, we took steps to make sure that Giuliano would become as comfortable in English as he was in Italian. After dropping off Giuliano, Victor came home to go marketing with me at Campo dei Fiori some mornings, close to the palazzo other times. When it was a mild day, we looked for a place where we could eat outdoors; otherwise we had lunch at home. The rest of the day, guidebooks and maps in hand, we visited Rome. We saw all of baroque Rome that we could find, every church of Borromini's, every carving of Bernini's, every painting of Caravaggio's. And we paid our respects to every other period of its long history, from the pre-Christian Forum, to the ghetto's medieval quarter, to the triumphant expression of the Renaissance that is the Vatican; from the beautiful art nouveau neighborhoods of the early 1900s to the neoimperial monuments of Mussolini's time.

Victor's father telephoned to say he was coming to see us. He came to Rome with a proposal. He and his wife had had a hard-working life, he said. They were longing for retirement to a warm climate, but first they had to sell the business. If Victor would come back and help make it very attractive to a good buyer, once the business was sold Victor would be able to retire as well and pursue his interests wherever they took him.

The apprehensions that possessed me when I had landed in Italy five years earlier had quickly been replaced by a life more complete than any I could have imagined. I had discovered my own country, taking full measure of its gifts. It hardly seemed possible to have to leave it. But my choice was either to continue to stay in Italy or to stay with my husband. I chose my husband. We didn't go to New York by plane. Victor felt we ought to go by sea, to have more time to adjust to the return to the States.

The hardest part of all for Victor was giving up our apartment. Twice before in his life when we moved—when he had had to leave the villa in the hills above Florence, and then, after Giuliano was born, when we exchanged the Sixty-fifth Street brownstone for an apartment on Central Park West—he felt that what he was leaving behind was part of himself. After the movers had emptied the apartment, before leaving for Naples to board the *Raffaello*, we climbed up to the *altana*, where Victor lingered to look once more on Rome, and cry.

Back to the New World

1967–1970

OUR BOOKS AND HOUSEHOLD EFFECTS were crossing the Atlantic, some of them for the fourth time. While waiting for them to arrive, we stayed in the house that Victor's parents owned in Atlantic Beach, on a sliver of land on Long Island that separates the ocean from an inlet known as Reynolds Channel. The ocean beach and the Atlantic's surf were a short walk away from the house, which had its own little patch of beach on the channel and a pier from which we could fish. It was a long commute to the city for Victor, but it was the beginning of summer and a pleasant place for Giuliano to be. He had terrific fun fishing from the pier, pulling up flounders, blowfish, and the strange-looking horseshoe crabs, and doing a ten-year-old's jig of triumph mixed with terror when he landed a thick, fiercely twisting eel.

We would soon be living in midtown Manhattan and we wanted Giuliano to continue his education in a private school not too far from us. He had had three years of grammar school in Italy, the last one in an English school, and we expected that he would be

On the S.S. *Raffaello*, 1967, the captain's
welcome ball

eligible for admission to the fourth grade. After the first few thorny
interviews in a language that he had scarcely begun to use, it became
obvious to us, to his examiners, and to Giuliano that it would be
to his advantage to step back a year and start his catching up at the
third-grade level.

As it turned out, language was the least of his problems. Lunch
was the problem. Giuliano had to have it at school, and at first,
I prepared the things he was accustomed to eating at home: veal
stews, *tortelloni* with ricotta and parsley, cannellini-bean soups, and
other similar dishes that I packed in a thermos container, along
with a separate container of fresh fruit. This didn't last too long.
Giuliano said the other children made fun of him for bringing such
peculiar food to school. The school had a cafeteria, so we decided
he should try it. Unfortunately, that didn't work either, because
there was hardly anything he could eat. He took a chance with the
macaroni and cheese because it sounded Italian, but one forkful of
it was all he could manage, again to the hilarity of his classmates.

I resigned myself to packing discreet-looking sandwiches for him. In his life up to then, it was not what he had been accustomed to thinking of as a meal, but it got him through the lunchtime recess without provoking curiosity and derision.

Neither I nor Victor wanted to give up having lunch at home, a decision that would, three years hence, play a strategic part in the birth of my cooking career. I narrowed my search for an apartment to within a few minutes' walking distance of West Fifty-seventh Street, forgetting about looking for the space, amenities, and architectural character that we had enjoyed in Italy. What I found, and what we could afford, was a compact but sunny two-bedroom on the tenth floor of a boxy, new, white-brick building on the corner of Sixth Avenue and Fifty-fifth Street, just two blocks away from Victor's work. When Giuliano came up to look, he raced through from the entrance to the end of the hall where his bedroom was. "*È tutto qui?*" he asked ("Is that all there is?").

Victor enrolled in a Japanese-language course at the New School. The pace wasn't fast enough for him, so he switched to a private tutor who had him prepare for their evening sessions with tapes that he would listen to every morning before going to work. He also took instruction in the tea ceremony ritual at the Urasenke Chanoyu Center, which had opened a branch near the United Nations. I had begun to take Japanese flower arrangement in Rome, intrigued by Victor's interest in Japanese arts and spurred by my own passion for nature in general, and for flowers in particular. The teacher was Jenny Banti, an Italian woman who had studied at the Ohara School of Ikebana in Japan. She had both a scholarly and an intuitive understanding of Japanese aesthetics and how they derive from the humble and patient observation of nature. Her teachings quickly found a welcome in my heart and mind. Italian regional cooking can claim no relationship to ikebana, nor can the look of our dishes, which hardly ever have any aesthetic objectives. Nevertheless, in ikebana's fidelity to natural values, in its disciplined improvisations, in its equilibrium of contrasts, there was a parallel, I thought, to my approach to ingredients and to my cooking. In New York, I enrolled in classes in the Ohara method, given by a Japanese master at the Algonquin Hotel.

In the spring of 1969, Victor arranged to have a month off from work and we flew to Tokyo, equipped with lists of everything: names, cities, restaurants, dishes, museums, temples. In Japan, we found beauty quite different in scale and character from that of Italy. Italy's beauties are often of the monumental kind, in settings encrusted with the country's multiple pasts. The beauty of Japan was almost self-effacing. It was usually in the immediate foreground: a garden of raked gravel and rocks; a scroll painting unrolled on a table; a tea alcove with an arrangement of flowers; the uncluttered, austere interior of a patrician house; a shop's wooden façade. It was the beauty of implements, of craftsmanship, of the softly robed women and men wearing their traditional costume. Everything looked ageless, as though it could have been made yesterday or a thousand years before.

I had been told of Japanese women's deference toward men, but my romantic Italian mentality, formed by tales of the age of chivalry and gallant knights, had refused to take it in. But I soon had to. In restaurants waitresses fawned over Victor, serving him first, and on the occasions when I would approach a door at the same time as a Japanese male, the man would rush past me to spare me the embarrassment of preceding him through it. I can still giggle now, as I did then, over an incident in the elevator of our hotel in Tokyo. When the elevator came to our floor, the top one, Victor and I were the only ones to get in. At the next floor, a big American man entered. At the floor below that, two Japanese women in kimonos, two living miniatures, came in. When the doors opened at the lobby level, the Japanese women stood aside, with a smile and a hint of a bow, waiting for the man to exit first. The tall American smiled back and waited for the ladies to go. We were stuck in the back. Nobody moved, the doors closed, and the elevator, with all its passengers still in place, rose to the uppermost floor again.

We roamed Tokyo on our own, visiting gardens, galleries, shops, playing pachinko, ducking into small restaurants, going to Kabuki and Noh theater. Looking back, it is hard to believe that we could have been so adventurous. Victor's rudimentary Japanese helped, of course, even though it didn't always work in the way he intended. He had become skillful and confident in giving taxi drivers directions. One driver threw him off balance by responding in English. He wanted to show off too. Victor, however, was concentrating so tightly on trying to understand Japanese that he could not make out what the man was saying. I translated into Italian for him, which threw Victor off even more. "When did you learn Japanese?" he asked me.

We were favored during our stay by excellent connections. Victor's old foreign service friend, Mark, had been consul in Tokyo and had recommended us to a Japanese woman who worked at the embassy. She in turn, when we departed for Kyoto, introduced us to the chief of police there, who became a helpful escort. In Kyoto, Victor also had an introduction to the Urasenke tea ceremony center, and I had an appointment later on in Kobe to meet a living national treasure, Houn Ohara, the head of the ikebana school I attended. I was also to call on a former ikebana classmate who lived in Nara, a Japanese woman whose husband had moved back to Japan to work for Toyota, then in its infancy.

We had allotted five days to Kyoto. We stayed ten. If Victor had still been the madcap bachelor I once knew, nothing would have prevented him from cashing in his return plane ticket and staying as long as he could. We took long walks, we spent hours in the temples looking at their gardens, and we shopped. Victor bought some ceramics and loaded up on hand-cut wooden combs. We bought scroll paintings and an eighteenth-century screen painting of a bamboo fence, chrysanthemums, and a misty landscape in the distance that Victor shipped to New York as a gift for his mother. It now takes up the end wall of our living room in Florida.

We also ate very well, with not a single dull or indifferent dish in all the time we were in Kyoto. The larger part of the thousands of meals that Victor and I have had in our travels have faded to a blur in my memory, and many are altogether beyond recall, but two of the ones we had in Kyoto remain in sharp focus as among the most dazzling of our lives.

Mark had given Victor an introduction to an antiques dealer from whom he bought a sixth-century Sui dynasty Chinese terracotta horse and rider. Upon completion of the transaction, the dealer asked us if we liked tempura, which we assured him we did, and invited us to join him that evening. We met at a small, modern two-story building that bore no indication that it might be a restaurant. He escorted us upstairs to a private room where we found a semicircular counter of brilliant scarlet lacquer. A woman standing behind it presided over copper cauldrons brimming with hot oil. There were three stools, one for each of us. "This is called *zashiki* tempura," our host said. "The woman will be cooking only for you, and you must not be in a hurry because she has many things to offer you." As a qualifier, "many" was hardly adequate. "Limitless" might have been more accurate, but I don't know for sure because we eventually had to say, "Please stop." The variety of seafood was startling even for me, who comes from a famous fishing town. Its freshness and flavor, as well as those of the vegetables that were part of the dinner, could not have been surpassed. Each morsel was fried, drained of any drop of fat, and tendered to us by the cook—Victor first, of course—only when we had consumed the previous one. Thus, every bite was at its most desirable point of crispness and heat. It was an ideal rhythm for the enjoyment of fried food. Neapolitans, who also fry formidably well, have described it as *frienno e magnanno*, which was exactly what we were doing, frying and eating.

On Victor's list, there was the name of the restaurant reputed to be Kyoto's greatest. It was the kind of restaurant, we were to learn, where before you can make a reservation you have to have an introduction. On a day when we had made no other plans, Victor suggested we go there for lunch. We hailed a taxi and gave the driver the address. He looked us over and asked, "Do you have a reservation?" "No," Victor said. "It's all right; take us there, please." It was rather on the outskirts of town, a plain but dignified, low, traditional-looking, wood-and-stone structure. Victor paid the man, but he didn't drive off; evidently the driver was waiting for us to have to get back into the car and return to where we had come from.

We rang and a woman in a kimono came to the door. "We would like to have lunch," Victor said. "What is the name?" "Hazan." "Do you have a reservation?" "No, but won't you please accommodate us anyway?" "Oh, I am so sorry." The Japanese think a flat "no" is impolite, so they rarely say it. They wave their hand in front of their face as though they are brushing away a fly—curiously, it is similar to an Italian gesture that means "you are crazy"—and they say they are sorry, *sumimasen*. But it was not the last word, as far as Victor was concerned. The woman spoke some English, and using English laced with a few appropriate Japanese words to show that we were not complete barbarians, Victor managed to get her to reconsider. She excused herself and went inside for a few minutes, leaving the door open a crack. When she came back, she opened the door wide to let us in, and we turned to see the taxi drive away.

We were shown into a large room decorated in Japanese style where the only furnishings were a large five-fold screen painted with a river-and-mountain landscape, a beautiful low lacquer table, and brightly colored silk pillows. We sat down cross-legged at the table. We were the room's only occupants. A woman in a kimono came and pulled open the shoji screens of the wall in front of us, revealing an exquisite garden beyond. The meal was served one small course at a time, on handsome ceramics and lacquer, each piece unlike any of the others. At one point, our waitress brought in an iron grill no larger than a shoebox, with hot coals below it. On it she placed two small fish the size of smelts or sardines. When they were done, she used her chopsticks to butterfly them and expose the bones, and continuing with only the chopsticks, she fully boned them and recomposed them as though they had never been touched. At first, we responded to each course with lively vocal appreciation of the flavors, so clear and delicious, but eventually, the stillness of the setting, the subdued beauty of the presentation, and the skill and silent grace of our server made us speechless, and we finished the meal in quietude.

When we next met our police chief friend, he could scarcely believe our exploit. There were only two days remaining for our stay in Kyoto, and he asked what we wanted to do before leaving. "We'd like to visit the Katsura Imperial Villa in the morning," Victor said. "Certainly," said the chief. Others subsequently pointed out to us that for a Japanese, a wait of several months to book admittance is not unusual. Katsura is a residential complex of wood buildings erected in the 1600s by a prince of the imperial line. Its spaces, which flow and seem to float, have both a lofty serenity and a close-to-the-earth plainness. It is architecture of consummate refinement, but it prizes informality, and while it exemplifies order, it springs surprises. It's a house deliberately empty, but not vacant, made to be adorned by the fullness and color of human life. It is not only one of the world's masterworks of architecture, but an absolute masterwork of the human spirit.

When, after other stops, we left Japan, we felt that we had come on an exploratory visit to the country where, as Victor had dreamed, we might someday live part of our lives. It remained a dream. Twenty years later, when I was on the way to Hong Kong to present a fortnight of Italian cooking at the Mandarin Hotel, we stayed briefly in Tokyo. But the once placid streets were jammed with cars, the affordable little restaurants had become very expensive little restaurants, we saw no men on the street wearing the handsome traditional costume, and only waitresses appeared to be wearing kimonos. It was no longer the same place.

I probably would not have had a food career to write about if my father-in-law had not been a devotee and favored customer of Pearl's, a smart uptown Chinese restaurant. Few, if any, among those patrons of Pearl's from the 1960s who are still around can have forgotten her deft interpretations of Chinese home cooking. I never have. At that time, I wasn't working, and repeated exposure to Pearl's repertory prompted me to put some of my abundant free time to good use by learning something about the cuisine. I signed up for a Chinese cooking class taught by Grace Chu, a woman whom I have never heard anyone call anything other than Madame Chu. Madame Chu opened two new worlds to me. One was the world of Chinese cooking, for which I have developed as much affection as I have for the cuisines of my own country. The other was the world of cooking classes. I had never imagined that cooking was something that could be taught in a class.

To my regret, that first Chinese cooking course was also my last.

Madame Chu announced that she was taking a sabbatical in China, and my classmates looked around for something different to cook until she came back. One of them asked me what I was cooking at home. "Normal food," I said. "What is normal food?" she asked. I mentioned *tagliatelle alla bolognese, fegato alla veneziana, risotto coi funghi,* and *rollatini di vitello con la pancetta,* to which she made no reply. During our next class session, she asked me if I had ever had any teaching experience. Thinking of the classes I had taught in Italy, I said of course, it was what I had been trained to do. During another session she borrowed my typewritten copy of the day's recipe, and when she returned it, I found written on the back of it "For Italian cooking classes," followed by the names and telephone numbers of six of the women in class. I consulted Victor, who was all for it. "Why not?" he said. "You like to teach, you like to cook, and you have plenty of spare time." In October 1969, in the tight space of our apartment's kitchen, I began to teach Italian cooking once a week to six of my Chinese cooking classmates.

I tried to model my classes after Madame Chu's, which were beautifully organized. But I had to adapt them to my circumstances. Grace Chu had a large kitchen with room for a large table where the students stood to do their prepping. My kitchen was practically a galley kitchen, short and narrow, and it had to accommodate six students plus Lucia, my housekeeper from Italy—now also my assistant—and me. The best the students could do was to stand very close to one another and watch what I was doing.

We had an antique dining table in a nook just outside the kitchen, and it was there that, with an oilcloth protecting the table-top, I prepped for our own meals. It was too low to work on standing up, so I did it sitting down, having discovered it to be the most comfortable way to prep. The dining nook became part of my teaching space. In the kitchen they stood and watched, at the table they sat and worked. It was where I sat my students down to discuss the lesson, to examine the ingredients together, and to prep. I bought individual cutting boards and knives for everyone, and by each place at table, I set a moist washcloth for wiping one's fingers. I found that working sitting down was so convenient that for most of my teaching career thereafter I adopted it whenever it was possible.

From the very beginning, each of my lessons was based on a complete menu: an appetizer, sometimes; always a first course— pasta, risotto, or soup—followed by a second course, meat or fish; a suitable accompanying vegetable course or a simple, refreshing salad; and a dessert, which frequently was marinated fruit, in one combination or another. We prepped and cooked and assembled the menu from scratch, and we ate it at table in proper sequence to demonstrate the timing of preparation and rhythm of consumption of a classic Italian meal. Time was a fundamental ingredient that students didn't always know how to handle efficiently. They all wanted terribly to cook, but they rarely could find time to do it except during long weekends. Italians cook full, fresh, unpretentious, but tasteful meals every day for their family, and to the very last class of my career, I have tried to show how it is done.

The first recipe I chose to demonstrate in each lesson was for the dish that required the least preparation but needed the most time to cook. While it was on the fire, we trimmed the vegetables, which take a lot of prepping but cook in a short time. If the vegetables had to be blanched, I would put a pot of water on the fire in advance so that it would already be boiling when I needed it. Waiting for water to boil is a horrible waste of time. I would always have something cooking while I was working on something else; the fricassee would be on the fire while I was preparing the pasta sauce, the pasta sauce would be cooking while I was making a dessert of fresh fruits, and the pasta might be cooking while I was deglazing the pan in which the meat had been cooked. I showed my students that if the preparation of several dishes overlapped, there would be no idle moments in the kitchen, and they could produce the several courses of a classic Italian meal in relatively little time.

I had described the food that we ate at home as "normal food," but little about it was normal to my students. Why do Italians eat so much? they wanted to know. They don't, I told them. But what about all those courses? they asked. I explained: We really don't have that many courses; the appetizer course would be part of a special holiday meal, as would the dessert. At home, seasonal fruit usually takes the place of a baked dessert. We do have two courses, a first and a second, instead of a main course. However, we have two courses not in order to eat more but in order to eat less and more frugally. The pasta course, when it is served Italian style rather than Italian-American style, is quite small and has a minimal amount of sauce. The meat or fish in the course that follows is an expensive ingredient, but if you have a pasta or risotto or soup first, a small portion of it is sufficient. With meat, we always have a tasty vegetable, with fish, a simple salad of greens or tomatoes dressed with vinegar and olive oil. The quantities are small, but it is a more satisfying and a better-balanced way to eat.

I also had to point out that when we say Italian cooking, what we are really talking about is the cooking of Italian regions. The iconic dish of Naples is linguine with clams; in Florence, it is bean-and-black-cabbage soup; in Bologna, it is homemade noodles with meat sauce; and in Venice, it is a risotto with either fish or vegetables. Moreover, up to recent times, the people living in one region would have had little experience of the cooking of another. When I was young, we didn't have spaghetti or other forms of factory-made pasta, which were not common in northern Italy until after the war.

Victor got a two-sided map of Italy to help me describe both the historical and the physical causes of the profound differences in regional cooking. One side showed the country divided into the territories that loosely correspond to the independent states into which Italy was divided before it became a nation, in 1861. The other side was a physical map that allowed me to point, for example, to the large plain in the northeast, where it was feasible to raise cows that produced milk for making the butter that is essential to those cuisines; or to the slopes of the predominantly hilly areas of the center and south, where, instead of raising cows for their butter, it was more practical to cultivate olive trees for their oil. There were so many such examples of the roots of regional cooking that when I eventually opened my cooking school in Bologna, I expanded that talk into a full-scale lecture, using two five-foot maps. I have since carried those maps around the world and given that lecture wherever I have taught a class and whenever I have been invited to talk about the cooking of Italy.

Italians, like other Latin people, eat almost everything. It had never occurred to me that parts of animals, or animals that for me were conventional and delicious fare, might provoke a case of nerves in others. That year was as filled with surprises for me as it was for my six ladies. The day I chose to do lamb kidneys was a grim one. If there had been a Fletcher Christian in my class, they would have mutinied. "What could possibly be wrong with eating lamb kidneys?" I wondered. It is a piece of meat like any other, and much tastier than most. I insisted that we prepare the meal as I had planned it, and they even admitted that the kidneys were quite tasty. But I have never made it again, except for Victor and myself, and for Italian guests.

A dish that has sometimes caused problems for students who keep kosher is a Bolognese pan-roast of pork and milk. A student once asked if she could make it with a different kind of meat. "Yes," I said, "you can use veal, but it won't have the same depth of flavor." "If I make it with veal, can I omit the milk?" "Why do you want to make it at all?" I asked her. I have never taken that pork and milk off my class menus. There is no other dish made in Italy that more neatly embodies the genius of the cuisine, reaching a pinnacle of flavor with the bare minimum of ingredients—only two, pork and milk—and the simplest of procedures.

I cannot count the number of students who recoiled from handling fish with its head on. "It is looking at me!" they cried. I cried back, "How can it look at you? It's dead!" Or those who shrank from eating rabbit: "The poor little bunny." I remember a man in one of my Bologna classes who, I noticed, ate perhaps less than half of all the dishes we cooked. I spoke to him discreetly, on the side. "Do you have a dietary problem?" I asked. "Oh, no, I can eat everything," he said. "Then why don't you?" "I hate the taste of anything made with olive oil." "You don't like olive oil and you have come all the way to Italy to eat and to cook?" I wanted to ask, but didn't. I had already acquired the reputation of being sharp with students, and I was trying not to add to it.

Perhaps the most dramatic confrontations I had were over squid. Squid is an extraordinary source of flavor when used in seafood risottos, pasta sauces, or fish soups. On its own, it makes the tastiest stew. A squid's elegant triangular sac is one of the most versatile and delicious containers for stuffing of all kinds. The most popular, but also the most neutral tasting, way to cook squid is to slice it into rings and fry it. In American restaurants, it is hardly ever served any other way, and on the menu, the dish is listed simply as calamari. "Calamari," however, happens to be the Italian word for squid, whether it is live or raw or cooked in any of its thousand possible ways. In Venice, I once took an American visitor to the celebrated restaurant Da Fiore, where, after a cursory look at the menu, she ordered calamari. When she was eventually presented with a plate of beautiful, burnished stuffed squid sacs, she was shocked. "I didn't order that," she said, "I ordered calamari."

I was determined that students become acquainted with squid's many delectable uses, so in almost all of my courses, I have had a lesson in which we cleaned squid and cooked it in some way, but not fried in rings. To bring a bowl of raw squid soaking in water and ask the ladies—men didn't mind—to plunge their naked, mani- cured hands into it, retrieve a whole slippery squid, and perform the necessary cleaning and trimming procedures was to provoke a battle of wills. It was a battle I never lost. Anyone who refused was asked to leave the class, and none ever did. It wasn't as futile an effort as one might think. From time to time, I would hear that someone was putting squid into their risotto, or stewing it with tomatoes and chili pepper as I had taught them, or making stuffed squid, as I had suggested, for a buffet. It made me so glad.

When we finished our first series of six lessons, the ladies asked for another series, then another, and then another. We had started in October; we finished in June. I said good-bye to them affectionately but decisively. We had been together a year, scholastically speaking, and they and I deserved to graduate to something else. I would love to see them again, I said, but not for a cooking class.

I had found a cheap flight to Italy. I longed to see my widowed mother, who in turn longed to see her grandson, and for the next few weeks, Giuliano and I were back in Cesenatico. When we returned in August, Victor asked me whether I wanted to continue giving cooking classes. "Of course," I said. I had never done anything that I enjoyed more, but I didn't see how I could recruit other students. No one, aside from those first six ladies, knew that I was avail- able to teach cooking. Victor recalled having seen a list of cooking schools come out in the *New York Times* food section toward the end of the summer. "I'll write to them," he said, "and perhaps they'll add your name to the list." Shortly thereafter, we received a letter from the *Times*. They were sorry, but the list had already been set and it was too late to include my classes in it. "That's that!" I said. My new career had been a short one, and I started to look around to see how, aside from doing ikebana, I could fill my time.

Two or three weeks later, I had a telephone call from a stranger. I was then—and to a degree, I am today—uncomfortable speaking English over the telephone. On the phone, a foreign language sounds even more foreign. It was a man from the *Times*. He wanted to come over and interview me about my cooking class.

"When would you like to come?" I asked.

"How about Wednesday?" he said.

"That's fine," I said. "What time?"

"Twelve thirty."

"Oh, at twelve thirty my husband and I are having lunch."

"Well, then, how about Thursday?"

"That's fine," I said. "What time?"

"Twelve thirty."

"But my husband comes home for lunch every day at twelve thirty. If you really want to come at that time, come for lunch."

He said he did not usually accept lunch invitations, but he was intrigued to hear that Victor would be there, and he accepted.

"Anything new this morning?" Victor asked at lunch. I told him about the call from the *Times*. "Who was it?" he asked. "Someone named Crec, Greg, I didn't catch the name." I have never been a good catcher of names. "Could it have been Craig Claiborne?" "That's it!" I said. "You know who he is," he said. "Don't you remember that you always read his columns in the food section of the *Times*? He is the most famous food writer in America." I did read Claiborne's

October 1970. Setting lunch for Craig Claiborne

pieces, but neither the name of the writer nor his reputation had ever registered with me.

I decided to serve Claiborne a complete Italian meal: appetizer, first course, second course, salad, dessert. For the appetizer, I made *Carciofi alla Romana*, artichokes served upside down with their stems pointing up, as I had learned to do in Rome. My first course was one we used to make often at home in Cesenatico, *Tortelloni di Bieta e Ricotta*, hand-rolled pasta shaped into tortelloni that were stuffed with Swiss chard and ricotta. The second course was *Rollatini di Vitello*, veal rolls stuffed with pancetta and Parmesan cheese, cooked in butter and tomatoes, and sauced with a few drops of their pan juices reduced with white wine. The salad was raw *finocchio* sliced very thin, seasoned with salt, olive oil, and black pepper. It was too much food to end in a sweet dessert, so I prepared one of my favorite fruit bowls, *Arance Marinate*, peeled, sliced oranges marinated with a little bit of sugar and served cold. It was a lovely meal. Nearly forty years have passed, but I don't think I can improve on it.

I knew nothing about interviews. To me, it was just a guest joining us for lunch. The food was the thing. In Italy, when someone comes to eat, you don't bother with preliminaries; you go straight to the table. When the doorman rang to let me know that Claiborne was coming up, I turned on the heat under the saucepan of water in which I was to cook the pasta and put the cooked veal rolls back in the pan to reheat them. When Claiborne came in, however, he said he wanted to interview me before we sat down to eat, so I rushed back to the kitchen to turn all the burners off. When the interview was over, I turned on the heat under all the pans again, and I brought the artichokes to the table. We had just started on the artichokes when the doorman rang to say that there was a photographer from the *Times* downstairs. Claiborne had him come up, saying that if I didn't mind, he would take some photographs before we continued with the meal. Back into the kitchen I went to turn off all the fires, convinced that the veal was going to be leather-hard by the time I finished warming it up again. Miraculously, every dish was very good, and Craig, who in the years to follow would become a close friend, was enchanted. On the following Thursday, Craig's story covered the better part of a page. He printed my telephone number, and my cooking classes sprang to life again. It was October 15, 1970. I have never since then had to be concerned about how to occupy my time.

A Book Born Twice
and Twice Reborn

1971–1980

$\mathcal{A}$ YEAR HAD PASSED since Craig Claiborne's visit when I had another telephone call from a stranger. As I understood it, he was from *Harper's Bazaar,* he had seen my cooking school listed in the *Times,* and he had something that he wanted to discuss with me. Nothing else he said was clear to me. I didn't feel like struggling with a puzzling conversation over the telephone, so I invited him to come for dinner, hoping that he would write about my school for the magazine.

I opened the door to a tall, lean man in his late thirties, with a full head of curly dark hair. He came in with a bright smile.

"Good evening, I am Peter Mollman. Thank you for having me, I am so happy to meet you."

"You are from *Harper's Bazaar?*" I asked.

"*Harper's Bazaar?* Oh, no. I am with Harper & Row."

"What is the difference?"

"We have no connection with the magazine. We are a book

publisher. I am in charge of production there, but I am also the publisher of Harper's Magazine Press, a separate Harper imprint."

I had no idea what he was talking about, but I tried to conceal my confusion, relying on Victor to explain it all to me later. In the meantime, I showed him in, and soon thereafter, to the table. I hadn't yet adopted the custom of engaging guests in lengthy conversation over drinks and nibbles before serving dinner.

"Why did you want to talk to me?" I asked, after we had begun to eat.

"You must have heard of the publisher Mondadori?" he began by saying.

"Of course, everyone in Italy knows Mondadori."

"I recently spent three months with them in Verona, and I couldn't believe how wonderful the food was there. It is so different from Italian food in America, don't you think?"

"Oh, sure, very, very different," I said.

"When I came back from Verona, I looked for a cookbook in English with recipes for dishes like the ones I had had in Italy, but there doesn't seem to be one. Have you ever come across any?"

Had he come over to ask me to recommend a cookbook? I wondered. "No, I never have," I said.

"Well then, wouldn't you like to write one?"

"No."

He responded with the explosive laugh that would punctuate the many meetings we had thereafter.

"Why not?"

"I can't write in English."

Victor broke in at this point. "That is no problem," he said. "I can put it into English for you."

Not too many days later, Peter called to say he had a contract ready for me to sign, but he needed to insert a delivery date.

"How long do you think it will take you?"

"I am not sure. How about three months?"

"Let us make it ten," he said.

I knew nothing about writing a cookbook, but I had been teaching full-time for two years, and I had learned how to help students grasp the sense and method of a recipe. Moreover, I didn't have to hunt for recipes. I had cooked scores of dishes for my family in my sixteen years of marriage, and many of those I had recently taught in class. I knew their workings backward and forward. I had brought my favorite cookbooks from Italy and I studied them now, not, as I had been wont to do, in search of cooking ideas, but to see how they were organized and how the recipes were set down. They were of no help. In Italy, cookbooks are written for a public already familiar with the procedures of the cuisine. The instructions are in a cooking shorthand that I would have loved to use, but if I had, my recipes would have been inaccessible to most American readers. Together with Victor, who from that moment became my inseparable collaborator, I looked at the recipe styles of several cookbooks popular in America, and we eventually adopted the model that Craig Claiborne had followed, in which everything was spelled out and each step was numbered. It seemed to us the clearest approach of all, and we have stayed with it through all my cookbooks.

I equipped myself with a batch of spiral notebooks and a box of ball-point pens, Victor bought a portable Smith Corona electric typewriter, and we got down to work. During the day, I wrote out my recipes by hand—just as I am now writing these recollections—and tested them in the kitchen for reliability and accurate measurements. In the evening, when Victor came home from work, he read the recipes I had written. My approach was spontaneous and intuitive, his was deliberate and rational. He had an inexhaustible, and sometimes infuriating, store of questions: "How much butter, how much onion? Here you say flour spread on a plate; why not tell them how much? How much basil for the pesto? I have always seen you snap the ends off the green beans, but you don't say anything here about doing that." Sometimes, to satisfy him, but not without irritation, I tested a recipe again on another day. The mayonnaise I had to redo from scratch because I had made it without measuring any of the ingredients except for the eggs. Unless I was baking a cake, I never measured ahead of time, because it would have interfered with my instincts. I measured after the fact, calculating from how much was left in the measuring cup how much oil I had used, or how much butter was missing from a whole stick. I repeatedly tested the recipe, obediently following my original measurements, a procedure that felt as awkward for me as it was necessary for Victor. Once Victor was comfortable with my instructions, he would turn on his Smith Corona and give English expression to my notes and to the observations that had emerged from our discussions.

The title we gave the book was *The Classic Italian Cook Book.* Its subtitle was *The Art of Italian Cooking and the Italian Art of Eating.* To illustrate what I meant by the art of eating, I appended menus to each recipe to serve as examples of well-conceived Italian family meals. We completed the manuscript in less than ten months. When it was done, Victor placed the thick stack of typewritten pages on a table and photographed it. We knew so little about book publishing that we never expected to see it again. He delivered it

February 1972. Believing our work had come to an end, we photographed the manuscript of *The Classic Italian Cook Book* before taking it to the publisher.

himself to Harper's, and as all thoughts of the cookbook vanished from our minds, we left for a two-week holiday at Club Med in Martinique.

Not too long after our return, a messenger brought our manuscript back. The once beautiful clean margins were cluttered with notations, and thus we became acquainted with what an editor does. I can remember only two of her observations. She pointed out that we had used the adjective "piquant" five times in as many recipes and wondered whether we were considering calling this *The Piquant Italian Cook Book*. Victor was mortified. I am not sure that he has ever again described anything as piquant. The other boner was the editor's. I had a recipe for mussels following one for clams, and she wondered why I didn't call both of them clams. "Aren't they the same thing?" she wrote.

We thought we were done when we had replied to all the editor's queries and returned the manuscript to Harper's, but it came back with a whole new set of notes, those of the copy editor. This is the person who catches everything that the editor misses, parses your sentences, and brings your errant syntax into line. You can meet an editor many times and even have lunch with her, but all you ever see of the copy editor are her remarks and corrections in colored pencil. I have never met the copy editors of any of my books, but although anonymous, they were never reticent. The margins of a manuscript and, if there was not sufficient space on them, the paper banners Scotch-taped to the edges of the page bore copious evidence of exchanges that, while courteous, could be sharp, but were also, on occasion, encouraging.

We had hoped this would be the last time we would see our marked-up pages, and it was. In the next phase, we were presented with long sheets of paper called galleys that bore our words set into type. We had to comb those for any errors that might have escaped the editor, the copy editor, the typesetter, and ourselves. We were even allowed a limited amount of rewriting. We were deeply moved by those first galleys of our publishing career, because what we had done was finally beginning to look like a book. But we weren't finished yet. The galleys were followed by page proofs, which were laid out and set like the pages of the finished book. It can be quite expensive to correct a page proof, so one hopes to find few errors and flees the temptation to do any rewriting. That was thirty-five years ago. Computers have since transformed the whole process, making it faster, more accurate, and more flexible.

Victor and I shared the burden of dealing with edits, but the task of working with the illustrator, and preparing all the food he had to draw, was mine alone. Peter had chosen a marvelous draftsman, a Japanese artist named George Koizumi. He made the best drawings I have ever seen in a cookbook, lively, clear, with vigorous line and powerful chiaroscuro. When recently I read Bill Buford's account in *Heat* of his pilgrimage to a mountain town near Bologna to learn the secret of turning tortellini on one's fingertip, I thought of how much trouble he might have spared himself by turning to page 156 of *The Classic Italian Cook Book* and studying George Koizumi's wonderful drawing of that step. The only problem George had came up when he had to draw chestnuts to accompany the illustration of Monte Bianco, a dessert made of a purée of chocolate and chestnuts. He had never seen a chestnut, and there were none in the stores because it wasn't their season. He used Chinese water chestnuts from a can as a model, but he drew them so large that they looked gigantic next to the dessert. He redrew them, but they have never looked quite right. When I wrote *More Classic Italian Cooking*, a sequel to the first book, we tried to get George to do the drawings. He wouldn't be persuaded, however. It took too much of his time, he said, and it distracted him from the art that he wanted to produce for himself. I had a good time working with George, and when he would finish a sketch and we sat down to eat the models I had prepared for him to draw, I believe he enjoyed himself too.

Peter had the book's jacket designed without discussing it with us. When he sent it over, both Victor and I were aghast. It was a bright tomato-red with green stripes, the title in white. It was the Italian colors. Except when they win a world soccer title, an event that may take place once or twice in a decade, Italians are not flag-wavers. They had enough of doing it during the twenty years of fascist rule. There are no flagpoles in front of private buildings, no flags fluttering from car fenders, no flag decals stuck to car windows, and save for Mr. Berlusconi, men do not wear lapel pins of the flag.

Peter's design provoked the only sharp exchange of words with him that we have ever had. We succeeded in getting the green stripes removed, but nothing else was changed. When the book was reissued by Knopf, we were elated to see that garish jacket discarded in favor of the elegant one that Judith Jones chose for us. Ironically, the Harper's Magazine Press edition of *The Classic Italian Cook Book* in its original wrapper has become a collector's item. I recently saw one offered at $150. Today, when I look at the tomato-red jacket of my first book, the resentment has gone, replaced by nostalgia for those young, tumultuous moments of my publishing career.

The Classic Italian Cook Book was published in the spring of 1973, collecting enthusiastic reviews from all quarters. I was as happy as I was incredulous at its extraordinary reception. Walking past the Doubleday bookstore on Fifth Avenue, I saw it featured in the window display, and it so thrilled me that I ran home to get my camera so that I could photograph it. My high spirits tumbled to the ground, however, during a small tour that the publisher had arranged for me. I went to Chicago, Seattle, San Francisco, and Los Angeles. I was interviewed by the local food editors, I was on a few radio talk programs, and I did some cooking on television. Wherever I was, I visited bookstores, looking for my book on the cookbook shelves. I never found one anywhere. "Why am I here promoting something that no one will be able to buy?" I wondered.

On my return home, Victor suggested we try to meet Julia Child and ask her advice. He wrote her a letter attached to a copy of my book, and she wrote a warm letter back, with a flattering comment on my work. We spoke on the phone and arranged for her and her husband, Paul, to come for lunch on their next visit to New York. I don't remember what I made for lunch, but I remember that we connected quickly and openly. Julia described how she got into cooking in Paris. Paul talked about the time he was a young man and always walked around with a chip on his shoulder. I didn't understand the expression, so he demonstrated by placing his knife on his shoulder and mimicking someone ill-advisedly knocking it off. The knife was part of a handmade set of close-to-pure silver, and its handle still bears the small dent that it acquired when it fell to the floor.

I described how the elation at reading the favorable reviews of my book had been counterbalanced by my disappointment at how poorly it had been distributed. Victor asked if Julia would let us quote from her letter so that we might persuade the publisher to use it in an ad promoting the book. Julia said she couldn't do that because it was her policy never to supply a quote for publication. She explained that once you do that, it opens a door that everyone will want to go through, and moreover, if it's a cookbook, people will assume you have tried the recipes and are vouching for them. "A sensible policy," I thought. "If, in the future, anyone should ask me for a quote, I'll follow her example." "What you need," Julia said, "is a good editor, and I am going to introduce you to mine, Judith Jones at Knopf."

Had I not met Judith, my career might well have ended when

the last copies of the Harper's Magazine Press edition of my cook-book had been sold or remaindered. I would learn, thanks to Judith, what it meant to be well-published. To work with her was to work with someone who wanted for you no less than what you wanted for yourself, and showed you how to get it.

"I would like to publish your next book," she said, "but no doubt Harper's Magazine Press has put a right to first refusal in your con-tract. A good agent can get you out of that. Have you got one?"

"No."

"I'll ask mine to get in touch with you. His name is Robert Lescher, and he is a good man. He can help you."

Bob—aside from Judith's first reference, I never heard him called Robert—had an office with a hospitably clubby feeling, filled with soft armchairs, a fireplace, and shelves and stacks of books, in a gar-den apartment a couple of blocks away from our new apartment on East Seventy-sixth Street. When I called on him, I immediately felt comfortable with Bob. He was tall, with a broad, playful, slightly gap-toothed smile; a warm voice; and a gentle, humorous turn to his conversation. We went to lunch. In the middle of a New York winter day he wore no overcoat, just a muffler looped around his throat. I don't know if he has ever owned an overcoat; I have never seen him with one. We talked about my relationship with Harper's Magazine Press, which was deteriorating fast.

Peter Mollman had left Harper's in January 1974 to head the production team at Random House. Larry Freundlich was the new boss, and as far as I could see, he could do nothing right. He sent me on a brief, ineffectual tour, choosing as my escort a man who would write out the programs we were to follow in incomprehen-sible longhand, and who booked us in first class so that he could have his fill of free liquor. He also booked adjoining rooms in the hotels, but my first move upstairs was to make sure the door from my room to his was securely locked. I was embarrassed to be seen with him. The most damaging thing that Larry did, however, was to sell the British rights to *The Classic Italian Cook Book* to W. H. Allen, without consulting me. The W. H. Allen edition was a facsimile of the American one, printed on cheap, thick paper. No attempt had been made to revise the measurements, ingredients, and vocabulary so that the recipes would be more comprehensible to British cooks. Now I had two books that weren't moving, one in America, another in Britain.

Bob smoothly negotiated a release from Harper's Magazine Press and drew up a contract with Knopf for a new cookbook. At this point Judith said, "We really should have both your books under our imprint." "How do we do that?" I asked. "Talk to Bob, he should be able to figure something out." He did. He got Larry Freundlich to name a price for the rights to the book. It was twenty thousand dollars. We didn't have twenty thousand; we had ten, our entire savings. We asked Bob to talk to Judith to see if Knopf was willing to contribute the other half of the purchase price. They were. I felt low when we went to the bank. I grew up in a family where there never had been any money, and it was hard to make out a withdrawal slip for practically everything we had been able to save. But Victor said, "This is exactly what savings are for." We believed in our cookbook, and we believed in Judith. It was the best investment of our lives. Thirty years later, it is still paying us back.

Judith and Knopf's designer did a masterful repackaging job. The jacket was in earthy hues, ochre and mustard; the title and my name were in white on a green cartouche. A sampling of quotes from the scores of enthusiastic reviews I had received filled both the front and back of the jacket. One of my favorites was by Roy Andries de Groot, who at the time was one of the most respected writers on food: "Marcella's book is the most authentic and best guide to Italian food ever written in the U.S. Where other authors failed, Marcella has brilliantly succeeded in capturing (and conveying to the reader on almost every page) the feel, the aromatic scent, the subtle nuances of fresh country flavors and, above all, the easy uncomplication of Italian food prepared in the Italian style." The first Knopf edition of *The Classic Italian Cook Book* was published February 27, 1976. It was reprinted twenty-two times until, in 1992, its contents, together with those of my second book, *More Classic Italian Cooking*, were absorbed by my fourth book, *Essentials of Classic Italian Cooking*.

It didn't cost us anything to repossess the British rights to my cookbook. W. H. Allen's lamentable edition could not and did not fare well. They let it go out of print, and Bob moved quickly to recover our rights. My new British publisher was Macmillan, and my English editor was Caroline Hobhouse.

Caro was everything that you can imagine a grand English literary lady might be: tall, handsome, amusing, aristocratic in speech and bearing. She had a beautiful house in London where she gave us dinner parties so that we could meet figures from the British food establishment, such as Alan Davidson. Unfortunately, I didn't take to Davidson, nor he to me. Caro engaged Anna Del Conte, an Italian writer who had married an Englishman, to adapt my book for English use, converting all the measurements from the American spoons and cups into both metric and British units, anglicizing the spelling and even the vocabulary—"aubergine" instead of "eggplant," for example—and where necessary replacing an ingredient unavailable in England with one that was. The Macmillan edition of *The Classic Italian Cook Book* was published in the spring of 1980; the venerable Hatchard's bookshop on Piccadilly filled its window with it, and I had a transatlantic hit to add to my stateside one.

1980, London. *The Classic Italian Cook Book* in the window of Hatchard's on Piccadilly

A Funny Thing Happened

1973-1975

*I*N THE FALL of the year my book was published, I was invited to do a demonstration on the Joyce Brothers television show. The producer looked through the cookbook and chose a recipe for striped bass stuffed with several kinds of shellfish and baked sealed in foil. I had five minutes in which to bone the fish; stuff it with clams, mussels, oysters, and shrimp; wrap it in foil; remove from the oven a similar fish previously prepared and already cooked; unwrap it and slice it, all the while chatting with Dr. Brothers, who was expected to drop in a plug for my book. Just to bone the fish would have taken me twenty minutes, so I boned it at home; then I put the bone back in its place and closed the fish over it. When I was on camera I opened up the fish, I went through the motions of running a knife under the bone, and presto! Off came the whole bone in just seconds.

There was another guest cooking, Enzo Stuarti, a Mario Lanza–style tenor who was going to cook spaghetti. The precooked spaghetti was in a pot of still-boiling water. The pot had a perforated insert for draining cooked pasta, a metal basket that Stu-

With Dr. Joyce Brothers, my
first television appearance

arti lifted and carried past me with
scalding water still dripping from it.
He let it drip all over my feet. It was
my first time on television, but it
became the last time that I allowed
a producer to choose what I was
to demonstrate, and the last time
I shared a cooking segment with
anyone else.

Like others who have been
nurtured by the settled life of a
small town, I have never felt a
strong urge to expand my habi-
tat. I am not a self-promoter,
but New York is a bellows that can fan
great flames from small sparks. In the
year that my cookbook was published,
I was invited to dinners and parties, and in a few months, I had
met nearly everyone in, or at the margins of, the city's food world.
I immediately felt strong empathy for and from James Beard. I was
startled at first by the open-air shower that he had in the back of
his house on West Twelfth Street, but I soon understood that it
wasn't crude exhibitionism; it was a manifestation of his natural
candor, of his aversion to cover-ups. I was amazed by what he knew
and remembered. He was my living encyclopedia: Whenever I had a
question, he had the answer. He had a sonorous voice that he used as
a foil for the mischief in his eyes. His laugh was magnificent, rising
from deep within his capacious belly. An example of it still rings in
my memory's ears. Sometime after we had become friends, we were
both giving cooking classes in Italy, Jim at the Gritti Palace in Venice
and I at my school in Bologna. Jim was always collecting recipes for

a syndicated column that he wrote. He phoned me in Bologna to ask a question about an ingredient.

"Marcella!" said the booming voice. "I came across a recipe in an Italian magazine that I would like to use, it's for shrimp with a beautiful pink sauce, and it sounds delicious, but it's driving me nuts."

"What's the problem?"

"There is a mysterious ingredient in it that has to be essential to the pink sauce because nothing else in the list has that color. I have looked it up everywhere, but there is no description of it in any of the sources. I hope you can help me out."

"I hope so too. What is it?"

"Rubra."

"Oh, sure, Jim, it's ketchup."

"*Ketchup?*"

"That's right. Rubra is the best-known Italian brand of ketchup."

Ho, ho, ho, the big laugh came rolling over the phone line, over and over, such a happy laugh, as though he had just heard the funniest joke in the world.

Tom Margittai and Paul Kovi, both Hungarians and both executives at Restaurant Associates, became the new operators of the Four Seasons and the Forum of the Twelve Caesars restaurants when their company divested itself of those two properties. Paul was very Old World, wearing well-tailored conservative three-piece suits, the vest, crossed by a gold watch chain, resting on a prosperous paunch. He spoke English with a suave accent and had an air of great connoisseurship, looking both paternal and shrewd. When he found out that I came from Cesenatico, he said, "I know it well. When I was young I played on a professional Italian soccer team, and we trained near there." He was the only person I had met in New York who had heard of and been in my hometown. Tom was jet-settish, fashionable, and briskly entrepreneurial. Both became generous friends, but I got to see more of Tom, perhaps because he was more likely to be away from the restaurant than Paul.

Tom had dinner with us at home and loved what I cooked. He offered to give my cookbook a boost by hosting a fortnight at the Forum of the Twelve Caesars restaurant based on my recipes. For $25, one could have an antipasto, a first course, a second course, salad, and dessert, choosing from a menu of nineteen dishes. One of the two fish dishes offered was the stuffed striped bass I had demonstrated on television. Three Italian wines were included. The event was to run from November 11 through November 23, but it was so successful that they held it over until December 7.

I was there every evening to talk to guests. One evening Tom told me to expect Danny Kaye, who was coming with his daughter Dena. Danny left me no opportunity to talk to anyone else that evening. I learned that cooking was one of his great loves. He had others, of course, including piloting airplanes and dabbling in a variety of medical subjects, but he was obviously an extremely well-informed and deeply committed cook. I discovered too that, aside from Italian cooking, we had another culinary passion in common, Chinese food. Danny described the special Chinese kitchen he had built in his Beverly Hills house. He had gas burners with several concentric rings able to reach such high temperatures that, to make getting close to them tolerable, he had had to install a steel trough in front of the stove with a stream of ice water circulating through it. "Do you know how the Chinese make chicken lollipops?" he asked me. "Come into the kitchen and I'll show you." If you are Danny Kaye, you can walk into a restaurant's busy kitchen unannounced and ask someone to give you a chicken thigh and a knife. He loosened the skin at the knob end of the bone, scraped the flesh upward to leave the bone clean, and turned the skin inside out over the thick part of the drumstick. "There! You now have a chicken lollipop ready for frying. Let me know if you come to California," Danny said. "I'll make you a Chinese dinner."

As it happened, I had already accepted an invitation to teach in the Napa Valley wine country in the spring of the following year. The courses were organized by Michael James, a long-haired, delicate-looking young man with a thin mustache, and his friend and associate, Billy Cross. Michael had been a student of Julia Child's old partner, Simone Beck, known to all as Simca. Simca was to launch the event, followed by Jacques Pépin, and I was to conclude it with a three-week stint.

The venue for the courses was a Victorian villa, but my accommodations were in an adjacent cottage. Students could sign up for a two-day or three-day course or for a full week. Evenings were free. I was puzzled to find that Michael and Billy, who did all the marketing, would come back with quantities of ingredients much greater than I had requested. "Why so much food?" I asked Michael. "There is going to be a lot left over." "Don't worry about it, Marcella; we don't want the students to think we are skimping." I was not too happy about it because I hate leftovers and try to avoid them. I have never had a microwave in my kitchens. Few are the dishes that taste as good reheated as they do when freshly cooked. Cold or warmed-over pasta, for example, is unspeakable. On our first Saturday evening, Michael asked me to join them for dinner in the villa. When I walked in, I discovered the reason for the large quantities of food I had cooked. All the dishes from my classes had been resuscitated, and friends of Michael and Billy were feasting on them. The room was filled with young men and votive candles, and I felt extremely uncomfortable. As soon as I could, I grabbed a piece of bread and some cheese and fled to my room.

One of our students was Dagmar Sullivan, whose grandfather,

Georges de Latour, had founded Beaulieu Vineyard. On Monday morning, she asked me how I had spent the weekend. "In my room," I said. "What a pity," she said. "We have to do something about that." She alerted everyone in the Valley, and from that moment, I was never alone for dinner in the evening. No one is more hospitable than wine people, and I enjoyed the company, the food, and the wines at table with the Heitzes, the Jaegers, the Mondavis, with Dagmar and her amusing husband, Walter, of course, and with many others whose names have now slipped away beyond recall.

Another of my students at the villa was a tall, blond, robust cooking teacher from San Francisco, Loni Kuhn. Soon after, when I opened a cooking school in Bologna, Loni was one of the first to attend. She invited me to come to San Francisco in the winter to give classes at her school, which I did for many years. I became then as much at home in San Francisco as I was in New York. For the entire time that I was there, Jim Nassikas, the general manager of the Stanford Court hotel, generously made available the suite that was always reserved for James Beard when he came to town. Nassikas used to joke that he carried cigarette butts in his pocket that he distributed in odd corners of the hallways to see how long it would take the staff to sweep them away. It was only a slight exaggeration, and I can't even be sure that it wasn't true. I have never known a more immaculate hotel than the Stanford Court of those early Jim Nassikas years. Jim liked to cook, but I was never able to persuade him that you can't make a true risotto unless you stir it.

Victor and I made a great many friends in California, and one of those whose company I most enjoyed was Jeremiah Tower. He had charm, good looks, and the poise of a gentleman. He was no longer cooking at Chez Panisse, but he used to take us for lunch to the café upstairs, driving us there in a marvelous car whose interior glowed with more polished wood than I had ever seen inside an automobile.

We talked a lot about cooking, of course, and although the places we had come from, Australia and Italy, were so distant from each other, our feelings about food had the same origin. We had a kindred devotion to taste, taste free of affectation, taste that was clear, bold, and simple, taste that wanted only to be good. The meals that Jeremiah cooked for us at the places he subsequently opened, the Santa Fe Café and Stars, were the most delectable seafood feasts I have ever had in America, comparable with the best that I have ever had in Italy or in Asia. He eventually left San Francisco; he was in Hong Kong for a while, and in New York, but after the publication of his idol-smashing memoir in 2003, I lost his tracks. Sometimes in my daydreams, Jeremiah and I are as young as we were then, and I am still licking my fingers over his crab, lobster, and shrimp.

I had finished my third week of teaching for Michael at the Napa Valley villa, and I was packing to leave for New York, looking forward to being with Victor again, when I got a telephone call. It was Danny Kaye. "I am in Seattle. Tonight I am conducting the Seattle Symphony; tomorrow morning early I am returning to Los Angeles." He then gave me the number and time of a flight that I was to take from San Francisco to Los Angeles. "You will land not too long after me," he said. "I'll wait for you at the gate, we'll go marketing, and in the evening I'll make dinner." "But Danny, I already have a ticket for New York and Victor is expecting me." I don't think he even heard. "Look for me at the gate," he said. "I'll be there waiting." And he hung up. When I called Victor, he said, "You don't want to stand him up. Go, you'll have a good time."

As I came off the plane, I had no trouble spotting Danny under his soft-brimmed hat with an outsize crocodile logo. He drove us home, where I was given just enough time to put my bag down and use the bathroom. Before heading for the farmer's market, he leafed through the book of menus he had served. "To jog my memory," he said. When we returned, he showed me his kitchens, one for Western cooking, one for Chinese. The stove of the latter was as he had described when we had talked in New York; when the burners were at their maximum setting, the gas came on like a blast from a jet engine.

Of the people at table, I remember Danny's wife, Sylvia Fine, a funny lady; the actor Roddy McDowall; and Olive Behrendt, a patron of the Los Angeles Symphony. I would see a lot of Olive in later years in Venice. She had passed the city's tough skipper's exam and piloted her own motorboat through the baffling shallows of the lagoon. A heart attack eventually landed her in Venice's hospital, where she died alone and neglected in a common ward. There were others, but I have forgotten who they were and there is no one left alive from that evening whom I could ask.

Danny never came to the table. He cooked a dish that his Chinese assistant served to us, and while we were eating, he sat in a pantry pulling hard on his pipe. When the assistant told him we had finished, he prepared another dish, and again he retired, through to the end of dinner. I wish I'd had the nerve to ask him when and what he ate, but Danny didn't respond gently to interrogation. My memories of food are some of my sharpest, and they go back to the earliest moments of my conscious life, yet while I recall being happy at Danny's dinner, I don't remember a single dish I had. It had been a long, restless, and anomalous day whose happenings, at its end, had become hazy.

My greatest concern, whenever I wake up in the morning away from home, is where and how soon I am going to get a cup of coffee. I had been lodged in Dena's room upstairs, and when I came out of my sleep early that morning, I wrapped a robe around me and I tiptoed quietly downstairs, headed for the kitchen. Danny was already there, blowing huge clouds of smoke from his pipe. "It's about time

Danny Kaye comes to class.

you came down," he said. "We have got a lot to do. We are going to make pasta and *fegato alla veneziana*" (sautéed liver and onions Venetian style). We cooked and finished lunch barely in time for me to make the flight to New York.

The next time I heard from Danny, I was teaching a class in my apartment. One of the students was Pamela Fiori, today the editor in chief of *Town & Country* magazine. She was then on the staff of *Travel & Leisure* magazine, for which she was taping the lesson.

"What are you doing?" said Danny on the phone.

"I am teaching."

"What are you teaching?"

"I am making pasta, a roast of veal, sautéed vegetables, and marinated oranges."

"What kind of sauce do you have on the pasta?"

I told him.

"How do you make the veal?"

"Where are you, Danny?" I asked.

"In New York."

"Look, I am in class now and I can't talk. If you really want to know what I am cooking, come over."

His apartment, at the Sherry-Netherland, was not too far from ours, and in a few minutes, he was at my door. I had never had him in a class, and I was concerned that he might distract us with his routines. I shouldn't have worried. He was quiet, attentive, and helpful. But he did get an opportunity to do an unscripted number. I was demonstrating the Italian method of cooking a roast on top of the stove. There were six students crowding around me in the kitchen, plus Danny, plus my corpulent new assistant, Maria. The wall telephone rang. He asked if he could answer it for me. "Yes, please," I said. Pamela kept her tape recorder running and the following is a transcript of Danny's side of that phone conversation:

Allo? Eh? Yah, mah, whosa callin?

Wha, whazza your name?

Misses Horowis? En you lika to talk to Misses Hazan?

You wanta ask a question about the cookoobook?

Ehh, today sheeza very busy now, yah, if you aska me I will be able to tell you.

Oh, in da recipe where you hava da meat sauce bolognes?

You mada da sauce?

Izza too salty?

Well, in dat case you want me to tell you what to do?

Why it waza too salty?

Eh, you puta two teaspoon of salt?

Ahah! Ehh, three-quarters pounda meat en two teaspoon salt is too mucha salt? Oh my!

I tell you whacha do, Misses Horowis. You hava . . . you hava kosher salt?

Izza da big salt . . . you hava dat?

Now da next time you maka dis dish you taka four teaspoons of salt. Four! Put three teaspoons in a cuppa water and put it in de icebox. Use half a teaspoona salt in de, in de sauce, en, iffa not too salty, putta little more salt, if not throw da water with da salt into da sink en den it will not be too salty.

Two teaspoona regular salt. I think datsa mistake. Yes. No, no in da book, izza mistake of da salt you are using. You're using too salty salt. There are different kinds of salt, you know. You can buy salty salt and not-so-salty salt.

Iffa you go to the place and you aska, "Mister, I lika to hava some salt, but not too salty," en den dey give dis, en den you can use two teaspoons.

It came outa nice? Ehh, you see Misses Horowis, yourra smart lady. Whatsa nice Jewish lady makin wit Italian food?

Aha! You see, mah, you not using da right salt! Kosher salt, dat izza da one, izza not too salty. Ma, if you usa no kosher salt, if you usa just kinda salt [mumbles] . . . *aha, aha?*

It say in da recipe two teaspoons of salt? Eh, heh . . . Misses Horowis, I lika to ask you a question, when you cook, you taste? Mah, when you taste, you finda izza too salty, and no usa so much!

Yeh, datsa right, you put a potato in de thing, if izza too salty, when it finishes throw outa da sauce an eata da potato.

Eheh . . . eheh . . . eheh . . . eheh . . . ahah . . . ahah . . . izza nice. I will teller becoz she willa be very happy to know dat you maka da sauce now.

All right. Bye bye, en tank you.

I laughed along with the others while wondering if it was my accent that Danny was mimicking. "Is that how I sound to others?" I thought. It is true that sometimes people misunderstood me, but I am not sure the fault was always mine. I was teaching a dessert, and when I asked a student to separate two eggs that had been put on the table, she just moved them apart. "Is it me or is it her?" I asked myself. "Isn't 'separate' the correct word?" When your grip on a language is uncertain, it is easy to think that you are the one who has slipped.

I had a call one morning from a woman at Giuliano's school who said she was organizing an event for parents and children.

"There is going to be a buffet," she said, "and I was hoping that you could contribute a dish."

"Certainly," I said.

"Could you bring some Swedish meatballs?"

"Oh, I don't know what they are."

"Can you make a tuna casserole?"

"I am afraid not."

"How about a chicken casserole?"

"I don't even know what you mean by 'casserole.'"

"Well, all right," she said, sounding somewhat cross. "Can you contribute a dozen bottles of Coke?"

"Certainly."

"Can you bring them next Thursday evening?"

"I'll have to send them with someone, because on Thursday evening I have a cooking class."

"Of course, I understand. I hope you are making progress."

On another occasion, I was giving a demonstration class at Boston University with a small tasting. The tasting portions were small, but the audience was large. I had a lot of cooking to do and a lot of prepping. It was my custom, in such circumstances, to cook everything in full view of the audience, but to complete all but a small part of the prepping backstage in advance, keeping the lesson within reasonable time limits. That evening in Boston I was doing a fish stew with squid, and I had earlier held back just enough squid to use for the prepping demonstration. I had put it away in the refrigerator in a steel bowl filled with cold water. As I was getting ready to start, one of the assistants asked me whether she was to leave the squid in the refrigerator. "No," I said. "Keep it outside." When the moment came to show how to prep squid, I asked the assistant to bring me the bowl. I was surprised to see her leave the auditorium, but she returned quickly.

"It's gone!" she cried.

"What's gone?" I asked.

"The squid. I put it where you told me, and it's gone, it's not there anymore."

"Where did you put it?"

"Where you told me, outside."

"Where outside?"

"In the parking lot."

It didn't seem possible. "In the parking lot? Why the parking lot?"

"Well, Marcella, you said outside, and 'outside' means outside of the building, which is where the parking lot is."

Victor and I hardly ever speak anything but Italian to each other. Somehow, one day, when we were discussing what I was going to teach the next day, I slipped into the language of the lesson, and I said at one point, "I am going to show them how to screw the shrimp."

"Say that again," Victor said.

I repeated the words.

"And you have been saying it all this time?" he asked.

"Sure."

"And no one has ever made a comment?"

"No, why, what's wrong with it?"

I never tried to use the word "skewer" again. I showed students how to make a brochette of shrimp.

The classes had begun to attract an ever more interesting group of students. A few were professionals, sometimes even too professional. Gael Greene arrived to take a pasta class equipped with a formidable array of knives. "You don't need knives for pasta, Gael," I said. "You need good hands and a rolling pin." Men began to come to the classes. Jamie Niven, Ronald Lauder, Michael Thomas were among the ones I remember. Ronald was the most carefully dressed man I have ever had in class, or that I have ever known, perhaps.

He was often going to or coming from a formal event, and then he would come in his dinner jacket. In one class, I had both James Beard and Joel Grey, colossal Jim and doll-like Joel, working side by side. Italian cooking was catching on with a rush, but the markets that were essential to it were missing still. Every time I started a lesson I would think, "If only I could have gone with the students to a real Italian market this morning, if only they could see what our vegetables are like, our fish, our tiny lambs; if only we had quality olive oil to cook with, and eggs with sunset-red yolks for our pasta." The only way to do it would have been to take the class to Italy. And then, it seemed so obvious: Of course, I must take the class to Italy. I discussed it with Victor. He was always ready to consider any plan that would involve going to Italy. He said, "Yes, yes, yes! Go to Italy, go this summer, and see how it can be done."

Bologna

1975-1987

$\mathcal{P}$RIMO GRASSI AND I lived, played, and grew up a few houses apart on the same street in Cesenatico. He lives there still, in his childhood home. After the war, like many Italian intellectuals of his generation, he joined the Communist Party, a party that so dominated the administrative affairs of my native Emilia-Romagna that its capital city, Bologna, was dubbed *la rossa*, Bologna "the red." Primo was in charge of tourist affairs, an important position in the busy resort area of which Cesenatico was part.

At the end of Giuliano's spring term, I went back to Cesenatico with him. I told my mother I had come to see Primo about setting up a cooking school in town for my American students. She thought it was the most implausible scheme she had ever heard. She lived another twenty-one years, to the age of 101, and to the end, she never really got the point of her university-educated daughter's cooking career.

Primo didn't think any better of my project. "*Sei matta?*" ("Are you crazy?") he said. "You expect people to cross the ocean and come to Cesenatico to learn how to make *ragù*, meat sauce?" The town owned several buildings that could have accommodated a teaching kitchen, but Primo wouldn't consider it. Romagnoli, the natives of my area, are famous for their stubbornness, but if Primo was a Romagnolo, I was a Romagnola, and no less stubborn than he. When I insisted that I could make my idea work and that it would draw a desirable class of tourists to the region, he said, "*Va bene*, okay. The man you should talk to is Gianpaolo Testa. You may be able to convince him. I'll give you an introduction." "Testa? Where is he?" "In Bologna."

My first memories of Bologna were the traumatic ones of my childhood and of the operations to save my right arm, but they did not darken my feelings now for the warmhearted and warm-looking city I had come back to. Bologna is most beautiful at sunset. The prevalent building material is red brick, which lights up, at the end of the day, with a scarlet glow that some liked to interpret as nature's endorsement of the city's political affiliation. *La rossa* is just one of Bologna's sobriquets. *La dotta*, "the learned," is another, a reference to its university, Europe's oldest. Bologna is also known as *la grassa*, "the fat," in affectionate recognition of the native elements of its rich cuisine, the butter, the cream, the Parmigiano, the prosciutto, the mortadella, the *zampone* and *cotechino*, the handmade egg pasta.

Primo's introduction got me an appointment with Gianpaolo Testa, the president of Bologna's department of tourism. He had his office in a modern building that had replaced one of the older structures destroyed during the air raids of the Second World War. He rose and came briskly around his large desk to greet me. A well-nourished man, he had a ruddy complexion, wavy brown hair, a smile lacking a tooth or two, and quick, compelling eyes. I told him my story, describing how I had ended up in New York and how I had gone from teaching science to teaching cooking. I had brought a copy of my cookbook and a stack of newspaper and magazine articles. I laid out the plan I had of leading my students to the markets, the vineyards, the restaurants, the cheese makers, the prosciutto curers, and of setting up a kitchen where they could cook Italian food with the fresh, native ingredients they had seen in the market. He was fascinated and listened without interrupting, which is unusual for an Italian. I couldn't have placed my hopes in better hands. Testa had entrepreneurial drive and the political connections to make it fruitful. He loved and understood food. He lost no time in agreeing that my proposal could create a new and welcome flow of visitors to Bologna.

"When do you want to start?" he asked.

"Next summer."

"What do you need?"

"A kitchen and a place where the students can stay."

"You will have them," he said. "Go back to New York and get yourself organized. I will let you know very quickly what I have found."

Testa telephoned at the end of that summer. "Mail your announcement," he said. "I have a hotel that will set aside rooms for your students and will provide the kitchen." We had a substantial list of people who, during the previous five years, had inquired about or come to my classes in New York and in California, or attended my demonstrations around the country. Victor and I worked on a general description of the courses in Bologna, and we put it into a letter that we mailed to our list, offering three one-week courses in the summer of 1976. When we dropped the envelopes into the box at the post office, I wondered if I had been too optimistic and if we would hear from enough people to be able to go through with the project. We had the answer in just a few days, when every course was fully subscribed.

I was anxious to see the hotel and the kitchen that Testa had found, but Victor and I couldn't leave New York yet: It was high season for Victor's business, Giuliano was in school, and my own classes at home were filled until the end of May. My Neapolitan friend Claudia was going home at Christmas, and she volunteered to go to Bologna and inspect the premises for me. The hotel, the Milano-Excelsior, was across the street from the railway station. It had a four-star rating. Claudia reported that the rooms were very comfortable, with new furniture, marble floors, and good private baths. She also brought back a floor plan of the kitchen, which looked spacious. It was a professional kitchen from before the war that she thought would work well for me, a vintage kitchen, she said, with many burners, two ovens, and a lot of counter space for the students to work on.

At the beginning of June, Victor, Giuliano, and I flew to Italy. We had an appointment with Testa at the Milano-Excelsior, where he introduced us to Signor Gallieri, the director of the hotel, a tall, bony, glum-looking man. He escorted us to our room, a sunny and commodious double with a large bath. It was nice, but I was aching to see the kitchen. Gallieri explained that it was in the hotel next door, the Hotel Bologna, which belonged to the same family that owned the Milano-Excelsior. The Bologna had been closed for several years, he said, and the kitchen, which was about forty years old, might need some sprucing up. I shouldn't worry about that, he added, because he had a skilled crew working for him that, if necessary, could rebuild the whole kitchen in no time.

Gallieri let Victor and me into the shuttered Bologna, followed by his two-man crew, Testa with his assistant, and an architect friend of Testa's who would provide technical advice, if it were required. We walked into the kitchen and I tried not to believe what I was seeing. Everything was covered by grime a decade old or more. The once-white enamel of the cabinets and oven doors was chipped and rusted. I opened one of the oven doors and it came unhinged. Corroded metal fittings crumbled at the touch. The white-tiled walls and floor had almost as many gaps as tiles, and most of the tiles that remained were cracked, the cracks black with petrified dirt. The icebox could have been exhibited in a museum of early kitchen equipment. *"È impossibile!"* ("This is impossible!") I said. "Don't be discouraged," Gallieri said. "My men can clean everything up, replace the missing tiles, repair the oven doors and anything else that needs to be fixed in plenty of time for your class." I wasn't discouraged. I was desperate. The kitchen was beyond reviving; it had been dead too long. There was a dirty old wooden chair by the door and I dropped onto it, barely suppressing tears. I saw my career crumbling like the equipment in that kitchen. The trailblazing venture that so many in the food world had been talking about was ending in failure before its start. The students who were enrolled in the first week would be coming over in not too many days, some of them might be traveling in Europe already, and I might not even be able to alert them in time that there was no kitchen, that there would be no classes, no cooking adventure for them in Italy. I moaned because I couldn't speak. Testa came over and put a hand on my shoulder. "Please," he said, "it's not hopeless. I have an idea. I am going to make a few calls and by tomorrow I'll let you know what we can do."

The following afternoon, Testa collected Victor, Giuliano, and me and drove us to the Fiera, Bologna's large, modern convention complex at the city's edge. From fall to spring, the huge trade fairs that were held there made it the busiest place in Bologna. The fair calendar had come to an end, and on that day, the Fiera was deserted. Testa led us to the restaurant building, where some men had been waiting for him. They unlocked the doors, and we went up to the second floor, where we found ourselves in an immense dining

room. From the dining room, we entered the largest kitchen I had
ever seen.

"*Ma cosè?*" ("What is this?") I asked Testa.

"It's the most up-to-date commercial kitchen in Bologna," he said.
"It serves over three thousand meals a day during the trade fairs."

"What am I to do with it?"

"Anything you like. It's yours, at no charge, with all its furniture
and equipment, for the three weeks of your courses."

"How will I find my way around? How will I know how things
work?"

"We have a man who is familiar with the operation, his name
is Bruno. He'll be here with you for the entire time that you will be
using the kitchen."

"How will I get my students here from the hotel?"

"With the same bus that you are going to be hiring for your
field trips."

To prevent our class from disappearing into the oceanic empti-
ness of the vast dining hall, we had to reconfigure the space. There
was a score or more of tall sideboards lining the walls. Victor, with
Bruno's help, pulled enough of them around to create a small,
screened dining cove near the entrance to the kitchen. He used the
open shelves of the upper halves of the sideboards to display all
the wines he had ordered for the class meals. He would be unable
to discuss the wines with the students because he had to return to
New York, to his work, and neither I nor anyone else there knew
very much about them. His solution to that problem was to write
descriptive cards that he placed alongside each wine. The cards led
to yet another unexpected career for Victor, that of wine writer.
Judith Jones, my editor at Knopf, came to Bologna to visit the class,
and she was moved by Victor's descriptions to suggest that he write
a book on the wines of Italy. He took his time doing it, but when

it was published by Knopf six years later, in 1982, *Italian Wine* was very well received. The subject was unfamiliar then to most wine lovers, and to make it more accessible, Victor organized the wines by categories of taste instead of following the conventional classification by place of origin. It was an unorthodox approach, but it caught on, and we have since seen many restaurants adopt it for their wine lists.

Cooking was only part of our program, perhaps no more than half of it. We wanted our students to experience Italian life as it was lived through food. In class, they ate what they had prepared, but for their meals outside of class, we took them to restaurants both in the city and in the countryside. In choosing the menus, we were careful never to repeat a dish or a wine that they had had elsewhere or in class. When my son, Giuliano, and I talked about this recently, he recalled the maddening time we had working with a large graph we had drawn, penciling in, and erasing, dishes and wines by date and place. One of the precepts that Victor tried to work by was "Never leave anything to chance." The experience of the antique kitchen that had so nearly shipwrecked us led him to modify it to "Never leave anything to someone else." He and I tasted every dish and poured every wine in advance of the students' visit. As the date of our arrival neared, we called the restaurants to remind them of their commitment, and on the day before our arrival, I telephoned the chef to review every dish and its preparation.

Our classes were large, often exceeding twenty students, and their makeup—whether judged by geographic origin or professional, social, or economic position—was extraordinarily diverse. To lower barriers and promote congeniality, we would organize, very early in the course, an informal evening in a farmhouse or rustic trattoria, with hearty food, free-flowing wine, and old-fashioned Italian country music.

Marketing with students in Bologna

The farm-country fare of Emilia-Romagna introduced our international guests to food that they were not likely even to have heard of, let alone eaten. Appetizers might have been *tigelle,* a sort of crumpet that was sliced in half and layered with a finely chopped mixture of lard, rosemary, and Parmigiano; *il gnocco fritto,* a palm-sized dough dumpling that, when crisply fried, puffed up to create a hollow suitable for stuffing with slices of incomparable handmade salami. The pasta, always homemade, was often *gramigna con la salsiccia,* small, curved macaroni, sauced with the farm's fresh pork sausages, or it could have been *garganelli,* hand-turned, ridged, short quill-like tubes sauced with prosciutto and peas. One of our farms made *porchetta,* a stuffed, roasted whole small pig brought to table stretched out on a plank. It was extraordinarily delicious, the skin crisp and savory, the flesh sweetly succulent. Instead of the pig, other hosts in other venues served roasted *faraona,* guinea fowl, or *coniglio in umido,* fricasseed rabbit. One of our country cooks, a woman named Perla, fried potatoes in lard and rosemary that so eclipsed all other versions of fried potatoes that one of our students returned for another course the following year, saying, "I came back just to have Perla's potatoes."

The music was provided by a foursome that we privately referred to as "*i quattro vecchietti*," the four old-timers. The leader and the youngest was a septuagenarian called Spartaco, with a shiny bald pate of the classic billiard-ball type. He played the *mandola*, a lute-like instrument with four double chords, and he sang. Mori, the mandolin player, was the oldest. He was extremely nearsighted and wore glasses with thicker lenses than any I had ever seen, although he took them off to play, playing "blind," so to speak. For him alone, we always made sure there was a bowl of tortellini in broth at dinner. He loved to eat them with large helpings of bread that he broke into the broth. Bagnoli, the smallest of the four, was completely toothless. His instrument was an *organino*, a small accordion, which he alternated with a twelve-stringed guitar. Scalera, grave-faced and

The old-timers' quartet. From left to right: Mori, Scalera, Bagnoli, Spartaco

somber, with a look of permanently suppressed anger, played a mandolin. After dinner, Spartaco sang old, romantic songs, and the group played country dance music, polkas, mazurkas, tarantellas. They always ended with a tarantella that the class danced, forming a line that snaked through the dining room, around the tables, and if we were on a farm, in and out of the yard.

It never failed to be a successful event, establishing a spirit of enthusiastic camaraderie that carried us for the rest of the course. Romantic liaisons may have developed during the evening, but I always shrank from learning the particulars. There was one exception, though, an open courtship of such charm that it touched us all. Juan was a distinguished, vigorous Cuban man in his eighties. His family had founded the Bacardi rum company. He had enrolled in the course because he wanted to take charge of the cooking on his yacht. The lady's name I have forgotten, but I remember her looks; she was a very handsome widow in her sixties. Juan fell instantly in love and courted the object of his passion with public yet mannerly displays of admiration, which at one dinner took the form of a serenade. A few months after the course, I received an invitation to their wedding in Puerto Rico.

At the end of one of our evenings in the country, when everyone piled into the bus to return to the hotel, some of the students brought along unfinished bottles of wine and continued to carouse during the ride home. The driver told us he was worried that some of his passengers might lose their balance and get hurt as they weaved unsteadily along the aisle while the bus was moving. To prevent a recurrence of the situation on other trips, Victor amplified the Italian traffic code with a rule of his own devising. He informed students that Italian laws forbade drinking and carrying open bottles of wine and liquor on buses, and that if they were caught, they and the driver would be brought down to the station and fined, and the driver's license would be suspended. Thereafter, when traveling back to the hotel in the evening, we had the bus lights dimmed, and people snoozed on the ride home.

It astonishes me, as I recall the scores of expeditions we undertook with groups so dissimilar, that everything always went off as planned, that no one was ever hurt or lost. Actually, something did get lost once: a denture. On the way to our country dinner one week, we had stopped to visit the patrician estate and taste the wines of a prominent producer. I had learned that during such tastings, my students would not limit themselves to just a short, thoughtful sip, and I wanted them to put down some ballast so that they could handle the alcohol better. I had arranged for one of the cooks of the estate to make *piadina*, the flat bread native to Romagna, the region we were in, and to layer it with soft cheese, or sautéed greens, or prosciutto. As the class was getting back into the bus, the cook came up to my assistant, Margherita, with something concealed in a napkin. With great embarrassment, she unfolded the napkin to expose its contents, a denture, which one of the students had dropped. Everyone got back into the bus, but no one looked troubled or said anything to us. "Whoever lost it," I said to Margherita, "will have a problem at dinner. Let's have each of us"—Victor and Giuliano were also there—"focus on a different section of the table and when we see who is having difficulty eating, we can go up to him or her and discreetly return the denture." We paid more attention to the students than to the food on our own plates, but we saw no one having trouble with anything that was served. We returned to the hotel, with Margherita still holding on to her little bundle. While we were all gathered in the lobby, good-nighting each other before going up to our respective rooms, one of the women spoke up, her voice ringing high above the chatter.

"Margherita! Has anyone found a denture?" So much for discretion. I wondered whether she was used to such mishaps and whether she always kept a spare in her bag.

In the second season of the school, while I was still teaching in the kitchen at the Fiera, Danny Kaye decided to come for a week, bringing his daughter Dena. I was fond of Danny, but I was concerned about class discipline, which was never easy to maintain. Would he slip into one of his acts and draw attention away from the lesson? It turned out to be quite the other way around. He was such a serious and attentive, respectful student that the rest of the class was influenced by his example. He also showed me how to overcome one of my problems. My low voice made it difficult to talk above the conversations that students would sometimes have on the side. Danny had a magnificent whistling technique that any doorman hailing taxis could have envied. With two fingers between his lips, he produced an ear-shattering call to attention that immediately stopped all the background chatter. My whistling, unfortunately, was no louder than my speaking voice, but when Danny left, Victor gave me a silver whistle that got me through my classes for the next thirty years.

That Danny was on his best behavior didn't prevent him from indulging in a little teasing. We had a woman in class, an Italian-American, whose family had a restaurant in upstate New York. It was astonishing to all of us how little she knew of basic Italian ingredients. The lesson one day included a roast of veal, and in describing the menu, which I always did before beginning to cook, I told the class that in an Italian kitchen, the aroma of rosemary sautéing was always associated with the making of a meat roast. Before I could go on, the woman interrupted me to ask, "Marcella, what is rosemary?" When I became persuaded that I was hearing the question correctly, I showed her a handful of sprigs. From that moment, Danny called

Lunch with Craig Claiborne and Tom Margittai at the San Domenico in Imola

her Rosemary, and he generated as many opportunities as he could to address her by the name he had bestowed on her.

Nor did he shrink from razzing me when my English gave him the chance. On the evening that we were going to go to the farm, I described it as having many beautiful pickups on its grounds. I meant "peacocks." "Oh, Marcella!" said Danny. "You are amazing. Pickups! You really want us to have a good time. How soon are we leaving?"

It was curious how my malapropisms often seemed to lead to ribald interpretations. I was at lunch with the class at a restaurant that was becoming famous in Italy and that would eventually be celebrated abroad, Imola's San Domenico. I was fond of its brilliant teenage chef, Valentino Mercatilli, whose cuisine was a hybrid of the savory dishes he had learned at home and French-accented cooking he had brought back from a stint in a Paris restaurant. I wanted my class to taste the splendid food that Valentino could cook. For me, he tried to tone down his acquired French accent, letting more of the local dialect come through. It was my custom whenever I took the class to a restaurant to introduce each course, describing its making and its place on the menu. We had just had a fine risotto as a first course, and guinea hen was coming up as the second course. In between, Valentino was serving a luscious onion tart. I stood up, described how it was made, and added, "In a simpler meal, it would be the second course, but today we shall have it for intercourse." A New York lawyer shot up out of his chair and exclaimed, "Marcella, I know that Italians are imaginative cooks, and I have heard that they are wonderful lovers, but I never thought they could combine both talents with a single dish." Lucky for me, Danny wasn't there that week.

In that second year at the Fiera, James Beard came with Marion Cunningham to take a week's course. His arrival at the hotel precipitated a small crisis. The bathroom in the room he had been given had a shower cabin that had been designed to take up the minimum amount of space, with sliding doors that, when pulled aside, left a small opening in the corner of the cabin to enter and exit by. Jim had somehow managed to wriggle inside the shower, but once he was done, he was unable to wriggle out. What happened next I have forgotten: Who helped extract him? Was he moved to a room with a larger shower or did Mr. Gallieri's maintenance crew adjust the cabin's opening so that he could get in and out of it on his own?

Jim had serious circulation problems, and he had been ordered by his doctor to avoid salt completely. I never made allowances for special diets—it would have been impossible to teach if I did—but

With Jim Beard in the kitchen of the Fiera, Bologna

Jim was dear to me; he was like a favorite uncle. I held back a portion of everything we cooked in class and made it for him without
salt. Jim tried to go along with that, but only for a very short while.
He loved flavorful food too much. I always put a special unsalted
portion on a dish for him, but he pushed it aside and served himself what everyone else was having. He had come down from Venice
with large, striped gondolier's T-shirts, which had to be changed
constantly because he ate with such abandon that you could deduce
from them everything that had been on the menu. His enthusiasm
kept everyone's spirits high. The class was one of the jolliest I have
ever given. On the last night, at the diploma dinner in my home-

town, Cesenatico, a few students surprised us with a musical tribute to Jim, Victor, and me. The words were their own; the melody was that of "Making Whoopee." One of those involved in that charming production was Lynne Rossetto Kasper, out of whose introduction to Emilia-Romagna came an important cookbook, *The Splendid Table*.

Victor and I had a meeting with Gianpaolo Testa. The school had had extraordinary press coverage, with stories running in many newspapers and magazines, including a two-page spread in *The New York Times Magazine*. There had already been a notable increase in American and other foreign visitors to Bologna. Gianpaolo agreed with us that we needed to find a permanent facility independent of the Fiera, where we could expand our season to the spring and fall and offer many more courses. "Let me talk to Gallieri," he said. "The hotel may have the space for a permanent kitchen for you, and I know how to find the funds to build it." In the courtyard in back of the hotel, there was a covered area where carriages had once been parked. It had subsequently been leased to the baggage handlers of the railway station, who used it to store their carts and other equipment. It was the rawest possible space: it had walls on three sides; the fourth side, facing the courtyard, was closed by battered plywood panels and a lopsided door; inside it had a low dropped ceiling and the floor was plain, hard earth. There were no utilities, no electricity, no water, no gas. The hotel ceded that area to the city for a period of ten years, and Testa got the city to budget the funds to build a kitchen on it to our specifications.

After we had given our last course at the Fiera, Victor and I met with a contractor that the hotel had chosen, and we drafted a fully detailed design for the kitchen. We asked that it be completed by early spring so that we could inaugurate it at the beginning of June. Back in New York, Victor told his father that he would be traveling to Italy frequently that winter to check on the building of the kitchen, and in the spring he would altogether stop working in the fur business.

Giuliano was no longer in New York—he was a freshman at Swarthmore—and I had stopped giving classes at home. I was working with Judith Jones, finishing up my second cookbook, the first that we had done together. When we were all but ready to go to press, we still didn't have a title for it.

"Why not call it 'Volume Two,' as Julia has done with hers?" I asked.

"No, no, 'Volume Two' doesn't sell well," Judith said.

"How about 'The Second Classic Italian Cook Book'?"

"That's terrible!" (As it turned out, that is the title Macmillan put on it when they published the book in England.)

"I can't think of anything else, Judith. This is just more classic Italian cooking."

"That's it! That's what we'll call it."

Victor and I returned to Bologna in April to make some last-minute decisions on the kitchen. A ceramics manufacturer in Modena offered us their tiles. For the walls, we chose one with a geometric border in brown and white with, in the center, a childlike drawing of a rooster in brown and ochre. On the floors, we had plain white tiles. It was the last time I put ceramic on a kitchen floor; it was torment for our feet. We had table linens done in a traditional grape-cluster pattern that was hand-printed with wooden blocks by Pascucci, a nineteenth-century workshop near my town. The color was that of real rust, shed by old pieces of iron submerged in vinegar. When we handed our departing students their diplomas, we also gave them an apron hand-printed with the same pattern.

Victor had the low plaster ceilings removed to expose the old, brick-faced, barrel-vaulted ceilings, raising the height of the room to

The new kitchen the city of Bologna built for us in 1978

fourteen feet. Where there had been plywood, he put in a wall of glass bricks that flooded the kitchen with light during daytime classes. In the evening, we turned on the modern Italian fixtures that Victor had chosen. For prepping and for hand-rolled-pasta workshops, we bought several industrial stainless-steel tables whose tops we capped with butcher block. All our china came from Richard Ginori. We still have a full set that we now use every day at home in Florida. Victor created a wine cellar by mounting two parallel layers of strong chicken wire spaced ten inches apart over the full height of one narrow wall. The wire, painted black, had four-inch-square openings into which he laid the bottles. It was a dazzling kitchen. We had ample space for twenty or more participating students and a staff of four. In 1978, it had cost the Communist-run city of Bologna $100,000 to build. Glowing with paternal pride, Testa brought Renato Zangheri, the mayor of Bologna, and the whole city council to see it.

My school finally had a home of its own. When I think of those years in Bologna, and of all the classes that succeeded one another, and all the people to whom I said hello and good-bye, whose names I learned and forgot, I imagine myself camped every spring and every fall by the bank of a great river, waiting for the periodic flow of a current that eddies before me to discharge its living freight and comes through again when it's time to retrieve it and deliver a fresh contingent. It felt as though the world itself was streaming through. When Victor and I once counted the countries our students were coming from, we counted twenty-eight. They came from Britain, Scandinavia, and every country in Western Europe; they came from the Middle East, from Africa, from Japan, India, Australia, Singa-

Students in Bologna gathered around me at the large stove of the new kitchen

pore, Hong Kong, South and Central America, Canada, and nearly all the states. One was from Montana, but I don't remember any from the Dakotas, or Nevada, or Wyoming.

Some of my students were there for professional reasons, many were serious amateurs, and others came, no doubt, only because going to Marcella's school in Bologna was the thing to do that year. Some among them were prominent in their fields, even world famous, but they blended smoothly with classmates who led unadvertised lives. I taught them how to make pasta dough using only eggs and flour, and how to roll it out by hand, ignoring the skepticism of those who didn't understand that it was worth the effort. Those who did understand bought the long, narrow, Bolognese hardwood pasta pin in the market and mailed back from home photographic proof of the skill they had mastered. I taught them how to make everything, from pickles to gelato. To demonstrate where the correct cut of meat for scaloppine came from, I had a butcher take apart a whole leg of veal in front of them. Giorgio Guazzaloca, my talented butcher, was a good-looking young man, and not all the attention directed at him focused on the technical details of his demonstration. Giorgio was as bright as he was attractive, and twenty years later he became Bologna's first non-Communist mayor. Once the students had grasped the fundamentals of muscle structure, I taught them how to cut a slice across the grain and pound it thin. It was another instance of having to overcome skepticism. I relied on taste to persuade my students that both the knowledge and the effort that were required could make a difference. They discovered that our scaloppine cooked flat, without curling, that they could be tender yet satisfyingly firm, and that their juices ran sweet.

In between courses, I received many visitors in Bologna: colleagues, journalists, restaurateurs, friends. Tom Margittai of the Four Seasons paid me the most influential visit, one that led to profound changes in my teaching career and in our private life in Italy. When the spring session was over, Tom had us join him at the Cipriani hotel in Venice, where he introduced us to its new director, Natale Rusconi. Things moved very quickly after we met Natale. He came with his family to Bologna to see our operation. The following year I was giving two classes at the Cipriani, and at the end of the year, we had put a down payment on a large apartment atop the roof of an early sixteenth-century palazzo in Venice.

My last class had been graduated and had left Bologna, and I was looking forward to the luxurious laziness of the pause before the next one checked in. Mimi Sheraton, who was then the restaurant critic for *The New York Times,* was on the phone from Florence.

"What brings you to Italy, Mimi?" I asked.

"I am writing a piece for the *Times* on the restaurants here, and I would like to come up and let you take me to the one you think is cooking the best food in Bologna."

"When would you like to come?" I was hoping she would choose a day when I was busy teaching.

"I checked with your office in New York, and they said you have no class next week. Are you available on Wednesday?" Unfortunately, I was.

I don't dislike Mimi. In fact, I admire her. No one writing about food has a broader store of knowledge, or a more perceptive palate, or a more deeply graven taste memory. I am also grateful to her for kind reviews of my cookbooks. But in my experience, when Mimi is at the table, things have an uncanny way of going wrong. Twice I had her for dinner at home in New York. Once I cooked a lamb shoulder to an unchewable state; another time a fish soup—one of the things that I do best—was more dreary in flavor than I would have thought was possible.

To play it safe, I chose the restaurant where I had most recently been taking my students. It was run by one of Bologna's steadiest restaurateurs, Pierantonio Zarotti. The food had been so consistently satisfying that it had become the favorite place for Victor and me to go to alone when we were not teaching. The chef, Nino, was a friend. "When you make the reservation," Mimi said, "don't let them know who I am or why I am there." I considered her request and then ignored it. How could I spring such a surprise on Zarotti, a man with whom I had worked so closely and who had never disappointed me? "Don't worry," said Pierantonio. *"Le farò fare una bellissima figura"* ("I am going to make you proud").

"May I recommend some of the specials we have this evening?" Zarotti said when he had shown us to our table. "No," said Mimi. "Please bring the menu." After he had left the menus with us, she said to me, "I don't like to order specials; they are usually leftovers the restaurant is eager to move." We were four, Mimi and her husband, and Victor and I. She had each of us order something different, from the appetizers, to the pastas, to the second course, to dessert. We ate glumly because there was not a single agreeable dish among them.

When we asked for the check, Zarotti brought one that had just a single figure on it. It was the kind of bill reserved for favored customers, and it represented a discount over what the meal would have cost if every dish had been itemized. Mimi would have none of it; she sent it back asking for an item-by-item accounting. While she was studying the bill, I ran over to Zarotti.

"Where is Nino? What happened to him tonight? The dinner was a disaster."

"Nino is no longer here, he quit."

"He's not in the kitchen? Who is cooking?"

"My son."

His son? I wondered. Zarotti couldn't have been forty yet.

"How old is your son?"

"Seventeen."

BY 1985, I HAD a full schedule of classes in Bologna, in Venice I was teaching at the Cipriani and in our new apartment, and back in New York, I was reviewing the edits of *Marcella's Italian Kitchen*, a new cookbook I had written for Knopf. I decided to give two last courses in Bologna in 1986. In 1987, I would turn over the Bologna operation to my son, Giuliano, and to my assistants, the Simili sisters, Margherita and Valeria. Two events took place in 1986 that persuaded most Americans who had planned to visit Europe to stay home: one was the radioactive fallout from the explosion at the nuclear reactor in Chernobyl, Russia; the other, the bombing raid on Colonel Gadhafi in Libya that President Reagan had ordered. There were hardly any Americans in Italy that year, except for students in my two courses, both of which were full.

It wasn't only Americans who had enrolled. Among the students from other countries, there was John Arthur Dove, from South Africa. He was exceedingly quiet, keeping to himself the whole week. He followed the lessons scrupulously and learned the techniques very quickly. All that I knew about him then was that he was a private chef. We got the full story several years later when, in Johannesburg, as I shall relate in another chapter, we were treated to a remarkable encounter in the house where John worked.

Burt Lancaster was also a student in that class. When he arrived at the hotel, he looked grizzled and old, with a brown soft cloth cap pulled down over his eyes. I didn't even recognize him. Everyone else standing there did, however. He didn't stay long in the hotel. Gallieri had done the best he could to glamorize one of the small suites similar to ours. He replaced the furniture with antiques, hung colored engravings of flowers on the walls, and laid an Oriental rug on the floor. But it wasn't spacious enough for Burt, and on the following day, he moved a few blocks away to the Carlton, then the only luxury hotel in Bologna.

My office in New York had advised me that Burt hoped to make his visit private and to please not inform the press of his arrival. It was exactly what I had hoped for. I did not want distractions in the class, I did not allow comings and goings during the lesson, and I did not accept anyone coming late. (It was a policy that on a much earlier occasion had led to a serious confrontation with a student, as I'll relate further on.) Burt had been in Bologna just one day when my telephone became overheated with calls from several Italian papers. Lancaster had starred as the Sicilian prince Don Fabrizio Salina in Luchino Visconti's *The Leopard* and had become the most popular American film actor in the country. I also had to take calls from journalists in other European countries. They all wanted to interview him; they all wanted to take photographs of him working in the kitchen. "Absolutely not," I said to every one of them. "Burt Lancaster doesn't want it and I won't allow it." I told the telephone operator not to let any other calls through, unless it was my mother. The last journalist I spoke to was calling from Rome, and I asked him how he had learned that the actor was taking my course. He had read it in *Variety*, he said. Burt had been playing chess with the editor of the paper and told him he was coming to Bologna to cook with me. *Variety* printed the story. "Well, Burt," I thought, "is that how you keep your movements secret from the press?"

In class, Burt was self-effacing and followed each lesson with great intensity. I understood, from watching him, how carefully he must have studied all the different characters he'd played, to slip into their skins so convincingly. On the evening we went to the country, I was startled to see motorcycle police following the bus. They waited while we dined and danced—it was my night to dance with Burt Lancaster—and when we got back into the bus, they escorted us to the hotel. It was my first and last police escort. I was told that anti-American feeling was running high after the Libya bombing, and they didn't want to risk an incident involving a high-profile personality.

Burt Lancaster was exceptionally kind to Victor and me, but I was puzzled to find him so much less vigorous in person than on the screen. I learned subsequently that just a few years earlier he had had a major heart attack and several bypasses. He unwound during our diploma dinner. On the last night of every class, I brought my students to my hometown, to a restaurant perched on a pier facing the sunset over the Adriatic. For that final get-together, I regularly engaged a small, local male chorus. Unnoticed by the students, the men of the chorus sat having dinner several tables away. At my signal, during a pause in the service, they broke into their first song. Their voices were magnificent, and they sang powerfully, with great feeling. That evening Burt allowed himself to have fun. During another pause, he sang for his fiancée, Susan Martin, who had come to Bologna with him. The song was "If You Knew Suzie (Like I Know Suzie)." Several of us joined him. A few years later, Susan became his third wife.

What we called a diploma was actually a certificate of attendance. Students weren't tested, and the course was too brief for me to judge and reward their proficiency. What mattered, for my self-respect and that of everyone in the class, was that each student participate fully

With Burt Lancaster and Susan Martin at the diploma
dinner in Cesenatico

and punctually in our activities. I made that clear to everyone when we
met at the beginning of the course. In the twelve years that we had the
school, only one student chose to ignore that requirement. His name
was Salvatore, and he was a restaurateur from the Midwest.

The kitchen was a brief elevator ride from everyone's rooms, but
Salvatore was ten minutes late for the first lesson. The second lesson
he didn't come to at all. During the third lesson he asked questions
about subjects we had discussed when he was absent, and I told him
I wouldn't answer him. When the class went on a field trip, he went
on a trip of his own. He missed one more lesson, without offering
explanations. He did come to the diploma dinner in Cesenatico.
After dinner, I called the students one by one to come up to receive
the diploma and their gift, the hand-printed apron. Only Salvatore
never got out of his chair, because I had nothing for him. Back at the
hotel, a few of the students insisted on seeing me inside my room
because Salvatore was acting truculently. The following morning,

when I went down to the lobby to see my students leave, I found pages torn out of my books strewn all over the floor. The desk clerk said that Salvatore, who had just checked out, had done that while shouting obscenities about my cooking.

The hotel's concession to the city for the space they had turned over to build our kitchen was to expire at the end of 1987. Our life and work were now firmly rooted in Venice, as firmly as any roots can take in its waters. I had no intention of traveling to Bologna to give classes, but it was Victor's thought that we could build on what we had created and establish the first English-speaking culinary academy in Italy for professionals. We tried out the idea in 1987, when students interested in professional training were offered a much longer and more complete curriculum. We put our son Giuliano in charge of a faculty of three. To teach bread making, desserts, and homemade pasta, he had Margherita and Valeria Simili, the twin sisters who had been my invaluable assistants. The Similis came from a baking family and had operated a celebrated bakery of their own in Bologna. The other member of the faculty was Anna Gennaro, an extraordinarily talented chef.

We attracted a very enthusiastic group of students and we felt encouraged to develop Victor's idea. Unfortunately, the hotel was sold to an outside group, Gallieri was gone, and the new director advised the city that the hotel would not renew the concession. What was even more unfortunate was that Testa had left his post. The head of the tourist department was now a woman named Gianna Spezia. We offered to finance the outfitting of a new kitchen designed for professional training if the city would find us a space for it. We could not afford to buy or lease a building ourselves, but Bologna, like every other city in Italy, had many unused municipal properties.

We were soon offered the premises of a kindergarten that had been closed for some time. The space was perfect and the location was enchanting, within Bologna's largest and greenest park. Victor's promotional wheels started to spin. He suggested we name the school L'Accademia. He found a head shot of me that he asked a graphic designer friend to transform into a logo. He would excitedly—and excitingly—describe how we could create a brand that would appear on a line of Italian foods and kitchen supplies for the American market.

Gianna called us in New York to say that the city's commissioner of education had denied the request to release the premises of the former kindergarten to us. "But don't worry," Gianna said. "There are many other places available." We were then offered a former firemen's social hall. We went to Bologna to look at it, and although it required extensive renovation, we said we would take it. The city council approved the plan and we thought we were on our way. But Gianna called again. The powerful head of the firemen's union had refused to turn over the building. Gianna had a third place in mind. We went to see it. It was at the edge of the city, a two-hundred-year-old building in ruinous condition. To restore it would have put *us* in a ruinous condition. In declining the offer, we said thank you to Gianna, and to Bologna *la rossa, la dotta, la grassa*, we bade good-bye, *addio*.

Other Worlds

1984–1992

THE MOST COMMONLY used herb in Italian cooking is parsley, *prez-zemolo*, and it is said of someone who turns up everywhere, *"É come il prezzemolo,"* "He's like parsley." In Venice, Peter Stafford was parsley. You were on your way to the food market, and Peter would cross your path on the Rialto Bridge, both his arms pulled down by bulging shopping bags. You were at Palazzo Barbaro for one of Patricia Curtis's receptions, and when you stepped out onto a balcony to gaze at the water traffic on the Grand Canal, Peter would already be there, doing the same. You went to a lecture at the Ateneo Veneto and there was Peter, sitting in the front row, wearing one of his perfectly fitting, ageless English suits, chatting with his neighbor on the right, the one on the left, and perhaps with the couple behind him. He was small, for an Australian, but he was lean, well-proportioned, and smart-looking. He had retired to Venice at the end of a notable career as the director of grand hotels like the Mandarin in Hong Kong and the Savoy and the Dorchester in London. It was Peter who started me globe-trotting.

Every year in Hong Kong, the Mandarin Hotel organized a gas-tronomic fortnight that featured the cooking of a well-known chef, invariably French. Peter, whom the hotel consulted periodically, sug-gested they try Italian cooking for a change, and he recommended that they get in touch with me. The Mandarin's executive chef, a Belgian named Michel, and the hotel's food and beverage manager, whose name I can't recall, came to Venice to meet me. Michel was charming, easy, and relaxed, with a young man's open smile. We had a few meals together, some at home, some in restaurants, and agreed on a long list of possible dishes and the ingredients that Michel would have to import. The following spring we were at the Manda-rin. Never in my career have I been favored with such a delightful business arrangement. In addition to my fee, there were first-class round-trip tickets to Hong Kong for Victor and me; a three-day stopover in Tokyo to recover from jet lag; a suite at the Mandarin, where we ended up staying for more than a month; and a ten-day stay at its sister hotel in Bangkok, the Oriental, to unwind before returning to Venice.

I had work to do at the Mandarin, but we had time to explore a different part of Asia from the one we had known almost twenty years earlier. It did not feel as far from our Eurocentric world as Japan had in the 1960s. Hong Kong was still a British colony then, hence there was no language barrier for English speakers. Its most notable buildings were the work of European architects, and its fashion was either French or Italian. Joyce Ma, a Hong Kong society woman, had a string of boutiques so crammed with French and Italian de-signer names that you might have been shopping in Paris or Milan, while the famous tailors and shirtmakers took pride in their English fabrics. Joyce became a good friend, but what shopping we did was of another sort. Victor presented me with a portable memento of our trip, a necklace of jade and Chinese lapis made by Kai Yin Lo, a well-known designer of such desirable things. From a dealer in Kowloon, we bought what is still one of our most treasured objects, a seventeenth-century bronze Laotian rain drum. Poking around in various small shops, we came away with Chinese ink paintings, ceramics, and household objects, such as an antique brush pot to hold my wooden spoons in the kitchen. Ever since, these beautiful things have been a prominent part of the places we've lived, to the puzzlement of many of our visitors who cannot reconcile our Italian origin with a predilection for Asian art and crafts.

What we loved most, however, we couldn't carry away: the restaurants and the food markets. I love Chinese food nearly as much as my own native cooking, and eating out in Hong Kong was a dream that kept coming true nearly every day. Whenever we chose to eat at the hotel, we were welcome at the Mandarin's own Chinese restaurant, the Man Wah, but we explored other restaurants, and teahouses, and the cavernous mah-jongg halls clattering with action at a dozen or more tables. We were expertly escorted by Kai Yin Lo, whose mother had founded Hong Kong's first cooking school; by Joyce Ma; and by two well-informed young international couples living in Hong Kong to whom we had been introduced. One was half French, half Chinese; the other half Austrian, half American. Allowing ourselves to be led by those who knew the way, every time we got up from the table we felt that we had just had the best of all possible meals.

One of the most exquisite meals, however, was memorable less for the food than for the encounter associated with it, an encounter that we have put into our "The Inscrutable Orient" file, inasmuch as we have never found an explanation for it. A New York friend of ours, Max Pine, who was then the president of Restaurant Associates, had suggested we get in touch with the owner of a group of regional restaurants in Hong Kong. Each restaurant had a regional

In Hong Kong, 1985

name, such as Shanghai or Canton, followed by the word "Garden." The owner's name was Wu. "He'll be delighted to meet you," Max assured me. "Wu has a beautiful boat, and I'll write to him and suggest that he take you for a sail around the bay." When we called Mr. Wu, he said nothing about the boat. He instructed us instead to show up at a restaurant he named, on a day and at a time that he determined. He added that we could bring friends. The Austrian-American couple was the one we chose to go with. Maya, a raven-haired beauty, was, like us, interested in Asian crafts, and Clint, her American husband, was an insurance executive who had been in Asia for several years.

Victor approached the restaurant's reservations desk and asked for Mr. Wu, which led to a routine reminiscent of Abbot and Costello:

"Who?" asked the woman at the desk.

"Mr. Wu."

"Mr. who?"

"Wu."

"Who?"

Chinese is a language whose meanings vary according to subtle inflections in tone, and evidently, Victor was stuck on the wrong one.

We were eventually shown to a table and our host soon joined us. He must have taken an immediate dislike to us. He sat dourly throughout the excellent meal he ordered for us, and lectured us, with unconcealed contempt for our ignorance, on Chinese flavors and Chinese table practices. There was a curt leave-taking at the end of the dinner. We didn't mention the boat. He didn't suggest meeting again. The following day, Victor and I were walking along one of the elevated passages that connect some of the downtown buildings when we saw Mr. Wu approaching from the opposite end. As he came abreast of us, we nodded. Mr. Wu walked past, making it obvious that to him we were invisible.

I was given ten days to work with Michel on the menu for the Mandarin's first Italian Fortnight. I had come prepared to help him produce seventy dishes, which we trimmed down to sixty. I was in the kitchen from eight thirty to eleven in the morning and from three to six in the afternoon, when the cooks were not filling orders for the restaurants. I prepped and cooked each dish while Michel and his two principal sous chefs, one Chinese, the other French, looked on. Michel translated for the Chinese chef. I taught them how to turn flour and boiled potatoes into fluffy, weightless gnocchi, something that even good Italian restaurants rarely do well. The pastry chef learned how to roll out handmade pasta on his first try. Michel was quick at grasping and responding, and we made steady progress. Many ingredients had to be imported and almost all ar-

With Chef Michel in the kitchen of the Mandarin Hotel, Hong Kong

rived in good condition, but in the case of the small-leaf basil for our pesto, which was flown in at considerable cost from the Italian Riviera, more than half of it was spoiled.

Two days before opening night, Michel asked to talk to me privately in his office. I had told him originally that as soon as a pasta dish was ready, it couldn't sit; it had to be served. He did not see how the cook at the pasta station could handle orders for up to six different pasta dishes at the same time. It was easier to demonstrate than to explain it in words, so we both went to the kitchen, where I showed him how it could be done. On the first day, Michel was at the pasta station, where he cooked all the orders for pasta himself. The kitchen brigade was flabbergasted. No one had ever before seen Michel cook on the line. An executive chef for a food operation as large as the Mandarin's, in whose three restaurants and employee dining room thousands of meals were served each day, must only direct, because he cannot spare time to cook. "Marcella," he said, "I had to prove to myself that it could be done and show my man how it could be done. Now I don't need to worry." I have never known a chef so modest, so courteous with his staff, so painstaking, and of such constantly agreeable humor.

I had one slight and short-lived confrontation, and predictably, it was with the French sous chef. The French like their fowl chewy and underdone; Italians like it cooked through and through until it comes softly off the bone. When the Frenchman read in my instructions for the squab dish that it had to cook at least forty-five minutes, he exclaimed, *"Ce n'est pas possible!"* "My dear," I said, "not only is it *possible,* it is exactly the way you are going to cook it."

Thanks to Michel, and the extraordinary intelligence and discipline of his Chinese staff, the Italian Fortnight was a great success. I came down every evening in one of my best gowns and, before going out myself for dinner, circulated around the tables. My greatest compliment came from an Italian couple. They were from Genoa, where pesto originated, and they had ordered gnocchi with pesto. "*Signora,*" they said, "*le dovrebbero fare un monumento*" ("They should build you a statue"). "We would never have believed that in Hong Kong we could have pesto as good as the one we make at home." They could not have imagined what it had cost us to produce it. The demand for tables was so great that the Fortnight was extended to three weeks, and without even thinking it over, I accepted an invitation to stay in Hong Kong an extra week.

Three years later, I was on a new continent, but in not wholly endearing circumstances. My third cookbook, *Marcella's Italian Kitchen*, had just appeared in Australia, and I was there as the guest of its British publisher, Macmillan. As it happened, I was more of a paying guest—paying in kind, that is. When Macmillan's Australian representative had arranged for me to go there for two weeks, he had asked that I make myself available for demonstrations to the press and on television. Subsequently, I learned that he had booked me to teach classes offered to the general public, a week of them in Sydney and a week in Melbourne. "We shall split the fees," he said, "and our share will in part defray the cost of your stay." I had never even been asked what I charged. "How much are they paying?" I asked. "The standard amount for cooking classes here," he said. The figure was a fraction of my established teaching fee, even without calculating that I was to keep only half of it.

"I am not going to do it," I said.

"Oh, you can't get out of it. We have tied in the book's promotion with these classes, the schools have publicized them, and they are fully booked."

"Well then, if I have to teach the classes, I am not going to surrender any part of the fee." And that is how it stood. I asked if there was going to be time for me to see something of Australia. "You have both weekends," the man said.

I had been so eager to go to Australia. The frequency with which I found Australians in my classes in Bologna and Venice surprised me, when I considered how far they had come and how small their country's population was. Their presence always added enthusiasm and energy to the class and encouragement to my efforts. I had expected to like their country very much. I hadn't expected to see little more than the inside of two cooking schools. What I did have an opportunity to enjoy was the seafood, starting with my first morning, when, even before I had unpacked, I was rushed to the glorious seafood market in Sydney to choose the fish for my classes. Twenty years and a great many good meals have come between then and now, but I can still clearly recall the day that Victor and I sat down to a whole large mud crab apiece and quietly demolished them, extracting and dispatching every succulent shred of flesh. Crab is my favorite crustacean, and I have feasted on crabs nearly everywhere I have been, in Venice on *granzevola*, *granciporro*, and *moleche*, on Dungeness in Seattle, on blue crabs in Long Island, on the stone crab claws of my Florida coast, on crabs whose acquaintance was too brief to remember their names. None has surpassed and few have compared with that Australian mud crab.

The most enjoyable parts of the voyage to Australia were the stopovers. We interrupted our flight in Singapore, where we hopped on an Indonesian plane to get to Bali. In Singapore, we allowed ourselves several days to visit people we knew. A member of Venice's Rocca family, with whom we were acquainted, had married Alessandro Vattani, Italy's ambassador to Singapore. We also knew Beatrice Tao, a regal, and regally accoutered, Chinese woman who had come to Venice with one of her daughters to take my class at the Cipriani hotel. Another of her daughters, who lived in Hong Kong with her French husband, had often been our dining companion and mentor when we were there.

People who welcome you to their country and are proud to exhibit its treasures may introduce you to its monuments, to the handsome streets and charming neighborhoods of its cities, to its spectacular coastline, to the poetry of its landscape, or to the majesty of its forests. Singapore lacks all of these, but that is no impediment to its hospitality, because in their place it has food—food so unfailingly wonderful in all its manifestations that I have known no place to equal it. The Vattanis and their friends and various members of the Tao clan formed two separate task forces with a single strategy: to make sure that we tasted everything and that we never stopped long enough to lose momentum. An afternoon nap, a swim in the hotel's pool, and a massage filled the interval that separated lunch from dinner. After-dinner conversation at the home of one of our hosts allowed us to recover in order to join the feasting at Singapore's greatest attraction, its late-night open-air food stalls.

The food of the stalls, although different in content and variety, was not dissimilar in spirit from our *cicheti*, the little plates of tasty things: fresh sardines, small soles, mussels, tiny octopi, sausages, meatballs, or eggs, served with soft or grilled polenta in the *bacari*, the wine bars of Venice. But Singapore's brightly lit stalls stay open late, whereas the *bacari* do most of their business in the light of morning, when Venetians prefer to do their drinking. Moreover, the stalls congregate gregariously outdoors, while *bacari* retreat behind closed doors and are scattered around the city at a distance from one another. You are not likely to have fruit in a Venetian wine bar, but the Singapore stalls glory in their honeyed tropical fruits. Of these, however, there is one that even devotees might not describe as honeyed. It is durian, which, when its ripeness is most expressive, smells to some like carrion. It was unlawful, we were told, to bring it into any enclosed public space. To my husband, durian's texture, taste, and smell were those of the funkiest cheese imaginable, to which add decadent sweetness. I recoiled from it, but Victor loved it, and at the end of a day long in gastronomic exploits, he ate it greedily over butcher paper standing on a street corner.

Some years later, when Darina Allen asked us to come to Ballymaloe, her school in Ireland, we accepted the invitation notwithstanding the discouraging descriptions we had heard of Irish food. To our surprise, the ingredients we found were superb. The seafood—I remember the Dublin Bay prawns (known as scampi in Italy), the turbot, the hake, the monkfish—was equal to the best and freshest we had ever had on the Adriatic. The cheeses, breads, and jams were wonderful. To this day, it is Irish butter that I use in my kitchen. We didn't know any of that, however, before going. What we knew was that we loved Darina, and we were grateful that she had forgiven the hard time she had had one day in Bologna when she had been our student.

In Bologna, it had been one of Victor's responsibilities to accompany the class on its field trips and to maintain strict observance of the schedules we had so laboriously worked out. Our longest trip was the one we made to Parma to observe the entire production cycle of Parmigiano Reggiano cheese, an eight-hundred-year-old process. We had arranged with a dairy to hold back, in the morning, a batch of the milk from which they made the cheese, so that the students could watch it being cooked in copper cauldrons of ancient design. They would then have the opportunity to follow the subsequent steps in the cycle, to see the cylindrical mold that shaped the soft mass of the previous day's cheese, a two-day-old cheese being unmolded, a firm month-old round soaking in its brine bath, and a year-old seventy-five-pound wheel of Parmigiano aging in the cathedral-like space of the maturation vaults. The class had to be on the bus no later than eight A.M. to leave for the one-hour drive to Parma where the dairy master was waiting. Victor had announced on the previous evening that the bus would pull out at exactly eight A.M., whether or not every student was on it.

No one had ever been late for that appointment—except for Darina. Diligent, dependable, respectful Darina. She had been in the lobby on time, but then she had returned to her room to look for her camera. Victor didn't know. When she returned, the bus had left. Poor Darina. She hired a taxi to take her to the dairy, but when she got there, the demonstration was over and the class was gone. She continued by taxi to all the other stops on the tour, always arriving too late. Fortunately, she did make it in time to the restaurant by the Po River where a midday banquet in grand Parma style awaited the class, and applause awaited her.

Darina and her husband, Tim, met us at Cork Airport and drove us first to her mother-in-law's inn at Ballymaloe, where we would be staying. When we had checked in, she asked, "Would you like to see the school now?" "Certainly," I said. She drove us to a large property in the country. "It was Tim's farm," she said. The stables had been converted into small but charming rustic rooms for resident students. Chickens scampered over the grounds. A disused truck had been filled with straw and turned into their roost. We passed by row after row of vegetables. "It's where we grow the produce for our classes," Darina said. We walked to the large main building. As I remember it, the first floor had the students' spacious kitchen, with six or more four-burner stoves; the teachers' room; a well-equipped pantry; an auditorium with closed-circuit T.V. monitors for lectures and demonstrations; and a beautiful dining veranda with many tables facing a flower garden. The second floor held a splendid library, Darina's office, and the administrative offices.

I had never seen a cooking school like it, and I was both awed and made uneasy by its scale. I had said that the classes I would teach would permit full participation by the students.

"How many people are you expecting?" I asked Darina.

"Sixty."

I thought the English language was tripping me up again. I have difficulty discriminating between the sounds of "sixty" and "sixteen." "Did you say six*teen*?" I asked.

"No, sixty, six-zero."

"How can that be? I have never done a full-participation class larger than twelve. You must do something. Return the deposits. Get the class down to no more than fifteen, fif*teen*."

Darina smiled. "There is no way I can do that. Many students are already here. Others are on the way. Some are coming from as far as Australia and South Africa. And everyone is so excited by your being here. It will be all right, you'll see."

Victor smiled too. *"Non fasciarti la testa,"* he said, alluding to the family proverb about not bandaging your head before it is broken. "I'll give you a hand."

And he did. I see him still, on the day we made risotto. All the stoves were going, and Victor was flying from pot to pot, making sure that everyone was stirring correctly and that when they ladled in the broth, it was neither too much nor too little. We came up with a new cooking statistic: Sixty pairs of hands can make wonderful risotto.

My course was the last of the school year at Ballymaloe. When all the students had left, Darina invited me to join her and her staff for a farewell dinner at an unusual restaurant. The chef opened only when he had a minimum of twelve guaranteed reservations. When fewer than those had booked, they were not confirmed until enough other bookings came in to complete the necessary number. The restaurant was on Hare Island, a stony lump breaking the surface of the Atlantic Ocean. Transportation to it was in an open dinghy. It would give us a feeling, Darina said, of what living on the wild west coast of Ireland could be like.

The day started out with a gray sky that soon produced that steady, light drizzle that the Irish affectionately call "soft rain." It may have been soft, but by the time we reached the shore and the dinghy's landing, it was a very wet and cold rain. Out of the trunks of our cars came blankets and towels, into which we snuggled up to our eyes. I felt like a refugee being driven to the sea. We stepped into the open dinghy, the water on its bottom an inch deep. I could see nothing but water: water above, water below, water ahead. By the time we had been rowed to the shore of what looked as inhabitable as a piece of the moon, I was as wet as I could ever be short of dissolving into a puddle. We made land, but our trek wasn't over. We were on a scraggly path, which we followed until we reached

On Hare Island, off the west coast of Ireland

the first white stone house, one of two on Hare Island. There still was water above, but at least we had solid land below. When we eventually came to the house, I went in not knowing what I might find or whether there would be any hope of returning to a less liquid state. It was cheerful inside, warm and cozy. We dropped our soaking blankets and, like puppies released from their bath, shook off as much water as we could. Dry towels appeared, and what was even more effective, whiskey and wine. The dinner—I remember a perfect lamb rack—was comfort and salvation. We ate, we drank, we sang, we were happy. On the way back, the sun came out.

Annette Kessler, a short, dark-haired, lively woman speaking clipped British English, was urging us to go to South Africa. Annette, an editor at *Fairlady*, a South African women's magazine, had come to Venice with a photographer to do a story about the Cipriani hotel, and one about me. I would be very happy to visit South Africa, I told her, but I couldn't consider it as long as the antiapartheid sanctions against her country were in force. In 1990, however, the South African president, Mr. de Klerk, launched the process of dismantling apartheid. Nelson Mandela was released from prison, and a year later, the United States government lifted its sanctions. We left for Cape Town at the end of February 1992. On March 17, the country voted on a referendum that asked whether or not it approved of the government's reforms and its intention to negotiate a new constitution. On that evening we were guests at a referendum party at a private house, and when the news came that a large majority had voted "yes," we were clasped to one another by sensations of relief, hope, and exultation.

On the *Fairlady* tour, I demonstrated a menu for a large audience, which was followed by a dinner based on that menu. I gave the same demonstration three times, each time in a different hotel in a different city. I started in Cape Town, went on to Durban, and finished in Johannesburg. The dinners were cooked by the chef and kitchen staff of each hotel, an arrangement that has always made me extremely uncomfortable. I usually decline to participate in such programs because it is a rare chef who cooks my dishes as I do. The one shining exception was Michel at the Hong Kong Mandarin. But I wanted to see South Africa. I had been promised some nice excursions—a stay in the mountains, another in a game park with a private guide—and it seemed worthwhile to ignore my misgivings. We added two weeks on our own to our stay, hoping to see more of the country.

It was time spent well, and if we hadn't had a class coming to Venice, we would have stayed longer. We were attracted by the towns on the coast east of Cape Town, which we discovered while driving to the Cape of Good Hope. Victor and I talked about finding a place there to stay during South Africa's long sunny winter, but life rushed by before we found time to go back. The Nederburg winery was one of the sponsors of our tour, and they generously introduced us to some of South Africa's best wine estates, in Constantia, Paarl, and Stellenbosch. Their vineyards are among the most beautiful in the world, framed by spectacular mountain scenery and graced by handsome, whitewashed seventeenth- and eighteenth-century Dutch Cape architecture. Victor, who regards a great sweet wine as the highest achievement of the wine-making art, was overjoyed to discover superb late-harvest, botrytised wine made from Riesling grapes, known there as Weisser Riesling. In his cellar, he still hides some bottles from the cache he took back with him to Venice, and on an extraordinarily deserving occasion, he may reluctantly pry one out. I was astonished by and powerfully drawn to this country close to the bottom of the world, a many-complexioned nation—African, European, Indian—whose vast territory can equally accommodate French wine grapes maturing in a Mediterranean climate and a bush that is home to lions and elephants, where one parks the Land Rover under a full moon, with a drink in hand, to watch lionesses lope by looking for dinner.

Alas, it was the cooking that let me down. The ingredients were marvelous, the fish and lobsters in particular, but in the month that we were there we hardly ever ate well. I spent a great deal of time in the kitchens of the hotels where I gave my demonstrations, and what I saw was disheartening. The vegetables they served came out of cans, and there was no thought of cooking something fresh to order. A grilled fish might have been cooked an hour or two earlier and reheated before it was sent to table. But it was the fate of the magnificent lobsters that all but filled my eyes with tears. They arrived at the kitchen fiercely alive, but they were immediately boiled. If you ordered a steamed lobster, they would plunge it in boiling water again. If you ordered it grilled, the already cooked lobster would be split and run under the broiler. It was pitiful that those splendid creatures had to surrender their lives for such sorry results.

The tears did rise to my eyes the evening of the first demonstration. I was demonstrating homemade egg pasta and how to use it for lasagne, which I had chosen as the pasta course. Because I didn't trust the kitchen to follow my recipes, I spent the entire afternoon with an assistant who had been assigned to me, making the Bolognese meat sauce, the béchamel, and all the pasta sheets necessary for the seven-layer lasagne that would be served at dinner. I showed the chef how he would later have to cook, assemble, and bake the lasagne. I went up to my room to change, and since I had time before the demonstration, I stopped in at the kitchen to check on the preparations. I asked where they had put the pasta I had made, and they brought out several steel basins filled with water. The pasta was inside, dissolving into glue. I summoned the chef and had him mobilize the full kitchen staff to make a new batch of pasta. I didn't leave for the demonstration until I had made sure that the basins of water had been banished from the kitchen, and that the chef and everyone else involved understood exactly how they were to proceed. When I finished the demonstration, I took advantage of the time it took the guests to have a glass of champagne before sitting down at the dinner table to dash into the kitchen and survey the situation. It was going well, and the lasagne turned out to be delicious, all seven thin layers of them.

In Durban, my next stop, I had words with Annette Kessler. My meat course was a lamb dish that I consider one of my tastiest. It calls for shoulder of lamb that skips the pre-browning and is cooked slowly with vegetables and juniper berries for two hours. On the plate, it isn't exceptionally beautiful to look at, but the meat is of a tenderness and richness of flavor that no other method can surpass. Annette had been disappointed by its appearance when it had been served in Cape Town and demanded that I use chops instead of the shoulder. I refused. I tried to explain that after two hours of cooking, the chops would not look particularly pretty—they might even come apart—and moreover, the meat would almost certainly be dry. We talked and talked, and I know she was not persuaded, but it didn't matter because it was the shoulder that we continued to use.

My last working stop was Johannesburg. In Cape Town and Durban, Victor and I would take long walks, but we were told it was not advisable to do so in Johannesburg. Most women carried guns in their purses, I was informed, and it would be prudent for us not to step out of the hotel. There was nothing on my schedule in Johannesburg aside from a reception, the demonstration, and the dinner, save for an appointment to have tea with a Mrs. Oppenheimer. I didn't know who Mrs. Oppenheimer was. We never asked and no one told us, assuming we knew. I was sure I had never met her, but when I traveled it was not unusual for me to receive invitations to people's homes, and I was happy to get out of the hotel. A car collected Annette, Victor, and me at the hotel and drove us quite a distance into a lovely, hilly suburban area. "What do you know about this Mrs. Oppenheimer?" I asked Victor. Victor, who had just learned it from Annette, said, "Her husband is the chairman of De Beers, the diamond company."

The tall iron gate where the car stopped was guarded by several men carrying machine guns. They asked us to show identification, then spoke on the intercom to someone in the villa, and the gate opened. After we had been shown inside, a tall, portly woman who walked with a cane greeted us: "I am Mrs. Oppenheimer, and I am so happy you could come." She was wearing a simple, loose-fitting black dress, her shoulder-length hair was black shot through with gray, and she had the most exquisite manners I have ever encountered. She looked at you straight, with a serene smile, and spoke gently, unaffectedly, as though we had had a long experience of talking to each other. The sitting room where tea had been laid held several works of art, of which I remember two tall Goya panels. After a few minutes of conversation, a man appeared carrying a silver tray with cookies. I didn't immediately recognize him, but I recognized the cookies as the ones we taught in Bologna. The man reminded me: He had been in Bologna in 1986 for the last course I taught, the one to which Burt Lancaster had come. He was John Arthur Dove and he was the Oppenheimers' chef.

We were shown Mr. Oppenheimer's study. A Renoir hung on the wall behind his desk. "He bought that when he was a student at Oxford. Don't you think that was clever of him?" said our hostess. I assented, thinking, "Clever, of course, and with a generous allowance besides." "Would you like to see the garden?" Mrs. Oppenheimer asked. It was more a park than a garden, and I thought how kind it was for her to take me there when it was evident that walking was hard for her. It had the informal, unregimented look of some English and Irish gardens, with something that other gardens didn't have, splendid sculptures. I remember a Moore and a Rodin, but not the others. And something else there was different. The path we walked on was paved with small, round, flat stones that glittered. "What are they?" I asked. "When they drill for diamonds," Mrs. Oppenheimer explained, "the cores that come up may contain minute diamond fragments. We have them sliced into paving stones."

In the car, on the way back to our hotel, Annette turned to us and said, "You have just been given tea by South Africa's royal family."

How Not to Get Rich

1972–1993

I KNOW HOW TO COOK, and I know how to teach, but I have never known how to make a great deal of money. Growing wealth should be like growing anything else: Drop the right seed on the right ground, and cultivate it. Many good seeds have flown out of our hands; a few have put down strong roots and become fruitful, but somehow it was never for us to harvest those fruits.

There was a time in America when, in culinary matters, if it was French it was good, and if it was good, it had to be French. Chuck Williams, the founder of Williams-Sonoma, came across to me as a dedicated exponent of that principle. I had never seen a shop like the early one he had opened in San Francisco, so white, so tidy, so pure, so dazzling. And so frightfully French! Except for ceramic jugs and other trifles, there was nothing seriously Italian in it. When I came to know Chuck a little better, I asked him, "Why don't you bring in some good things from Italy?" "What is there in Italy?" he shot back. His was a flippant and dismissive reply, to which I chose to make none of my own. Nonetheless, the question rankled.

Some months later, I returned from Italy with samples of *aceto balsamico*, balsamic vinegar, a product that I had been unfamiliar with and that, as far as I knew, was completely unknown in America. In fact, it was then also completely unknown in Italy, except to the people living in a small territory whose center was Modena, a city just northwest of Bologna. Every year at harvesttime for nearly the past thousand years, families in that area boiled down the juice of white grapes, poured it into small barrels, and let it sleep in the warm attics of their farmhouses. Fitfully, the sugary juice would awaken and ferment. Part of the sugar turned into alcohol, which was in turn converted into vinegar by airborne bacteria. For each batch, the process continued over a span of several generations, for a hundred years even, yielding a sublimely sweet vinegar, dense, dark brown, and complex. This priceless extract had transformative powers when drops of it were used as a condiment over salad greens and certain berries. It was too precious to be sold or given as a present, although a tiny cask of it might be included in a daughter's dowry.

I have forgotten the exact year that I became acquainted with balsamic vinegar, but it happened in the early 1970s on a visit to Bologna, when the Fini food company of Modena announced its tradition-breaking intention to bottle it and release it commercially. Like all land-owning families in Modena, the Finis had been making balsamic vinegar for their own use for generations, and through marriage, inheritance, and acquisition, they had amassed a substantial stock of it. A small quantity was very old, and that was not for sale. What they intended to market was a good-quality five-year-old product, whose tasting characteristics were representative of, although not equal to, those of the venerable heirloom balsamics.

Giorgio Fini, the head of the family and of the company, hoping that I might help get the word out in the States about this ancient and yet new product, gave me a few samples of the vinegar and a prototype of the eight-sided bottle they were going to put it into. I never asked what was in it for me. I was happy to have the opportunity to approach my friends with a small spoonful of the elixir and say, "Here, try this, you have never tasted anything like it!" Craig Claiborne came over for one of our periodic lunches during which we chatted about our world, and he became the first person in America to taste it. "This will be a sensation," he said. When two men I knew from Williams-Sonoma were in New York, I had them to lunch, and they also had their first taste of balsamic vinegar at my table. As their eyes opened wide, I brought up Chuck's remark about Italy. Not too long thereafter, while turning the pages of the new Williams-Sonoma catalogue, I was startled to come upon an illustration of the Fini octagonal bottle. It was offered at $15, a not inconsiderable price for a small bottle of an unfamiliar, curious vinegar from Italy. Nonetheless, its sales took off, and thus began America's infatuation with balsamic vinegar.

I have no way of knowing whether my informal presentations at home had a connection with the appearance of Fini's vinegar in the Williams-Sonoma catalogue. An acknowledgment that might have confirmed it never came from Chuck. The ones who thought I was owed some recognition were the people at Fini, who wrote me a warm letter of thanks, and who, to express their appreciation, liberally supplied my school in Bologna with complimentary samples of choice *balsamico*.

Jim Beard introduced me to Burt Wolf, a former mutual funds broker, around 1975. Burt was a captivating man who had begun to apply his adventurous salesmanship to food. When I met him, he was assembling a team, guided by the omniscient Barbara Kafka, that would produce *The Cooks' Catalogue*, the first comprehensive, and still unrivaled, guide to cooking equipment. At the Stanford Court in San Francisco, I observed some of the classes that Barbara taught for Jim Beard, and she was dazzling. She had an unassailable command of her topics and her students. She handled questions with what in tennis terms would be described as a crackling return of service, fast and well-placed.

During that decade, Bloomingdale's food department was the talk of the town. In addition to a floor stocked with an assortment of packaged foods from all over the world, they had begun to put specialized food boutiques into their storefront on Fifty-ninth Street. I remember the bakery, where we often got our bread, and the Petrossian fresh caviar and smoked salmon shop, where Victor risked sliding from self-indulgence to costly addiction. It was Burt's idea that Bloomingdale's should use one of those storefronts for an

The window of my Bloomingdale's boutique on Fifty-ninth Street.

Italian food boutique to be called Marcella Hazan's Italian Kitchen. He sold the idea to Lester Gribetz, a marketing manager, who sold it to Marvin Traub, the president of the store.

The pasta for my shop was going to be made in-house, and I was determined that it would be the best that New Yorkers had ever been offered. Unfortunately, Bloomingdale's bought the wrong machine, one made for speed. In their machine, a mass of rapidly kneaded dough was forced through rollers that thinned it in a single step. It produced the same limp, gummy, nerveless pasta found in every pasta shop and Italian restaurant in town. It wasn't easy to persuade a department store to dump a $10,000 piece of equipment they had just bought. I did it with a sketch. I drew a figure standing on the roof of a six-story building. "There are two ways for that man to get to the sidewalk," I said. "He can jump off and land on it, breaking his bones. Or he can take the stairs and reach ground level one floor at a time, with his body in good shape." I explained that pasta must be judged by its body, and it develops a good one when well-kneaded dough is thinned out in as many steps as possible. We didn't make any pasta at Bloomingdale's until they replaced the machine they had bought with an Italian one that could do the job I had described.

We opened the shop with my good Bolognese-style homemade pasta and a few other carefully chosen products. I cashed my chips at Fini, asking them to dip into their reserves to produce a special edition of balsamic vinegar for me. They came through with a beautiful little bottle that could have been designed to contain a small quantity of very expensive perfume, and filled it with twenty-five-year-old vinegar, the first time that *balsamico* of that quality had been offered for sale in this country. The Martelli family of Lari, in Tuscany, produced some of the finest dried factory pasta in Italy. They were good friends and offered me the exclusive for the United States on their excellent spaghetti, penne, and *maccheroncini*. Bloomingdale's was not prepared for that kind of commitment, so when we introduced the bright yellow packages of Martelli pasta to America, we were not alone. We shared that distinction with Dean & DeLuca, the company started by a former student of mine, Giorgio DeLuca. We also sold a superb extra-virgin olive oil produced in Tuscany by the same artisan grower who supplied my school.

The shop did well, and Bloomingdale's asked that I stock it with many other products. I had just taken possession of the beautiful kitchen the city of Bologna had built for me, and there I collected scores of honeys, jams, pickles, canned tuna, and other products from high-quality artisans. During a week I didn't teach, Bloomingdale's sent Pamela Krausman, one of its food buyers, to Bologna to help me select and assemble a line for my Italian Kitchen. Tasting a score of jams and honeys is a terrible way to spend a morning, and it took a few years before I felt again any desire for either. Bloomingdale's commissioned a graphic design studio to produce special packaging for my foods, and I was elated when the design they created won an award as the best in its category.

I was not elated, however, when on my return to New York a year later, I found that my shop had been moved away from street traffic to an underground corner by an escalator, while the storefront on the sidewalk level had been turned over to Michel Guérard and his Cuisine Minceur. I had a fierce discussion with Lester Gribetz:

"But, Lester," I cried, "we had an understanding! That was supposed to be my window on the street!"

"It's Bloomingdale's window, not yours, and we decide where to put our merchandise so that it will do us the most good."

"I thought you were doing very well with Italian food. Is Michel Guérard doing any better?"

"It doesn't matter how much he sells. He's good for Bloomingdale's. Even if we lose a million dollars a year on him, he is still good for Bloomingdale's."

Other problems developed. The in-house kitchen had a constant personnel turnover; the people I had trained were no longer there, and the ones who replaced them did not follow my instructions. I had originally allowed them to sell some of my soups and sauces, but they had become unrecognizable and I had them removed from the line. I was also upset to find that they were selling olive oil that had been standing next to a bright fluorescent light, turning rancid. Moreover, complaints about the pasta had begun to reach me. Each time I came back to New York from Italy, I had to retrain the people making the pasta because Bloomingdale's kept shifting personnel to different departments. When I was back in Italy, I wondered how many people would have taken a turn at the pasta station by the time I returned to New York.

I was approached by a major food importer who was interested in national distribution of Italian products bearing my name. Together with Pamela Krausman, Victor and I went to their offices in New Jersey, where we discussed the outline of a collaborative venture and reached a tentative agreement. They asked that Pamela serve as the consulting brand manager for the line on a commission basis. I liked and trusted her, and I had no objections. They did not want to proceed, however, while a competitive line with my name was selling at Bloomingdale's. My contract there was coming up for renewal, and I had had too many disappointments over the way my shop was run, so I opted to exercise the escape clause and ended my relationship with the store. Pamela, Victor, and I took one last ride to New Jersey to put our agreement on paper. The company's senior executive, with whom we had been negotiating, sat across from the three of us at the conference table.

"You have to understand," he said, "that our margins are small and we cannot absorb Pamela's commission."

"You can't? Then who will?" I asked.

"You will. We shall deduct it from your percentage of sales."

"And how much is it?" The figure was so close to my own percentage that it was hard to tell them apart. We got up and left, possibly without saying good-bye.

Another project would have put my sauces on the shelves of every good food store, but it never got to be more than a project. Phil Teverow sent a charming letter to me in Venice saying that he had enjoyed cooking from my books and would like to make some of my sauces available commercially. He wrote that he had already done as much for Pino Luongo and other well-known figures, and that he had the technical knowledge necessary to transform home-made food into industrially packaged food.

We signed reciprocal letters of understanding, and Phil set to work applying his industrial formulas to three or four sauces we had selected from my books. When I was briefly in New York, he brought the results to the Beekman Tower, a hotel near the United Nations where I had taken a housekeeping suite. I tasted them and they were terrible. I made the sauces myself in the suite's kitchen to demonstrate how they should taste. "They are delicious," Phil said. "I need to go back and figure out how to develop an industrial approach to making them."

He tried one more time, bringing the samples to Longboat Key, Florida, where Victor and I had just acquired an apartment. They didn't work; they were not my sauces, and I could never let them go out into the world with my name on them, even if I were to sell a million jars.

"Look, Phil, I am going to make a basic tomato sauce from scratch," I said. "Follow me carefully and tell me why you can't make yours to taste like mine."

When I was done, he said, "I can make it like yours, with the same ingredients, in small, hand-cooked batches. But I wouldn't be able to sell it."

"Why not?"

"Because I would have to charge twenty-five dollars a jar."

Phil Teverow was a gentlemanly, intelligent, soft-spoken young man with excellent manners. He was good company. We had a very pleasant lunch before he caught the late afternoon plane for New York. I have never heard from him again.

I have worked with restaurants often, contributing what I know about producing good Italian food. In each case, I have hoped that I was taking the first step with my client on a profitable road that we could continue to travel together. But that first step always seemed to be as much propulsion as my clients needed from me. From then on, they moved forward on their own. Finally, it was one of my former students who came to see me in New York bringing a proposal that held the promise of long-term involvement and reward.

Susie Hurwitt and Mary Murray were friends and neighbors from Darien, Connecticut, who took my class in Bologna. Mary owned The Complete Kitchen, a cookware store and cooking school in Darien and Nantucket. Susie had long since answered the call of the entrepreneurial spirit. What she liked to do best was to buy, restore, and sell houses. I had a good relationship with her that soon became friendship. We still stay in touch, and from time to time, Susie and her husband, David, come to visit us in Longboat Key. When she came to see me in New York, she had been working with Mary's husband, Ian, on a project for a gelato shop, but her thoughts then moved on to something else.

"Marcella," she said, "what we don't have here yet is a restaurant that serves the simple, flavorful, light-handed food we had in Italy and that you taught us how to make. Don't you think we could do that, have a restaurant that is authentically Italian and set it in a spare, cleanly designed, modern space as they do in Italy? I don't want a restaurant with trendy food and a trendy look. What do you think?"

"Why not, Susie? I know how to produce true Italian food in America, but everyone involved has to believe in it very strongly."

"I believe, I believe! If I can get the funding, would you like to come in with us? You can do it as a consultant or, if you prefer, as a general partner."

Victor broke into the conversation. "*Basta* with consulting, enough of working on someone else's restaurant," he said. "We want a partnership."

Susie came back much sooner than I had expected. I had been disappointed enough times not to expect her back at all. Ian, who had moved to Toronto to take an executive position with Nestlé, was coming in as an investor, and two Canadian attorneys, John Kime and Bill Macdonald, were chipping in too. Kime's wife and Bill Macdonald had both attended my classes in Italy.

We agreed to offer a partnership to the designer, who was to be Emily Summers. Emily has since acquired a major reputation in her profession and was named in January 2007 as one of *Architectural Digest*'s one hundred best designers in the world. She had a long-standing connection to Susie. Her mom and Susie's had been best friends, and her sister and Susie had been best friends when they were kids. Emily was from Dallas and she suggested that a friend of hers from Dallas, Janet Colgin, be brought in to help plan and to manage the restaurant. We gave Janet a partnership too.

Research pointed to Atlanta as the most promising place for our launch, which we optimistically envisioned as the first of several. A large, open space in a new building in midtown Atlanta would house the restaurant. There was a broad lawn beside it that was turned into a bocce court. More research turned up a chef, a young man named

Joey Venezia. We had established our lives in Venice by then, and I thought his name was a good omen.

Joey came to Venice and stayed two weeks with me, marketing, cooking, tasting, talking Italian food. He was a nice-looking young man with a ready smile, attentive and respectful. He amused me with his Italian-American habit of dropping the last vowel from Italian nouns, "prosciut" for prosciutto, "mozzarel" for mozzarella, "Trevis" for Treviso (the radicchio). When he left me, he spent two weeks in restaurants I had selected for him to try in other regions. He gave me huge encouragement, because he demonstrated a natural flair for producing dishes with genuine, light-handed Italian flavor.

In the spring of 1990, when the construction of the restaurant was completed, Victor and I went to Atlanta. We stayed for a month, until after the opening, in an apartment that we had been provided in a suburb called Smyrna. In another intriguing coincidence, Smyrna was the name of the city in Turkey where Victor's father and mother had been born. We weren't always so happily surprised by names, however. We had our first disagreement with some of the partners over the name of the restaurant. We had submitted many Italian ones, but they were rejected in favor of Veni Vidi Vici, which was not even Italian and did not appeal to us.

My son, Giuliano, who had been studying drama in Providence, Rhode Island, at the Trinity Square Repertory Theater, had become persuaded that he would be more likely to eat pursuing a culinary career rather than a theatrical one. He joined the kitchen staff in Atlanta, where he was put in charge of the pasta station, a tidy little room with a window that passersby could look into.

We tested and retested the dishes that Joey and I had agreed upon, and I was completely satisfied that they were going to work. We had a magnificent opening. Emily had done well by us; the restaurant looked serene, uncluttered, and inviting. Susie's husband,

Enjoying a few after-dinner puffs with Chef Joey

David, an accomplished amateur photographer, gave us many fine black-and-white photographs of Italy for the walls. They are still hanging there, I understand. We opened on the week that the American Institute of Wine and Food was meeting in Atlanta. Julia Child and Robert Mondavi came to a private lunch we gave for the institute and addressed us with extremely warm and heartening words. The mayor of Atlanta was there and presented me with an honorary citizenship in the city of Atlanta.

The restaurant was an immediate and clamorous success. It was filled for every lunch and dinner. Customers played bocce on our lawn. John Kime wrote joyfully to all the partners: "Veni Vidi Vici is successful beyond our wildest dreams." *Esquire* magazine listed it as one of the ten best new restaurants of the year. Even dishes that had been viewed with skepticism when I proposed them, such as an artichoke and calamari soup, became popular. I left for Venice deeply gratified at having demonstrated the broad appeal of the food and the flavors that I believed in.

A month later, I was informed that Joey had been fired and summarily removed from the premises. I never learned what had gone wrong with Joey. Neither Joey nor Janet told me. The end of our partnership came two years later. Although Veni Vidi Vici was doing excellent business, we heard that vendors would deliver goods only for cash. We also learned that the landlord, who had advanced funds for construction and was owed more than half a million dollars, was not being repaid. Janet wanted to open a branch in Dallas. The investors felt it was too soon and that it might imperil the operation in Atlanta. Janet, however, did open her own restaurant in Dallas, and Ian and Mary Murray moved from Toronto to Atlanta to take charge of Veni Vidi Vici. It was too late. The landlord was not paid, and he foreclosed, selling our restaurant to an Atlanta group. Veni Vidi Vici is still in place, and doing well, I am told.

Of all these missed opportunities and fruitless ventures, the collapse of the Atlanta restaurant is the one I most regret. It is not about the money, although I would not have objected if it had brought in some. I was drawn to the project as one may be drawn to compete in some sporting event. I was weary of hearing that Italian cooking, as it is practiced in Italy, would not be successful in a mainstream American city. I was as weary of the clichés of so-called northern Italian as I was of the garlicky, over-sauced, overflowing portions of presumed southern-style Italian. I was eager to prove that judiciously balanced classic dishes, based on genuine regional traditions, could win the game. I had the satisfaction, which I shall carry with me always, of knowing that they would have. I was ahead when the game was called.

Venice

1978–1995

THE CIRCUMSTANCES THAT put me in Venice during the latter decades of my teaching and writing life were probably set in motion
one summer weekend in 1936. When Victor was eight years old,
and his parents lived in Bologna, the family rose early on a Sunday
morning and took the train to Venice, to have lunch there and spend
the day. It is a two-hour trip now, even less with a super-express
train, but in the 1930s it may have taken slightly longer. As Victor
told it in a story he wrote for a magazine a few years ago, he came
down the steps of the Venice railway station with his parents to
board the *vaporetto*, the Venetian water bus, and as the *vaporetto* pushed
off from its landing and churned up the Grand Canal, he knew that
this was a place where he would have to live one day.

Tom Margittai, our friend from the Four Seasons restaurant,
was on the telephone. We had just finished the final course of the
inaugural spring-to-summer term in our brand-new kitchen in Bologna.

"Where are you, Tom?"

"In Venice, at the Cipriani hotel. Are you still teaching?" he asked.

"No, thank heaven! We are all finished with school until September," I said. "We are leaving for Cesenatico, and I am going straight to the beach to lie on the hot sand."

"There is no sand here, Marcella, but there is a world-class pool and a terrific buffet lunch. The new general manager, Natale Rusconi, is an old friend. I told him about your school and he would like to meet you and talk to you about it. Why don't you come up for a few days? He has a room for you."

When Victor hears a piece of good news, his green eyes widen and look even greener, and his cheeks become flushed. A trip to Venice was very, very good news. It had been more than ten years since we had been to Venice. Our return was in much grander style than on any of our previous visits. Natale sent a launch to meet us at the station and put us up in a room on the top floor with a dormer

On the Cipriani launch

window and a view of the Lido in the distance. In the morning, we swam in the huge pool filled with warm seawater and stayed poolside for the buffet lunch. Tom had not misspoken. The buffet was laid with all the seafood we loved, the shrimplike *canoce*, scampi, miniature octopus, cuttlefish, and the Venetian classic *sarde in saor*, fried fresh sardines marinated in vinegar with raisins and pine nuts. The afternoons were for long walks and the evenings for chatty dinners at one of the trattorias favored by Tom and his friends.

Natale was exceedingly charming. He wore serious suits and serious eyeglasses, but he entertained us with naughty tales from his long career in grand hotels. Before taking charge of the Cipriani he had been the general manager of the Gritti Palace, where he had launched the idea of the cooking vacation, inviting James Beard and other celebrated cooks to give courses. An American, James Sherwood, had bought the Cipriani from its owners, the Guinness sisters, who had built it to showcase the cuisine of Giuseppe Cipriani, the founder of the restaurant family that bears his name. Sherwood plucked Natale from the Gritti and set him down on the Giudecca to run his new hotel.

Natale had heard about me from Tom, James Beard, and others, and was curious about my school in Bologna. I invited him to stay at our hotel for a weekend and see for himself. He came down with Connie, his American wife, and his two younger children, Pietro and Elisa, who are twins. Pietro, who has become a tall, handsome young man, is now an assistant manager at the Hilton hotel at the opposite end of Giudecca Island from the Cipriani. The twins were still quite little then, and I remember them squealing with excitement in our car when Victor was taking the Rusconis around Bologna. Victor was a vivacious driver in the Italian mold, while I suspected that their father's driving was as circumspect as his suits.

I gave Natale a tour of my newly inaugurated kitchen. He was astonished to learn that the city of Bologna had paid for its construction. I outlined our program, described the field trips, told him about Victor's popular wine and cheese lectures, and gave him a rundown of the curriculum that I covered during a single course. What he saw and heard appeared to excite him greatly. Later, during a subsequent stay at the Cipriani, I discovered that food was his passion. As our acquaintance deepened into friendship, I found that it was also one of his talents. Some of the best meals I had in the years that we lived in Venice were the ones that Natale cooked for us at his house on the Zattere. I was amazed when he converted my husband to the pleasures of tripe, the only thing aside from chicken that Victor had always refused to eat. "Wouldn't you like to bring your cooking to the Cipriani?" Natale asked me before he left Bologna. It meant squeezing classes in Venice into the intervals that we had between our Bologna courses, sweetly indolent intervals that I would become desperate for when each course ended and the students went home. To dip our toes into Venetian life, however, was an opportunity we couldn't pass up. Nor did it stop at the toes. It wasn't long before we were fully submerged.

It was 1978 and we had begun to spend most of the year in Italy, returning to the States only late in the fall. Peering into the future, it seemed likely that we would live in Italy full-time. Dividing our life between the hotel suite above the kitchen and the small apartment we had in Cesenatico was not going to work for much longer. We had begun to look around for a permanent place in Bologna, but nothing we saw had clicked with us yet. On a spring day of the following year, Victor and I were sitting across from each other in a compartment of the train that was taking us to Venice, where I would teach the first of the two spring courses that I had agreed to give at the Cipriani. When Victor is dreaming up something that I have not been prepared for, he falls into an intensively meditative silence and you believe that you are seeing streams of thought sweep across his face.

"What are you thinking about, Victor?"

"Ummm . . ."

"I know that you are cooking something up. What is it?"

"Why do we have to live in Bologna?"

"It's obvious, that's where our school is."

"But that's only for three months of the year, four maximum."

"If not Bologna, where then?" I asked, but I had already guessed.

"In Venice! Is there any other place like it?"

While we were at the Cipriani, we inquired about apartments for sale. Most of the buildings in Venice are between four hundred and six hundred years old, and in the 1970s, only a small number of the apartments in them had been modernized. It was unthinkable to take a chance on an apartment that needed radical restoration and renovation. There was no way one could predict if and when work permits would be issued or, once they were obtained, foresee the full costs of reconstructing a centuries-old structure. We would consider a place only if it had already been brought up to date with modern utilities, bathrooms, and a kitchen. Of those, only a few of their owners were willing to sell. We had a course coming up in Bologna, so we put off our research to a few weeks later, when I was to teach at the Cipriani again.

On our return, everything we were shown was discouragingly unattractive, except for one magnificent apartment that, sadly, was not a good fit for us. It was a piano nobile, a typical sixteenth-century Venetian layout that took you from a second-floor landing into a monumental high-beamed reception room that ran uninterrupted for nearly the whole depth of the building, from a tall loggia overlooking the canal in front almost to the back of the palazzo. Concealed at the back and side were the rooms for everyday life, the bedrooms, library, kitchen, and bathrooms. We saw no practical way for us to employ the huge ballroom-like space that commandeered half the area of the apartment. It would have been suitable for an embassy's formal receptions, and in fact, the owner who was showing us around was a retired ambassador. He was Sir Ashley Clarke, once the British ambassador to Italy and subsequently head of one of the international committees that had been formed after the catastrophic floods of 1966 to raise funds to repair the damage to the churches and artworks of Venice.

Sir Ashley was very kind. He was tall and portly but slightly hunched over, which made him seem even more courtly. He sympathized with our reluctance to consider his apartment, and he suggested we try to see the less formal apartment of a Mrs. Kaley, who lived with her daughter Diana on the top floor of a palazzo near the hospital. It had been perfectly restored, he said, with excellent facilities and two splendid terraces. "How can we arrange to see it?" we asked. "Unfortunately, she is away, somewhere in Finland," he said, "and it is hard to say when she might be back." He took our telephone number, however, and promised to have Mrs. Kaley call us on her return to Venice. "Do you know this Mrs. Kaley?" we asked Natale. "Flora? Certainly. Everyone in Venice knows her and her wonderful apartment near the hospital. It has marvelous views over the rooftops. And it is fully restored. You wouldn't have much to change there, except for the kitchen."

We heard nothing for the next several months. Our teaching year was coming to an end, and we would soon be returning to the States. Reluctantly, we concluded that the Venetian apartment we had dreamt of finding would remain just a dream, and we fell back on our original idea. We went house-hunting in Bologna again. The week before leaving for New York, we were shown a fine, large apartment near the old market, in the center of the city. It was late in the day when we saw it, so we told the agent we'd think it over and let her know in the morning. We called at eight in the morning, but the apartment had already been taken by someone else. I suspected that our show of interest had been used to leverage a decision by the other party. *"Mettiamoci il cuore in pace"* ("Let us put it out of our minds"), I said to Victor. "We'll find something when we come back in the spring."

On the day before we were to leave for Milan to take the plane to New York, Mrs. Kaley telephoned. It was close to lunchtime. Victor took the call.

"This is Flora Kaley," the woman said. "I am about to list my apartment for sale in the *Gazzettino* [Venice's local paper], but Sir Ashley insisted that I call you first."

"I wish you had called sooner," Victor said. "We are packing to go to New York tomorrow."

"Come up today then."

Victor turned to me, and we made a quick decision. "All right, we'll be there this afternoon," he said into the telephone.

We called Natale, who agreed to meet us at the station with a launch from the hotel and take us directly to Mrs. Kaley's place. "We shall have to move fast," he said, "because it will get dark soon and you won't be able to see much." It was the beginning of November, and Venice is dimly lit after dark.

At four P.M., we rang the Kaley bell in Calle della Testa. When Natale spoke his name into the intercom, the latch of the *portone*—the tall, heavy wooden entrance door—was released, the *portone* swung aside, and we stepped onto a nearly intact sixteenth-century courtyard framed by the four wings of a palazzo, but open above to the sky. It was so beautiful my breath stopped. There was a wellhead in the center of the courtyard and two large oleander trees. The floor, an uneven survivor of episodes of flooding and subsidence beyond our ken, was soft underfoot from the moss on the old bricks that paved it. The tallest of the buildings, at the rear, rested on a columned portico. Beyond the columns, below a wrought-iron gate, a canal rippled with the dying light of the fall afternoon. Natale led us through an arch in the far right corner of the portico and up a marble stairway. After the first two flights, my euphoria began to ebb. By the time we reached the top, I had counted eighty-two steps, and the beauty of the courtyard was no longer my most prominent impression. "How can I live here?" I thought. "I can't possibly climb eighty-two steps every time I come home."

At the top of the stairs there was another bell, another wooden door. Flora Kaley opened it. "Fiamma" would have been a better-fitting name for her. Her red hair, her burning eyes, the energy with which she spoke, and the contained sensuality with which she moved made you think of flames, not flowers. Mrs. Kaley showed us into her *salone,* the apartment's main room. It was long and very high-ceilinged for an attic. Its far end was framed and crossed by polished wooden beams. There the floor went up one step to form a dais that led to double dormer windows on the sunset side of the house. On another side of the *salone,* there were two double French doors that opened onto a large terrace. The height of the building allowed us to look down on the neighboring roofs and beyond them to the spire of the campanile in St. Mark's square and various church cupolas and other bell towers. The terrace was large enough to accommodate several potted trees with space to spare for a dining table.

The views from the terrace on the other side of the apartment were equally dazzling. There was the hospital square, the Gothic basilica of Saints John and Paul, the Renaissance façade of the hospital, and the bronze statue of Bartlomeo Colleoni, the Venetian republic's greatest general, astride a rearing horse, by Verrocchio, the

At the railing of my bedroom terrace in Venice; behind me is the church where we were married

Renaissance sculptor. The apartment, which occupied the entire top floor of the large palazzo, had twenty-eight windows, and when one walked past them, each brought up a different framed view of Venice. It was like being inside a magic lantern.

I forgot about the stairs. I was drinking in the beauty of the apartment, of its terraces, of its views. Victor was in a trance. We couldn't bear to leave for New York without knowing that when we came back, the place would be ours. We accepted the asking price, Victor gave Mrs. Kaley a check for earnest money, and we agreed to a closing immediately upon our return in the spring. Going back down, I was not aware of the stairs.

The Cipriani became yet another setting for my cooking school, after the New York apartments, the Fiera, and the new kitchen in Bologna. Many of my students were seeing Venice for the first time, and few of those who had been in the city before had been to the Cipriani. I thought how overwhelming it must have been for them to land in a city that for centuries had astonished its visitors, to board a launch in order to reach, across the dreamlike lagoon, the secluded hotel, itself an enchantment set in gardens thick with flowers, flanked by a vineyard the nuns next door had planted four hundred years earlier. I wondered too how it must have felt, that first, soundless night, when they turned in, reflecting on the wonders they had seen, to lie between freshly starched, crisp linen sheets, experiencing at the end of their first day in Venice one of the rarest of domestic luxuries. Could my classes measure up?

My first class meeting was not in the kitchen, but in the open-air market that has existed for close to one thousand years at the foot of the Rialto Bridge. The produce stalls there are set up on an embankment along a curve of the Grand Canal where the boatmen dock to unload their cargo. Much of the produce that is brought to Rialto—chard, green beans, spinach, purple cardoons, zucchini with their blossoms still attached, aspar-agus, tiny artichokes, fist-size cauliflowers, blushing pink beets only slightly larger than radishes, minia-ture salad greens—is harvested by growers in the outlying islands of the lagoon, some-times even on the same morning that they bring it to

A mess of spider crab at the Venice fish market

the market. It is farm-fresh in the literal sense of that abused term, and its flavors benefit from one of Venice's unique environments, the salt-bearing breezes of the lagoon.

The students were always fascinated by the variety of artichokes, from the bite-size, rosebud-like, and frightfully expensive *castraure* to the oversize ones that the sellers stripped of everything but their bottoms. When they observed the stall keeper swiftly decapitate a huge artichoke, entirely removing its leafy head, cut off its stem, and discard everything but the remaining thin disk of its bottom into a basin containing water and a few lemon halves, invariably someone would ask, "Why is he throwing so much of that artichoke away?" "He's not throwing away anything that you could use," I had to ex-plain. "Those artichokes are overgrown and the leaves are too tough to eat. What he keeps to sell are the delicious, creamy bottoms. They are called *i fondi*, a specialty of Venetian cooking."

Rialto's greatest glory, and one of the liveliest spectacles that Venice can offer, is the *pescheria*, the fish market. Venetians are sharp-eyed and dedicated consumers of seafood, and even though there were only a few more than sixty thousand residents left at last count, they support a fish market that in quality and variety has few rivals among metropolitan areas of any size. Of the scores of varieties of seafood that the market offers, the most sought-after—and consequently the most expensive—are the local ones, native to the northern Adriatic or, even closer, to the lagoon. I asked the students to notice the word *nostrani* that appeared from time to time along with the price. It means "local," hence more desirable both because it is fresher and because its flavor is familiar. "Look at that salmon," I said. "It is flown here all the way from Norway and costs one-third the price of these small, locally caught soles." Salmon in Venice is for the economy-minded. I have never known a self-respecting restaurant in Venice to serve it.

I identified some of the fish for them, pairing the English name with the corresponding Italian or Venetian: turbot, *rombo*; sole, *sogliola*; bream, *orata*; sea bass, *branzino*; monkfish, *coda di rospo*; gray

Squid-cleaning time in Venice, on the kitchen terrace

mullet, *otregan*; and indigenous crustceans such as *canoce*, a flat, silvery, sweet-fleshed creature whose folded pincers vaguely resemble those of a praying mantis; *schie*, a minute shrimp with brown, nut-flavored flesh; assorted clams, whelks, and periwinkles, *caparozzoli, garusoli, lumachine*; the silver dollar-size *moleche*, soft-shell crabs, which Venetians were the first to cultivate; *seppie*, cuttlefish, whose ink, rather than that of squid, as many believe, is what we use in Venice to make black risotto and pasta.

It was curious to observe how some of the students had difficulty connecting the fillets or fish steaks they were accustomed to eating to the anatomically complete creatures they saw in the market. How surprised they were to find that sardines and anchovies had heads, eyes, fins, and tails. And how startled they were when the soft-shell crabs, which were always sold live, would sometimes crawl out of their baskets, or the live shrimp would jump out of their bins. They were taken aback at the sight of a carcass of beef hanging in one of the market's butcher shops. I thought it useful for them to understand that the steaks, chops, roasts, veal scallops, or shanks that they bought, cooked, and ate were muscles coming from specific portions of an animal's body. "Muscles?" they would cry. "Of course, muscles. You are not eating bones and skin. You are eating muscles." Organs I chose not to discuss, never having forgotten the crisis I had provoked at the start of my teaching career when I brought out a bowl of kidneys for my class to prepare.

My kitchen at the Cipriani hotel was set up on a large, glass-walled terrace that faced a broad expanse of the lagoon toward the Lido. The building code did not countenance enclosing the terrace under a permanent roof. We had a temporary one that had to be dismantled at the end of every season. It was shaped like a tent, the interior made of heavy silk draperies protected on the outside by heavy, waterproof canvas. It was festive and luxurious—no other kitchen has ever looked like that—but during a downpour, the canvas cladding became a soundboard for the rain, which drummed out my voice. After I stopped teaching, the Cipriani obtained permission to build a solid roof, and my former kitchen space has been transformed into the hotel's fanciest apartment.

Rain did not provide the only surprise during the lessons. I was once demonstrating how to fry broad zucchini slices in flour-and-water batter. They can hold their own against the crispest tempura. I was slipping the zucchini into the hot oil of the skillet when suddenly the gas went out. I tried another burner, but it was just as dead. I called the concierge, who sent up one of his assistants, a nice young man, but he was as baffled as I. He left and returned with a maintenance man, who had the solution to the mystery. "It's simple. You are working with bottled gas," he said, "and your bottle is empty." He extracted a fresh bottle from a concealed storage compartment, hooked it up, and I was cooking again, with gas!

Aside from the tour of the Rialto market the first day, we scheduled just one expedition outside of Venice. Midway through the course, Victor took the class to Lake Garda to acquaint them with one of Italy's singular environments. Garda is a vast lake whose surface, like that of a giant mirror, bounces intense light over the vine-growing and olive-grove-studded slopes that encircle it. The light has a profound influence on the personality of such local wines as valpolicella, amarone, Bardolino, Soave—all of them brilliant in hue and fresh on the palate—and on the oil pressed from the olives grown on those slopes. The olive oil from the western shore of Lake Garda is my favorite Italian oil, owing its fragrance and its ingratiating texture to the radiance that comes from the lake. It is neither as aggressive as some of the pressings of Tuscany and the south, nor as bland as some of the Ligurian oils. A pity that there is so little of it, and that it costs so much. It was an instructive excursion, I thought. There is so much speculation about the role of territory in the character of wines and the flavor of food, about *terroir*, to use the French expression. On the shores of Lake Garda, my students had the opportunity to observe, to taste, and to identify the territorial connection right as it was taking place.

Frankly, I looked forward to their going out of town because it gave me a hugely welcome day off. Class days at the Cipriani were very long for me. The lessons started at five thirty in the evening, and with dinner at the end, they lasted four hours, and occasionally longer. While the students had the day free to explore Venice, I had to organize the lesson, do the marketing, look after personal matters at home, and make a good lunch, because it would be my only meal of the day.

My curriculum at the Cipriani was still the basic one I had developed when I taught in New York. Within the context of a menu, I explored Italian cooking through both its classic structure and its improvisational opportunities. Victor conducted his wine tastings. There were no shortcuts. But there was an aura about the courses at the Cipriani that set them apart from the cooking schools I conducted elsewhere. No one came to class in shorts or jeans or T-shirts. It would have been unthinkable to appear in such garb in that hotel in the evening. The men wore jackets, the women cocktail attire, and there were occasional displays of serious jewelry. By the glass wall overlooking the lagoon, the dining staff had set up a beautiful long banquet table laid with Cipriani linens, china, and crystal and exuberant flower arrangements. We served some of the dishes we made buffet-style from the cooking counter, but whenever it was more appropriate, I rang the dining room and a pair of uniformed waiters came up to take over the service.

Obviously, some of my students slipped more easily than others into the formal Venetian mode of the course at the hotel. A couple that fit into it with grace and good humor were Vincent Price and his wife, Coral Browne. Of all the students who have ever attended my classes, there are none whom I remember more fondly. Vincent was a marvelous gentleman, unaffectedly elegant in character no less than in dress. He was an accomplished cook who had written a substantial cookbook of his own. I believe that cooking and art—he

At the Cipriani kitchen with Simone Beck and Anne Willan. The man at my right is Natale Rusconi.

had majored in art history at Yale—engaged his feelings at a far deeper level than acting. He had formed so firm a bond with Coral that after she died of cancer, he continued to sign his Christmas cards "Vincent and Coral."

Coral had a devastating wit. One of her remarks that dates to her earlier years in the theater has become legendary. She was with a troupe in England whose members, both female and male, were perplexed about the sexuality of one of the actors, a very handsome man. He appeared to have neither girlfriends nor boyfriends, nor any interest in acquiring either. "He's asexual," the director told Coral. "Some English men are like that." "He's only shy," she replied. "I'll bet you twenty pounds that I can draw him out of his shell." The director accepted the wager, and after that evening's performance, Coral and the actor went off together. When she came back the following day, Coral went to the director and said, "You owe me only eight pounds six."

After the course, we continued to see Vincent and Coral at home in Venice, later on in the apartment we then kept in New York, and during book tours, in Beverly Hills. They were regulars at Spago, but Coral, who loved pizza, deplored Wolfgang Puck's version with goat cheese. "Please, Wolfgang," she said when he came to the table, "anything but goat cheese!" My feelings precisely. The year after Vincent died, I had a call from a woman who said she was Victoria Price, Vincent's daughter. She was in Venice and she had something that, before he died, her father had asked her to bring me. It was his working copy of his own cookbook, an imposing tome, with many additional recipes stuffed between the leaves and the margins densely annotated in his hand.

The last class I taught at the Cipriani I did not teach alone. A few years earlier, I had met Nobu Matsuhisa at a Masters of Food and Wine event at the Highlands Inn in Carmel, California, where we had been invited to demonstrate some of our dishes. At that time, he had only a small restaurant in Beverly Hills called Matsuhisa. By the time he opened Nobu in New York, we had become good friends. I asked him if he had ever been in Venice. He said he had never been to Europe, but that he was hoping to go soon. "You must come to Venice then, and see our fish market," I said. He did come, together with that marvelous wife and partner of his, Yoko. I took them to the fish market, which opened his eyes. He was fascinated to see live *canoce* there, which exist also in Japan, where they are called *shako*. Nobu, Yoko, Victor, and I spent several days together, eating out and cooking at home, and we had such a good time that we decided to organize an encore the following year.

I was working on a new cookbook and teaching many classes at home, which made it hard for me to continue teaching at the hotel. "I am going to teach one last class at the Cipriani; why don't you come and we'll do it together?" I said to Nobu. I asked my son to join us, and we worked out a program in which we each had a number to do. Giuliano, Nobu, and I taught a class on consecutive evenings, and on the final evening, we cooked together, producing an Italian-Japanese buffet to which the three of us contributed two or three dishes apiece. It was an immense success. More than forty people came, packing the terrace kitchen to capacity.

It was such a celebratory occasion, my farewell to the Cipriani classes, that we decided the welcome reception and dinner on the evening before the course should be in black tie. Our students had come from around the world, some of the women bringing exotic gowns. Yoko and another Japanese lady had spectacular kimonos, and there was a vaporous sari and a lustrous, richly embroidered, full-length black cheongsam. The glamorous spectacle contrasted with memories of the homey gatherings where my career had started, prepping vegetables with six matrons in cardigans around the din-

On the way to the fish market, stopping on the Rialto bridge with Nobu

ing table of a modest Fifty-fifth Street apartment in Manhattan. "There's certainly been a major scene change," I thought, "but as far as the substance of what I have been cooking and teaching, nothing has changed." Nothing ever would.

Natale was not quite ready to accept the end of my classes for the hotel. "Can't you think of some format where you don't have to prepare or cook anything, where you just act as the hostess?" he asked me. Victor agreed. "Yes, let's have other people do the cooking. It can be one of our friends in the kitchen of her palazzo, or a restaurateur friend taking the group into the kitchen of his restaurant. We can call the course 'Behind the Scenes with Marcella Hazan.'" With that, I found myself bidding one more farewell to the Cipriani—and, if it hadn't been for a fast-moving guest at our final dinner, possibly to my career or even my life.

We recruited a few of our friends who were good cooks, persuading them to bring our group into their kitchens, where they cooked some of their special dishes, which they then served in their dining rooms. The Cipriani provided service staff and logistical support. One of my favorite seafood restaurants of that period was Al Ponte del Diavolo, on the island of Torcello. Corrado, the manager-owner and a most accommodating man, agreed to have the chef demonstrate one of their specialties, which would then be included in the meal for our students. I was not required to do any cooking, but I was always present to translate, give full explanations of the procedures, and answer questions. Victor took the class for a day's outing in Friuli, where they visited a small elite winery not generally open to visitors and then had the typical dishes of the region in a local restaurant. One of the men in the class is now a neighbor in Longboat Key, and he stills mentions the borlotti beans and barley soup he had that day.

For the last day of "Behind the Scenes," I planned a grand finale in two parts. Piero Mainardis, a distinguished architect, and his wife, Silvana, a wine producer celebrated in Venice for her cooking, lived on the Grand Canal in the meticulously restored Palazzo Tiepolo. In the morning, Silvana would demonstrate in her palatial kitchen what she would cook for dinner. Dinner, in black tie, was served in the formal dining salon, which was lit only by candlelight. I wore a new gown for the occasion, with billowy green chiffon sleeves emerging from a long, narrow, vestlike tunic made from a piece of antique silk that Victor had bought in Thailand.

One of Silvana's first courses was *gnocchetti alle alghe*, little gnocchi with seaweed. The recipe had come down from Silvana's grandmother, who had trained a laborer engaged in clearing the banks of the canals to collect young, tender fronds of seaweed for her. Silvana got hers from a fisherman who, she said, thought it rather odd to cook with seaweed, but since he was being paid to procure it, he was happy to humor her.

There were candlesticks everywhere in the dining salon. If you have enough candles in a room, the illumination can be brilliant. The dinner was a huge success. The *gnocchetti* were delicious, tasting as though they had been made with a nuttier, brinier kind of spinach. I got up at the end, moving away from the table, to thank our hosts and to thank the participants. I had my evening bag in my hand, and I reached back toward a console behind me to put it down. I saw Victor, at the far end of the table, turning white. At that instant, a man who had been sitting beside me leaped out of his chair, overturning it, and rushed toward me, vigorously slapping my arm. In that moment, I noticed that the sleeve was smoking. Evidently, it had come too near one of the candles on the console. With his hands, the man quickly squelched the flames that were just starting to form. Silvana moistened his palms with aloe from a plant in the kitchen, but he did not seem to have been hurt. In what was now a one-sleeved dress, I returned to my farewell speech, adding a tribute to my savior, and with that, my final performance for the Cipriani came to a close.

We took possession of Mrs. Kaley's apartment in April 1980, but it was more than two years before we obtained the permits we needed and completed the renovations we had decided on. In Venice, you cannot alter the configuration of a room in a historically registered building. Our kitchen was jammed in under the eaves of a corner of the roof, and to transform it to suit my requirements was a challenge for our ingenuity and that of our architect. We also found we had to install a modern heating system. When we'd walked through the apartment before the closing, Mrs. Kaley's daughter Diana had shown us a contraption, explaining that to turn it on when it was cold, we had to turn a lever on it toward Finland, and turn it toward Africa to shut it off when it was hot. In the uncertainty about where either place lay with respect to the spot where we stood, we replaced the machinery with up-to-date gas boilers and a thermostat. We put in air-conditioning, hiding individual compressors for each room under the roof tiles. We had to rewire the apartment because the tangle of old wires was not up to code.

We could have stopped there. I would have. But Victor is a man who rearranges the furniture of a hotel room where he is going to spend two nights. His passion for altering and shaping the place where he lives had found in this apartment enough kindling to stoke it to fever heat. We had two bathrooms, neither of which he found suitable. The bathroom that was to be his had a tub. He wanted a stall shower. He didn't just put in a stall shower; he chucked the tub and replaced the sink, the commode, Flora Kaley's faux-silver fittings, and the tiles, and had the whole bathroom—the floor, the walls, and the interior of the shower—lined in marine mahogany. I was perfectly happy with my bathroom, which had a gorgeous cobalt-blue bathtub and tiny tiles that Flora had chosen because they reminded her of the colors of Monet's lily ponds. He allowed me to keep the tub, but everything else had to go, and on the principle he enunciated that in a bathroom, what goes on the walls goes on the floor, he had it all lined—saving part of a wall for mirrors—in slabs of Portuguese marble shot with pink and pale blue. It was lovely, I must admit.

We moved in, in the fall of 1982, almost three years after the November afternoon on which we had first seen the apartment. I longed to return to the intimate format of the classes I had originally given in New York. Just six students and me, sitting around a table, preparing dinner together. For the time being I was committed to the large classes in Bologna and at the Cipriani, where I had to speak into a microphone clipped to my apron to make my low voice heard, but I knew that those were coming to the end of their time, and I had hoped that I could spend the final years of my teaching career in quieter circumstances at home. We offered our first classes at home the year after we moved in. We called them Master Classes, to suggest a close tie between teacher and student. At home, I was able to return to my favorite prepping position, sitting at a table. The kitchen had French doors that gave onto the large terrace, where we put a long table on which the students and I could work. What we didn't know was that previous tenants were still at home in the terrace. Whenever I was doing a fish lesson, within seconds after I had put the fish on the table, a swarm of wasps tried to join the class. Victor became extraordinarily skillful at sucking them into a dust buster, using the narrow tube attachment. He soon followed them to their nest, inside one of the beams. He sealed it, and we were free of their company. In mild weather, if we didn't have a class, it was at that prepping table that Victor and I had lunch alfresco.

The classes started at ten in the morning, and by the time we had finished eating what we had prepared, it was close to four in the afternoon. The students had to arrange for their own accommodations, and there were no excursions, except for the tour of the Rialto market with which I launched every course. At the end of the market tour, I wanted the students to taste a representative sample of the encyclopedic variety of seafood they had just seen. I usually arranged for them to have a banquet lunch at a restaurant called Da Fiore—which was able to serve them a dozen or more kinds of seafood prepared in traditional style.

Da Fiore's tale is one of pluck, luck, and storybook success. It was once a grimy, working-class wine bar, whose sign is still nailed to the wall above the door. A very young couple, Maurizio and Mara—he may have been twenty, and she eighteen—came to Venice from the outlying farm country to find fortune. They found Da Fiore—it was for sale, they borrowed the money and bought it. The interior and the cuisine have since undergone several renovations, and both are quite chic these days. Then, both were very chaste.

We discovered Da Fiore soon after we had started coming to the Cipriani. What we liked immediately on entering the first time were the sounds of Venetian talk that filled the room. Venetians know fish. "If they come here to eat," we thought, "could it be bad?" Not only was it not bad, it was pure and unforgettable. Thanks perhaps to her innocence of professional experience, to the artlessness of her youth, and certainly to her natural talent, what distinguished Mara's cooking in those years was something ineffable that might be described as invisibility of the process, as the cook's trust in the ability of the ingredients to speak for themselves, eliciting from

In Venice on the kitchen terrace, a quick consultation

them the purest, clearest, brightest flavors that they were capable of expressing.

We took not just our classes to Da Fiore, but also every food and wine person who came to visit us in Venice, from Julia Child, to Robert Mondavi, to Nobu. The visitor who proved most important to Da Fiore's ascent was Patricia Wells. She had come to Venice twice, once to interview me for *Metropolitan Home* magazine, another time on holiday with her husband, Walter, and twice we took her to have Mara's cooking. Eventually, Pat traveled the world for the *International Herald Tribune* to assemble a list of the ten restaurants she considered the best. When her list of the world's ten best appeared, Da Fiore was on it. You can still eat exceptionally well at Da Fiore, if you have booked long in advance, but the sounds you are likely to hear from the other tables now are no longer those of the neighborhood, but those of the world.

My students feel very bad when they discover that my memories of them are usually vague. It happens again and again that someone will come up to my table at a restaurant, or stop me in the lobby of a theater, or park her cart alongside mine in a supermarket, to say, "Marcella! Remember me? I was in your class in Bologna." "When?" "Twenty-five years ago." How can I remember? She has had only one of me, but I have had a few thousand of her.

It has been ten years since I taught the last of my classes at home in Italy. Perhaps because there were never any more than six students in any of them, I can still clearly recollect some of the participants, although not their names necessarily. I recall the attractive young woman from Australia who lived on a ranch the size of Rhode Island. She lived there alone with twenty thousand cows and a few ranch hands. Her nearest neighbor lived six hundred miles away, she said. "What do you do if you need a doctor?" I asked. "That's not a problem. We have a flying doctor who makes house calls. We get better attention out on the ranch than people in cities do."

I am haunted by the memory of two women who were so determined to take the class that they ignored, in each case, a devastating and eventually fatal physical condition. One of them had advanced multiple sclerosis, yet she negotiated the eighty-two steps on our stairs all six mornings of the course. Another was anorexic. When she walked in the first day, I thought I was seeing an apparition from a horror movie, not an ordinary flesh-and-blood being. She tasted what we cooked in the minutest quantities imaginable, such as taking a single piece of penne pasta, dividing it in four, and eating one of the fourths. She loved to entertain, she said.

There have always been men in my classes, but at home there seemed to have been more of them, and more doctors among them. One of them rescued me when I got stuck midway through the preparation of a dessert. I was making peach halves stuffed with amaretto cookies, which then I would cook on the charcoal grill we had in the terrace. Victor did all the marketing every morning before class, rising very early to be there when the Rialto market opened, bringing back vegetables, fruit, meat, or fish over four bridges and through many narrow streets at amazing speed. He was always home early enough for me to inspect and organize my ingredients before the students arrived. On the morning that I was doing peaches for dessert, I had asked for freestones, but what he had brought were clings. I tried to separate a peach into two halves free of the pit, but I ended up with useless shreds. One student, a distinguished, tall older man, volunteered to help. "You are welcome to try," I said skeptically. He asked for a soup spoon. He slowly worked the spoon inside the peach, turning it steadily but with great delicacy. In not too long, he extracted the spoon, bearing the pit. The peach was intact. "Where did you learn to do that?" I asked. "In the hospital. It's simple. It's how I remove tumors from a brain."

Another brain surgeon from Chicago entertained us with his anecdotes. In one of the stories, he told us that one of his pastimes was owning a hot dog stand. Whenever he could, he loved working the stand himself. On one occasion, he saw a woman approaching whom he recognized as the daughter of someone on whose brain he had performed a long and complicated operation. He turned his head away when he handed her the hot dogs she had ordered, but she came closer to peer at him. He pulled his cap down lower over his face.

"Don't I know you from somewhere?" she asked.

"I don't know. I don't think so," he mumbled.

"What is your name?"

"Ummm, Lenny."

"Lenny?" She came closer. Her voice rose, "I know who you are! You operated on my mother!"

I have never, in any of my own classes, given out printed recipes. If you give students a printed something, they will stop to read it and forget to pay attention to what you are doing or saying. If they take notes, however, that helps them focus on the lesson. Nearly all of my students kept a notebook, but there was one who took notes in the form of sketches, which he drew incessantly. He sketched the dishes, the ingredients, my silver flatware. I had hoped to add a page from his notebook to the illustrations in this memoir, but when I asked, he said he had hundreds of notebooks and had forgotten where he had stored the one from our cooking class. He was Norman Foster, Lord Foster now that Queen Elizabeth has bestowed a peerage on him. As one of the world's most famous architects, his name should have been as familiar to his classmates as that of a rock star. It's curious how few people read architectural news even

Working under the eaves in my Venice kitchen

when it lands on their paper's front page. As soon as we had introduced ourselves to each other when we met in my sitting room, one of the other students asked, "What do you do, Norman?" "I am an architect." "Do you have your own practice or do you work for someone?" "I have my own practice. I have five hundred architects working for me."

Victor and I continued to differ, sometimes wrathfully, leaving deep wounds, about which alterations in the apartment were necessary and which were not. It always went Victor's way. Victor is a study in contrasts. He is gentle and considerate to a degree that few men are. He has unshakable faith in his judgment, however, and if he is persuaded of the correctness of his ideas, not even the Lord of the universe could budge him. He felt extremely proprietary about his bathroom, which he did not like to share. He therefore had a guest bathroom built, which had to be laboriously covered in a trio of tiny, round tiles colored chestnut-brown, fawn, and white. Victor loathes sharp edges. Wherever possible, every right angle had to be replaced by a curve. Flora Kaley's dropped ceilings over the bedrooms and my study oppressed him. "There are five-hundred-year-old beams imprisoned up there," he said. "There is air, there is space that wants to be let out." And so each year, another ceiling was taken down; antique beams were scraped, repaired, waxed, or replaced entirely when necessary; the walls of another room were finished in *marmorino*, the famous marble-smooth Venetian finish applied with a small spatula that takes two workmen ten days to do; and another large hole was poked into our bank account. We then had hand-troweled plaster in Venice rather than drywall, and I felt I was suffocating when plaster dust fogged the air I breathed; the noise of hammering, sawing, and of power tools twists my nerves almost beyond endurance; and I was irritated to see workmen come through the door and start their work early in the morning, when I was still in my bed clothes and had not yet had my coffee.

I was in agreement, however, on the necessity of the messiest and most ruinously expensive job we undertook, the installation of an elevator. After the Second World War, when Italy's cities and towns were aching to modernize, draconian laws were put into place to protect historic places (too feebly enforced, unfortunately, to save the coast of Naples and of part of the Riviera). To keep Venice from being erased by the rush to build and modernize, it had been all but frozen in place. We had become good friends with Francesco Valcanover, Venice's superintendent of fine arts, who lived on the floor above Sir Ashley Clark's old place. Valcanover facilitated our application for a permit to install an elevator, putting in a good word with his friend and colleague, the formidable superintendent of monuments, Margherita Asso, who then had all construction and renovation in Venice under her iron thumb. In a short time—short, that is, when judged by Venice's languid bureaucratic pace—we obtained one of the city's rarest privileges, the permit to build an elevator. All we lacked was the required unanimous consent of the owners. One owner, a café singer who had the smallest percentage of the voting shares, refused to grant it. The elevator, he said, would alter the architectural integrity of the stairs. It took six years to bring him around and another year to build the elevator.

During construction, the contractor had to remove part of the roof and the door to our apartment. To keep out the dust, we had heavy plastic sheets instead of a front door. It looked like the entry to an intensive care unit. Every night before they left, the workmen put up a temporary plywood door that we could lock. We couldn't cancel a year's classes, so we shared the noise, dust, and discomfort with our students. After six years of wrangling and one year of building, the elevator was done. It opened right into our apartment onto a small vestibule with a star-shaped marble floor in various colors that Victor had designed. For yet another year, we had to be satisfied just to look at it and admire it. There was only one elevator inspector for Venice and its surrounding territory, and it took him that long to come by. We were consoled to learn that the hospital near us also had had to wait a year for the same inspector to come to certify the elevator that went up to the operating room floor.

I was raised in a Catholic family that was both believing and observant. My grandmother Adele had come close to taking vows, stopping just one step away from becoming a nun. Yet, when we got married, we had a civil ceremony, in the effort to spare Victor's parents the offending news that their son had been married in church. After his parents' death, Victor said that even though his own feelings were profoundly antireligious, if I still cared to be married in church, he would go along with it. For me, it was a dream come true.

We lived across from one of Venice's great churches, the Gothic Santi Giovanni e Paolo, Saints John and Paul. I had occasionally gone to mass there, where I enjoyed listening to the plainspoken and engaging sermons of Padre Pio, the Dominican parish priest. I asked him if he could marry us. "Certainly!" he said. Did it matter that my husband was Jewish and a nonbeliever? That he was Jewish did not bother him at all, but he hoped that he could help Victor acquire faith and become a good Jew.

Because I had already been married in a civil ceremony, I needed to bring Padre Pio a copy of that certificate from my town's city hall.

"What is the purpose of this certificate?" asked the woman at the records office.

"In order to get married."

"In that case, I must first have a copy of your divorce decree."

Getting married again

"I am not divorced."

"If you are not divorced, you can't get married again, and I am unable to give you a certificate."

"I don't need a divorce. It's my husband that I am marrying!"

It was an intimate wedding, held in a beautiful small, candy box of a chapel that Padre Pio had chosen for us. It is called *la cappella della Madonna della Pace*, the chapel of the Madonna of Peace. The Madonna is a Byzantine icon painted sometime between the twelfth and thirteenth centuries. From her place above the altar, she looked down benevolently and, it seemed to me, encouragingly on us. I had invited two of my friends from Cesenatico, and Natale and his wife, Connie. Connie came alone because Natale was in London for a meeting of Sherwood's hotel group. The other guest was our son. Padre Pio had the organist play an air of Bach's, married us, and concluded with a charming sermon. He said, "It's my duty to instruct you on the steps you can take to make your marriage a sound one, but you have already been doing that for thirty years. I should also offer my counsel on how to raise the children you'll have, but your child, who is here, is already grown, and he has grown well." He concluded by saying that we should continue to do exactly what we had been doing. My eyes were teary the entire time.

We went home, where Padre Pio blessed our house, and although neither Victor nor I usually drink champagne—Victor says that the only thing it has ever done for him is to give him a headache—we unbent and drained a glass of it in toasts to each other, to our guests, and to Venice. We walked over to a good local trattoria for the wedding lunch, at the conclusion of which all the guests departed. Victor told me that he had booked a gondola for later that evening to take the two of us into the small inner canals, safe from encounters with tourists. We climbed into the gondola at a landing across from our house, and I settled back in expectation of the long ride through the black, untraveled canals of Venice. I was puzzled to see the gondolier head the boat toward the most central part of town and pull up at the landing of one of the restaurants we then used to patronize. The restaurant's owner came to greet us, and behind him came two waiters carrying a small table that they lowered into the gondola. Soon there were dishes on the table; silver; glasses; a platter with two cold boiled lobsters; small boiled potatoes; a sauceboat with homemade mayonnaise; two bowls of caviar on ice; two dessert cups filled with chocolate mousse; and an ice bucket with vodka. An accordion player boarded the gondola, seating himself at the far end from us. Then we pushed off into the dark.

It wasn't so dark that we weren't noticed. But then, nothing one does in Venice goes unnoticed, although people don't always get all the details right. Not long after, Pamela Fiori, our editor friend who, years before in our New York apartment, had taped the Danny Kaye conversation with Mrs. Horowitz, was in Venice and ran into the general manager of the Gritti Palace Hotel. "You will be amazed to learn," he told her, "that Marcella and Victor have finally got married."

The decade after our church wedding was the happiest and most relaxed time we spent in Venice. I no longer had to commute to teach in Bologna, and we were not in the States very much. We had a more active social life than we had ever had before or have had since. Cities can have surprisingly different social personalities. Bologna is the capital of its region, it is industrious and prosperous, it has a famous and ancient university, yet it is as inward-looking and provincial as any small farm town. We had worked there twelve years, we had brought several thousand students and as many other visitors who followed in their wake, and directly or indirectly, we contributed significantly to the city's economy. However, except for the people who did business with our school, who we were and what we were doing in Bologna was a subject of no interest to anyone.

Venice, on the contrary, has been an old hand at hospitality since the Crusades. When I think back on those years, they become a blurred sequence of dinners, receptions, and jaunts to the outlying islands on someone's boat. I think of the deliciously lazy mornings by the Cipriani pool and the incomparable seafood buffets. I remember the communal events when the lagoon and Grand Canal closed down, and everyone turned up in someone's house or boat to watch the great fireworks show in July at Redentore, the

Filming with Charlie Gibson on Piazza San Marco during the 1986 summit meeting in Venice

feast of the Redeemer, celebrating the city's deliverance from the plague, and the Regata Storica in September, to mark the city's symbolic nuptials with the sea.

A good friend at that time was Patricia Curtis, who lived in Palazzo Barbaro, the fifteenth-century palazzo that her Bostonian great-grandfather, Daniel Curtis, had bought in the late 1800s. Henry James, who was a friend of Daniel Curtis, stayed often at

Palazzo Barbaro and used it as the template for the palazzo that figures in *Wings of the Dove*. To join the jovial parties that Patricia gave in the piano nobile, or the small dinners in Patricia's upstairs apartment, when she would set up a table for four just outside the library where Henry James had worked, stimulated one's compliant imagination into hearing distant echoes of that moment in Venice's history when Palazzo Barbaro had been the center of its literary and artistic life.

We also had very good times at home, where I would make dinner for one friend or forty. The one might have been Padre Pio, an unwavering devotee of my cooking, or a neighbor, Donna Leon, an English teacher at the air force base in Aviano who would become known as a writer of mysteries. It was moreover a fortunate time for eating out. There were good restaurants everywhere in Venice. It proved to be the last happy period for my legs, which were still strong and agile enough to climb the bridges and take me wherever in the city Victor chose to go, either to try a new restaurant or return to a favorite. Whenever we are in Venice again, it is a comforting reminder of a precious and vigorous period of our lives to sit at the corner table by the window at Fiaschetteria Toscana, or in one of Ivo's banquettes, and find that we can still eat as well as we did so many years ago.

Most of the restaurants that we admired then, however, are better not mentioned, even though they are still around. One of them has given rise to an expression that we use now whenever we have a notably unsatisfactory meal. A trio of close friends from the States, the painter Hector Leonardi, Karl Mann, and the late Ruth Birnkrant, were spending a long visit with us. On one of the evenings, when we had a commitment elsewhere, we directed them to a small restaurant where we had always eaten very well. The following day, when I asked them how it had gone, Ruth, always outspoken, said, "Terrible! Atrocious! The worst we have ever had!" I was mortified, but we had eaten there so often and so well that I had to find out for myself what could have gone wrong. A few evenings later, they agreed to let me take them all there. Our meal was flawless. "If I had been brought here blindfolded, I would have sworn on my life that this could not have been the place we came to before," Ruth said. I called the owner, who was also the chef, over to our table. "Cesco, there is something I don't understand. Were you not here when my friends came for dinner three nights ago?" He thought a moment, then said, "No, that was the day my wife was taken to the hospital." "Who was doing the cooking?" "Our dishwasher." Ever since then, when we have a particularly deplorable meal out, Victor and I look at each other and say, "It must be the dishwasher's night at the stove."

My Three Graces
Lucia, Maria, Nadia

1963–1999

$\mathcal{A}$s FAR BACK as I can remember, and to the end of her very long life, my mother always had full-time domestic help. So did her sister, her sister-in-law, and all of her friends. Some among them may have been wealthy, but many were not. To enjoy the services of a woman who kept your house in order, who hand-washed everything and pressed it, who looked after your young children or your old parents, who may or may not have cooked, but certainly did all the cleaning up after meals, wasn't related to the money you had but to your social position. From the middle class upwards, nearly every family had servants. My parents never had any money, but the uneducated and close-to-illiterate young women who came from the farms to work in town had even less. Their cash salary was only slightly better than symbolic, but what they got they saved, and from time to time they took home some food staples, a bottle of olive oil, a piece of Parmigiano, and good used clothes.

Italy's semifeudal agricultural system, which populated the

farms with sharecropping families that had too many mouths to feed, was a source of abundant and cheap domestic labor. It didn't begin to change until some years after the Second World War, when profound social reforms were enacted. An Italian farm is now a business like any other, staffed with well-paid hired help. Today, Italian matrons who want to land a housekeeper must cast their net far from home, to Eastern Europe, to Africa, to the Philippines. When I returned to Italy in 1962, the new order had not yet completely supplanted the old one. Soon after we had established ourselves in Milan, and Victor had settled into what appeared to be a stable career, I looked for what I could not have afforded in New York—a woman who would live with us and help me take care of the house and my son. Not too many years later, the job description would have had to include "cooking school assistant." I followed the still valid custom of my elders, leaving word with neighbors and friends that I was looking for a country girl to come work for me in Milan. Several came forward, but the first two or three I tried did not stay long. They were too young, and one, who had never been to a big city, became homesick; whereas another, on her free evenings, made imprudent use of the city's diversions. Then Lucia turned up.

Lucia came from a hamlet high on one of the tall hills west of Cesenatico. She was astride of her late thirties and early forties, and unmarried, with no changes to her status in sight. She had the taut body and the sun- and wind-darkened skin of mountain people. Her smile was shy, and her eyes kind but sad. Sometimes, they looked spooked. She neither smoked nor drank. I remember how gently she broke the news to me, when we were living in Milan, and we had come back late from an evening out, that Papi had died. She was proud yet deferential. She immediately formed a deep attachment for Giuliano, then just six years old, an affection that lasted well beyond the years of her employment. Lucia was not a terrific cook, but like other women in Romagna of her age, she could roll out a fine sheet of pasta by hand.

We were fond of Lucia, but she was extremely reticent, reluctant to yield any clues to her feelings or thoughts. There was a cloud of mystery around her that never completely cleared away. On Lucia's day off, whether we were living in Milan, in Rome, or later in New York, and during the nonworking stops of a book or teaching tour in America, she disappeared and returned home late in the evening without a word about where she had been or what she had seen. It was particularly puzzling in the States because she neither spoke nor understood English. I think with amusement of the time in New York when I sent her to D'Agostino to buy a chicken. Victor, who does not eat fowl and is uncomfortable even to see it on the table, was out of town, and I greatly anticipated the uninhibited pleasure of a chicken fricassee done my way, the meat falling off the bones, its unctuous juices running down my fingers. I told Lucia to buy a small bird because there would be only the two of us eating. She came back with a portly roaster that might have fed four. "Lucia," I said, "*questo è un pollo per quattro,* this is a chicken for four!" "*No, signora, guardi qui,* not so madam, look here, *è un pollo per due,* it's a chicken for two." And she pointed to the label that said "Perdue," for two, if read as Italian.

Our disagreements always arose when she misunderstood my instructions. The final one was about artichokes. I was going to show a class how to trim artichokes the Italian way. I have never had a student who knew how to do it. Italians cut away most of the artichoke, keeping only those parts that are tender. When you cook it, all of it is edible. I found that others leave everything on when they cook an artichoke, which obliges you, when eating it, to scrape the tender bits off the leaves with your teeth. I needed seven artichokes, one for each of the six students to work on, and one for me to demonstrate the technique. It was a procedure with which Lucia was well acquainted. On that morning, I found that, inexplicably, she had failed to get artichokes when she had marketed for the class. The students had already arrived when I asked Lucia to rush back to the market for the artichokes. She returned after an awkwardly long time with only six artichokes. It was late, I was upset, but she became even more upset and closeted herself in her room, never to come out again for the duration of the class. My mother, who had come to stay with me at that time, went out herself to buy the seventh artichoke. I did not intend to fire Lucia, but I spoke sharply to her and she construed my remarks as a dismissal. It was late spring, close to the beginning of the summer break in my courses. At the end of the last course, Lucia packed all her things and returned to Italy. She had been with me for twelve years.

I wrote to nearly every one of my friends and acquaintances throughout Italy, asking if they knew of a mature woman who would be willing to come to New York to work for me. I specified that she had to be able to roll out pasta by hand. Soon I had a reply from my former landlady in Ferrara, with whom I had lodged when I was going to the university. She knew of someone from a village on the Veneto mainland near Venice who said she would come. She was single, in her forties, and a dependable, strong, hard worker. Her manner was gruff, I was warned, but she was good-hearted and loyal. Her name was Maria. I was spending most of my summer in a small town on the coast of the Italian Riviera, where I hoped to learn more about Ligurian cooking. One of the most popular recipes I ever published, the chicken with two lemons, came out of that trip. I immediately wrote to Ferrara: "I want to meet Maria as soon as possible. Have her come to see me in Liguria."

She was a short, stout woman in tight-fitting clothes. I would learn that she didn't think of herself as fat, and wore the tightest clothes she could get into to prove it. She was not exhibiting her gruffness that day, but I would get large doses of it ever after. She was in fact very pleasant, with a ready smile. It was one of the few smiles I was to see on her face in the twenty-one years that Maria lived with us. I asked her why she was willing to leave Italy. "I want to make a change in my life," she said. Her mother had died when she was still a very young girl, and she had worked hard ever since. She had had to take charge of the household, to bring up her younger brothers and sister, and when she was older, she moved from one tough job to another. I explained what I was doing and what her duties would be. She was incredulous and thought it rather funny that a doctor, actor, or businessman would take cooking instruction, but she was sure that whatever the work required she could handle it. "Can you roll out pasta by hand?" I asked. "*Faccio di tutto in cucina*" ("I can do everything in the kitchen"), she replied. I offered her a glass of wine, which she accepted and drained, and she lit a cigarette. "That's a change from Lucia," I thought.

When we moved back from Italy in 1967, we had taken a two-bedroom apartment on West Fifty-fifth Street. When Lucia came over, she had to share a bedroom with Giuliano. As soon as we were able, we moved to a larger apartment, where she had a bedroom of her own. The kitchen was larger too, and it was bright with a tall window facing south on East Seventy-sixth Street. There was even room in it for a four-foot-long butcher-block table that was perfect for rolling out pasta. I gave Maria my long Bolognese rolling pin, eggs, and flour, and asked her to show me how she made pasta.

"I have never made pasta," she said.

"Why did you tell me you did?"

"I didn't think it was important. Why do we have to make pasta? Don't you have stores where you can buy it?"

I was vexed by the deception, but it was not surprising that she had never made pasta. The boundaries sealing off one regional cooking tradition from another in Italy have long since suffered many breaches, but in Maria's youth the people of her native Veneto region did not eat pasta; they ate rice. "You may think this cooking course is a joke, but it's no joke," I said to her. "It's a serious business and we have serious customers who expect to learn, among other things, how to make pasta. I don't intend to make a *brutta figura*, to look bad, on your account. I am going to teach you how to roll out fresh pasta dough with a rolling pin, and no matter how many eggs it takes and how much flour, you are going to learn before the next course starts." Maria set her features into that joyless mask that I came to accept as her face, but she learned how to roll out pasta dough. And she learned it well.

I found that no expression of pleasure, of curiosity, of approbation, of enthusiasm, of mirth was likely to escape Maria. She would turn over one's most commonplace observation in order to expose its dark side. If in looking out the window one morning, I would say, "What a pretty day it's going to be," she would respond, "It will rain in the afternoon." In her movements, there was the brusqueness of unappeasable anger. She would not put something down if it could be slammed down instead. In her first month in New York, she chipped every single piece of Victor's favorite dinner service. In our school in Bologna, we had as much breakage of glass as a small restaurant's. She passed through people in a room with the undeviating trajectory of a bowling ball headed for a strike. In Venice, we had to forbid her to leave her room in the morning before we were up. Despite their monumental exteriors, the interiors of the palazzi of Venice are built of the lightest possible materials so they won't weigh too heavily on the pilings that support them. When Maria stomped down the corridor alongside our bedroom, the rumble and vibrations of the flimsy floorboards could just as easily have been produced by jackbooted soldiers on patrol. To describe Maria, I used to say she was a cross between Mussolini and a bulldozer.

After spending one summer's end on Long Island, we returned to Venice to prepare for the first course of the fall semester. As always, when we were away, Maria looked after the house and polished it to a high luster for our return. We went to bed early that night, having lost the previous night's sleep on the transatlantic crossing. I had been asleep for about two hours when I heard a tremendous slamming of drawers and the trembling of the house from stomping feet. Reluctantly, I pushed the bedclothes aside and rose. I went where the noises were coming from, at the end of the hall, in Maria's room. I found her fully dressed. She clutched her chest. "I am having an attack," she said. "I am going to the hospital." "*Calma, calma,* hold on," I said. "I'll call the litter carriers." The hospital was on the other side of our canal, and an ambulance boat was unnecessary. Emergency transport to the hospital, in such cases, required a hand-carried sedan chair. I gave our house number when I called, but because house numbers don't follow an easily comprehended pattern in Venice, I got dressed and went down outside the house to hail the chair carriers as soon as they appeared on the street. I had told Maria to sit down upstairs and wait, but she had taken the elevator after me and came down to our courtyard with her good Sunday coat on. She paced furiously back and forth. When the men carrying the chair entered our courtyard, they looked from me to Maria asking, "Who is the patient?"

Maria did have a minor heart attack, which she overcame handily. She never returned to work. Years before, she had bought and furnished a modern apartment in her old town, where she retired. There she still lives.

There was a classful of students coming in two weeks, and I

had no one to help me. I called Mara Martìn, who, with her husband, Maurizio, owned the celebrated restaurant Da Fiore. Mara and Maurizio came from a farm town outside Venice, and I thought that they would be the most likely people to know someone interested in the job. Mara phoned the next day. "We are in luck," she said. "I have the perfect girl for you. She is from our town and I have known her all my life. Can I bring her to meet you in the morning?" Nadia had never worked in anyone's house before. In her middle thirties, she had worked for the previous fifteen years as a bookkeeper. The company where she had most recently been working had gone bankrupt. She was tall, slim, and comely, with long black hair and a ready smile. She was skeptical at first about accepting the decline in status that doing housework for others implied, but she liked to cook and was bright and adventurous enough to be intrigued by the descriptions of my cooking classes and of the people who came from all over the world to attend them. She could not live in with us, however. She had a husband and a young son and had to be back home before evening. We were not unhappy about that. The conveniences of having a live-in housekeeper are paid for with a loss of privacy. I offered her the job and she accepted.

For Maria, cooking had been another of life's toilsome tasks that she had been sentenced to perform. She was indubitably a hard and productive worker, but lacking any enthusiasm for what we did, or for anything else for that matter, she worked with a scowl and a heavy heart. When Nadia joined me in the kitchen, I felt an immense weight slipping away from me. For the first time, the person I shared my work with was someone who enjoyed it. At last, there was space and time for levity in the kitchen. When I heard Nadia's happy laugh, I felt that I was being compensated by Providence for the two humorless decades I had passed with her predecessor. I wish that Providence had gotten around to it earlier, before some of that glumness had started to rub off on me.

Maria about to break eggs for the pasta lesson

Parting with Knopf

1975-1993

*I*T WAS A FORTUNATE day for my career when Julia Child brought Judith Jones and me together. It's what I thought then and what I think now. I was immensely taken with Judith. She was both different and familiar. She was different from all the publishing and newspaper people I had met until then. Her voice was husky and her diction, to my Italian ears, had what I took to be the inflections of cultivated American speech. Her light-colored eyes had an amused and comforting twinkle; they sparkled with intelligence and, it seemed, lively empathy. It was the way in which she dressed and put herself together that was familiar to me. Judith reminded me of the style of certain well-bred, conservative Italian women. I never saw her wearing pants or a dress but always skirts of modest length, a blouse, and a sweater. She wore very little makeup. Her hair then, which I remember as an ash blond, fell with girlish softness to her shoulders. We were born a month apart in the same year.

If I was at first intimidated by seeing in her office the books and photographs of the eminent authors she was editing, she soon put me at ease. When an author hands her book to a publisher, it's as though she were handing over her infant. A book can be so defenseless. When Judith took the Harper's Magazine Press edition of *The Classic Italian Cook Book* in hand, I felt as a mother might when she thinks she has found a doctor who can make her ailing child well and strong. And Judith did.

At the beginning, Victor and I had a cordial relationship with Judith and her simpatico husband, Evan, in which we thought we saw the makings of friendship. We shared several meals, at my place and hers, and exchanged little gifts. She once gave me a delicious terrine she had made, molded into a small terra-cotta-glazed lidded dish. We still have the dish and use it every morning. Victor likes a dollop of whipped heavy cream with his espresso. He whips up a week's supply and stows it in Judith's dish. It's good for a week in the refrigerator.

I can't say exactly when the warm feelings that we had once enjoyed began to cool. It was a perplexing turn of events that pains me to this day. It may have started with a dinner party I gave at home for a story *People* magazine wanted to do. The magazine had asked if I could organize a small dinner for Julia and Paul Child and James Beard, and round it out with two or three other friends or prominent students. I invited a television producer from PBS, whom I never saw again and whose name I have forgotten, and two students, the singer and actor Joel Grey and Ronald Lauder, who came with their wives. I suggested that we include Judith and Evan. The magazine said no, it might make the dinner too much of a publisher's party, and for their story, they preferred a more varied mix. Judith felt she should have been included and took offense.

Judith had no input on the content of *The Classic Italian Cook Book*, which Knopf reissued leaving the text and illustrations unchanged. *More Classic Italian Cooking*, my second cookbook, was the first book

Julia, Paul, and Jim Beard at the dinner for *People* magazine

that Judith edited. Inexplicably to me, it didn't go smoothly. I felt I was matched against an antagonist rather than paired with an editor. She complained that when she sautéed onion following my recipes, the onions in the pan were burned because I hadn't said anything about stirring. I can remember her taking strong exception to a recipe for gratinéed cauliflower with béchamel. "It's just old cauliflower with white sauce, so trite," she said dismissively. "There is nothing Italian about it." I could not allow even Judith to tell me what was or was not Italian. "You call it white sauce; we call it *balsamella*," I said, "and we have been using it forever. Without *balsamella*, there wouldn't be any *lasagne alla bolognese*, and there is nothing un-Italian about lasagne. Moreover, I have never had cauliflower in this country that tastes in the least like mine. Make it and see." Judith claimed that she often tested recipes with her authors in their kitchens. She never came into mine. Nor did she ever attend any of my courses.

We had puzzling, inconclusive discussions about my bread recipes. I am admittedly not a baker. When I entered the kitchen, I left chemistry behind in the laboratory. In addition, Judith made it clear that bread was a subject she knew a great deal about. She had an issue with a recipe for *mantovane*, a roll popular in northern Italy, but to this day, I don't know what her problem was. With all her

Judith Jones and Wolfgang Puck present me with the Who's Who in Cooking award

bread expertise, she never made a single specific suggestion. I made the rolls several times and they looked and tasted the way they were supposed to. She made them and they neither looked nor tasted good. James Beard was celebrated for his work on bread, and on an evening that we were to have dinner together at the Four Seasons restaurant, I made a few of my rolls for him to try, following my own recipe. When I put them on the table, the Italian maître d', Oreste, recognized them immediately. *"Ah, le mantovane!"* he exclaimed. For reasons too deep perhaps for me to plumb, this episode did not sit well with Judith.

The antagonisms from *More Classic Italian Cooking* carried over to *Marcella's Italian Kitchen*, my third cookbook. I remember a telephone conversation in which Judith had been so unpleasant that when I put the phone down I thought it would become impossible for me to go on with the book. Yet it became, like a child born in a time of crisis, the cookbook closest to my heart. I use it all the time. There was no fondness for it on Knopf's part, however. The first printing was so niggardly that stores were instantly out of it. The small printing adversely affected the publisher's cost-to-profit ratio, and we had to take a cut in royalties. The initial demand for that book exceeded Knopf's ability to print and ship it in time, and they had to fill orders with copies borrowed from the Book-of-the-Month Club. *Marcella's Italian Kitchen* is still in print, but in a softcover edition. It never fully recovered from its stunted launch.

Two or three years after its publication, Victor and I were lunching with Bob Lescher, our excellent agent, who put on the table a sheet of paper with some figures. "Look at these sales figures for *The Classic Italian Cook Book* and *More Classic Italian Cooking*," Bob said. They had started declining, and the decline in the most recent years was steep. "Perhaps you should think about revising both books and reissuing them to boost sales."

At home, Victor and I reflected on it. The two books contained a unique treasury of tested, workable, delicious Italian recipes. Pulled together into one volume, Victor suggested, they would form an immensely useful compendium that no one doing Italian cooking would want to be without. I would revise those recipes that I thought could stand clarification; update them, capitalizing on the vastly increased availability of Italian ingredients; and where possible, reduce the amount of fat I used. We would add a broad variety of background information on ingredients and a deeper discussion of fundamental Italian techniques.

There would also be many new recipes, of which I already had a few. When Victor and I lunched alone, I often came up with a different way of doing things. If a dish turned out well, I made notes that I put aside, saying, "I'll keep this one for the next book." I am retired, and there are no cookbooks in my future, but even now when I make something different—just today for lunch we had a tasty new pasta sauce of zucchini, caramelized onions, tomato dice, and lemon juice—Victor, who is a tease, will say, "Make a note of it for the next book."

Knopf wanted to talk to us about a new book of regional Italian recipes. We made an appointment to see Judith, having resolved that we would embark on a new book only if Knopf would first bring out a combined edition of the first two books. Jane Friedman, who was then vice president of marketing at Knopf, I believe, and who is now president of HarperCollins, came to Judith's office to discuss our proposal. Neither Jane nor Judith gave our idea a warm reception. "What you are suggesting," they said, "is to take two books off the market and replace them with one. It doesn't make sense. If the combined sales for two books are low, how are the sales of one book going to be better?" Publishers always know best, of course, but authors often know better. We agreed to do a new book, but it was to be delivered only after they published the revised and augmented version of the first two books as a single volume. Our title for it was *Essentials of Classic Italian Cooking*.

It was apparent from that two-book contract that Knopf didn't believe in *Essentials*. Not only was the advance for *Essentials* so low that it was little short of an insult, but it was leveraged against the earnings of the book that was to follow it. If Judith was aware of all the new material we had put into *Essentials*, she never gave any sign of it. Without consulting us, she moved ahead with her choice of a jacket, a feeble, frumpy, vapid design whose description of the book made no reference to the new recipes and the fresh introductory material it contained. We rejected it and demanded one that, with elegance and dignity, would have something inviting to say about the contents around which it was wrapped. Another tangible example of the lack of respect that *Essentials* and its author enjoyed in their publisher's eyes are the book's crowded pages, dense with text. They were a surprise to us. The sample pages we had been shown and were asked to sign off on had fewer lines and more white space.

One of an editor's tasks is to present her new list of books and their jackets to the sales force and ignite its enthusiasm. After the presentation, the salespeople submit the size of the printing they recommend, signaling thus the number of copies that they think they can sell. I do not know how enthusiastically Judith may have introduced *Essentials* to the sales force or whether the jacket she had to show was still that insignificant first design. What I do know is that, notwithstanding my track record of nearly half a million cookbooks sold in hardcover, notwithstanding that *Essentials* was the Book-of-the-Month's Homestyle Club main selection, notwithstanding the potent push from the many pages that *Food & Wine* magazine was running on the book, the salespeople apparently didn't think they could sell very much of it. The printing decided on was so pitifully small that within the first ten days of publication there were no copies left in the bookstores. We were getting close to Christmas, so Knopf rushed out another small printing and then another. At Christmas, the stores were out of books. The ad that had been scheduled to run then had to be postponed for several months because the major chains had no copies to sell.

It is fifteen years now since it was published, and *Essentials* is still selling very well, having established itself, as we had intended, as the basic handbook for Italian cooking. The last time we looked, it was in its eighteenth printing. It is also a very strong seller in its German-language edition, and it has been published in Dutch, Czech, and Portuguese, not to mention British English. Fifteen years later, a panel of prominent publishing figures chosen by the James Beard Foundation selected it as one of the twenty books essential to any kitchen. It was the only Italian book on that list.

The incident that transformed disappointment and irritation into unappeasable rancor, and made it impossible for us to continue to publish with Judith, came later. I had a telephone call from someone at the James Beard Foundation who was on the committee that selected the books for that year's best-of awards.

"Marcella," she asked, "don't you want *Essentials* to be considered for an award this year?"

"Of course."

"Well, it hasn't been submitted yet, and there isn't much time left."

"Who does the submitting?"

"Usually it's the publisher, but the author can submit her own book if the publisher fails to do it."

I telephoned Judith. "Do you know why *Essentials* was not submitted for a James Beard Award?"

"Those awards are for new books, Marcella, and I cannot in good conscience submit it as a new book."

"Don't you think you should have told me?"

"I am sorry, but I didn't think there was any point because the book is clearly ineligible."

I rushed a copy over to the foundation with the necessary documentation. When the awards were announced, *Essentials* had been chosen as the best Italian cookbook of the year.

To discuss what steps we could take, we met the Leschers, Bob and his wife and partner, Susan, at Montrachet, a restaurant in downtown Manhattan. As we reviewed the history of my relations with Judith Jones, I was so overcome by sadness that, giving no thought to the public place in which I found myself, I no longer controlled my feelings; I wept openly and copiously. It was inconceivable that I should do another book with Knopf. Bob asked that Victor send him a letter specifying the reasons why we wanted him to extricate us from our contract.

Once again, Bob had to negotiate a release from a publisher for us. He had done it skillfully and smoothly almost twenty years earlier, when he had obtained from Harper's Magazine Press not only our release, but also the rights to the book they had already published. He now had to take that path again, but with internal conflicts that he did not have then. Judith and Evan were his very good friends and he was their agent as well. Nonetheless, putting his relationship with the Joneses at risk, he wrote a letter to Judith that enumerated the slights we had suffered and stated, with clarity and force, the reasons for which it had become necessary to end our contractual obligations. I reread that letter when I started to write this chapter, and I remembered why I had put it away for so many years. It still has the power to roil me. My ties to Knopf were loosed soon thereafter.

Leaving Venice

1993–1999

WHEN KNOPF RELEASED ME from my contract, it was the first time in more than twenty years that I didn't have an American publisher. I dallied briefly with the notion of retiring from cookbook writing, but there was still at least one more book left in me, a book of the food that had brought so much flavor into our life in Venice. Susan Lescher put out the proposal for bids, and presently I experienced how it felt to become a commodity up for auction. All that was lacking was to have been rolled out on Sotheby's or Christie's stage and exhibited like a painting or an antique desk. The bidding was brisk, and finally two competitors were left, Morrow and Harper-Collins. The editors, Maria Guarnaschelli for Morrow and Susan Friedland for HarperCollins, came separately to Venice, where we spent a few days at table and at the market becoming acquainted with each other. Eventually, HarperCollins came in with the winning bid. Up to then, it was the largest advance ever paid in America for a cookbook.

The title of the new book was *Marcella Cucina*. In English, it can be mystifying, but in Italian it means "Marcella Cooks." What else would I be doing? Susan Friedland devoted herself, beyond her blue-pencil role, to the supervision and production of an elegant and personal book. She chose a designer of great gifts and remarkable sensitivity, Joel Avirom, from New York. We had agreed that it would be my first book fully illustrated with color photographs running through the text. We examined the portfolios of many photographers and even traveled to London to meet one. After nearly twenty years, what I remember best about that trip was a tasty Chinese dinner at a place called Now and Zen. It was a friend of ours in Venice who led us to the photographer we eventually chose, Alison Harris, an American who lived in Paris.

Alison and Joel were an ideal match. They came twice to Venice, each time for two weeks, in the spring and the fall. Alison shot all the photographs in natural light, and except for those of the market, they were all taken in our apartment. Joel was the stylist who designed each shot with understanding for the feeling of the dish and with respect for its ingredients, composing it with inexhaustible wit and variety. The light of Venice became Alison's genial assistant, pouring such brilliance over Joel's compositions that each acquired the intense life of a character portrait.

Our apartment and its contents were the props. Nothing appears in the photographs of *Marcella Cucina* that was not a part of our life in Venice. My notebooks became the endpapers, my implements kitchen sculpture, our doorbell a signpost indicating the entrance to the book. The sun-struck floor of a terrace, lined with forty pounds of ice that Victor had carried from the market, displayed fish for a double-page spread. The parapet of a terrace, with Venetian rooftops in the background, became a pedestal for an arrangement of appetizers. Joel's roving eye settled on the grape-leaf-and-cluster pattern printed in rust on my apron and transformed it into a graphic device that appears throughout the book. Joel demanded to see everything we owned that could be used as a container or a prop. And everything we owned—platters, dishes, vases, carafes, flatware, baskets, curiosities of every kind—had to come out of our cupboards. For each entire two-week period, every level surface in our apartment, including part of the floor, was populated by objects awaiting Joel's selection. In other circumstances, it would have been maddening. But we were watching Joel and Alison exercise their considerable talents to make something I had produced look beautiful and true. It was going to be the cookbook that I had long hoped a publisher would do for me. Victor and I were so happy we were giddy.

When I set off on the tour that HarperCollins and their publicist, Lisa Ekus, organized to publicize *Marcella Cucina*, I was seventy-three years old, and my body was fraying from a long and restless life. I felt as though I had led a few lives too many. Too many sharp changes of course, too many packing and moving days, too many years on my feet, too many road stops, too many performances in too many venues. I nonetheless worked the full schedule that Lisa planned for me, shuttling from coast to coast four times, touching what I was told was every significant book market in the States and in Canada. Jet lag seemed never to subside entirely; there were strings of one-night and two-night stands and very few decent meals at normal hours. What encouraged and spurred me on was the enthusiasm and affection of the crowds that turned out for me at my demonstrations and book signings.

It was at a signing in Pasadena that I had the most heartening encounter of the whole tour. I am completely helpless at spelling correctly any name but an Italian one, and an assistant always handed me a slip of paper with the name I was to inscribe in the book. There was a very long line in Pasadena, and I barely had enough time to raise my head and see whom I was signing the next book for. My assistant handed me a slip of paper that had "Marcella" written on it. Outside of Italy, it is not a common name and I don't recall ever having inscribed a book with it. I assumed it was a misunderstanding. I looked up to see a young woman with an infant girl in her arms. "Excuse me," I said, "I would like to sign this book for you, but the slip I have has only my name on it. Could you please write your own name on it?" "But the book *is* for Marcella," she said. "Marcella is my little girl. Your books have done so much for my family that when she was born we gave her your name. I hope you don't mind." I was tired and I was touched so deeply that I needed to cry, but I held back the tears. I had to keep my eyes clear to sign books for the scores of people still in line behind baby Marcella.

I started the tour in San Francisco in September and, after zig-zagging across the country for two months, ended it in Orlando. My ankles had become so swollen that I had to get in a wheelchair to take the VIP tour of Epcot that I had been offered. After Orlando, we took the winter off, repairing to a condo we had bought two years earlier in Longboat Key, on the Gulf Coast of Florida, where we had decided we would eventually retire. I was happy in Venice and content to be in my native country, to speak my native language, to be with the friends of my youth, but I had begun to find it hard to do all the walking and the climbing of bridges that life in Venice requires. I no longer took the students to the market and to the welcome banquet on the first day of the course. Victor had taken my place. We know that people get old but do not expect that it could happen to us. It was happening, however, and we did not want suddenly to find ourselves at the mercy of Italy's national-ized health care. When an expatriate in Venice asks another expatri-ate, "Where do you go when you need a good doctor?" the reply is

"To the airport." That is a joke, of course, but the problem is not a joke. We had to make serious plans to live in America again.

We had always kept a place in New York, in Manhattan. The last one was a one-bedroom condominium on a very high floor, in a building across the way from Bloomingdale's. We considered buying the apartment next door to it, thinking to break through and combine the two. During the same period, our son, who had been working as a chef in Portland, Oregon, went through a career and matrimonial crisis. After a visit to Sarasota, Florida, he decided he'd had enough of Portland weather and of restaurant kitchens, and he left Portland for Sarasota. His wife, instead, decided she'd had enough of marriage. He moved to Florida alone at Christmastime, he was depressed, and we came over from Venice to buy him some presents and cheer him up. We stayed at a hotel on Longboat Key, on the Gulf of Mexico, enjoying the perfect soft, white beach every day and a ravishingly different sunset every evening. The weather that winter was perfect. At the end of January, we returned suntanned to Venice.

Victor was at the Rialto market on a February morning, buying fish for our lunch. It was sleeting and cold. He called me from a telephone booth. "Go out on the terrace for a moment and then come right back to the telephone," he said. "Did you see what kind of weather you have out there? That's the weather we are going to get if we move to New York. Why do we have to live in New York? Why can't we live in Longboat Key?" When he tells the story now, he says it is the only suggestion he made in our entire married life with which I agreed instantly. The following year, 1995, we returned to Longboat Key in December and bought an apartment overlooking that soft, white beach, facing the sunsets. We weren't quite ready to move yet, however. We had people who had been waiting very long to take a class, and we gave ourselves another two years in

Venice, until the end of 1998, to accommodate as many of them as we could.

When I felt sufficiently recovered from the book tour, we returned to Venice to prepare for the 1998 spring courses and to find an agency with which to list our apartment. While I was teaching the first of the spring courses, the producer of the *Today* show telephoned. Matt Lauer was doing a series of shows from surprise destinations abroad. He would be in Venice the following week. Would I be willing to prepare typical Venetian dishes that I could discuss with Matt? Had I been teaching then, I would have said no, but I had a free week and I accepted. NBC set up the taping on the embankment by the Ducal Palace, the draftiest place in Venice. It was cold, gray, and wet, precisely the kind of day that we were going to Longboat Key to escape.

Shooting in the rain with Matt Lauer and the *Today* show

I had prepared several platters of *cicheti*, the tapas-like specialties of the wine bars, the *bacari*, so that I could talk to Matt about
that peculiarly Venetian institution and its cuisine. I don't remember
how long the actual segment was, no more than eight minutes without a doubt, but I waited for hours outdoors that morning before
they were ready to tape. We were wearing yellow slickers, courtesy
of NBC, but I was wet and cold through to my core. I cannot say
whether it was the book tour that undermined my strength, but my
resistance crumbled. The day after the taping of the *Today* show, I
became ill. For the first time in my teaching career, I had to cancel a
course, and then another, and then another, canceling every course
remaining in my spring semester.

A banker from Milan made an offer for the apartment that we
accepted. They were the wrong couple for it, though. The first thing
his wife did was ask to come to measure the windows for drapes.
Those marvelous windows, saturated with light, filled with images
of the city, every luminous square inch of them more precious to
us than gemstones, were to be hemmed in by fabric. We requested a
closing for no sooner than the following February. We did not want
to cancel any of the fall classes, we had to dispose of a houseful
of objects and furniture for which we had no room in Florida, and
we needed time to pack the remainder. We sold seventeen pieces
of period furniture as a single lot to a Venetian antiques dealer.
We did not strike a very good bargain, but I doubt that anyone has
ever struck a good bargain selling something to a Venetian antiques
dealer.

Life is a collection of stories, and every piece we owned had one
to narrate. Those storytellers were sent away and silenced. Of the
tales they once told, only the echoes continue to reach us, but growing fainter, across ever-lengthening stretches of memory. We sold
six nineteenth-century solid walnut dining chairs, the best things

my father had ever owned, that had survived the dispersions and the pillaging of the war. There were some early-seventeenth-century chairs and a small table that Victor had astutely collected during his bachelor stay in Tuscany, the first important purchases of his life. There was a chest and a small armoire that we had bought for the apartment in Milan where we lived during Victor's brief, brilliant, and improbable career in advertising. There was a majestic Renaissance credenza that we had bought in New York at Sotheby's, in exultant anticipation of our move to Venice. There was a prie-dieu, a kneeling bench for prayer, which had been converted into a small bedroom chest with very convenient drawers for my small articles. We had bought it during one of Victor's tours of the Chianti wine country, when we attended an auction of the contents of a house where it was claimed the model for the *Mona Lisa* once lived. She might even have said her devotions kneeling on that prie-dieu. I had written *Marcella Cucina* on the dented but handsome old walnut-and-wrought-iron desk that came out of my study. The most precious of the objects was a life-size seated Madonna in wood, carved more or less at the time that Columbus was landing on Hispaniola. Victor had bought her very soon after we had moved into our Venice apartment; we had set her on a pedestal by the large dining table where we ate with students and guests, and she presided benevolently over every meal we took there. She was precious not for her value, although it was not indifferent, but for her beauty. She had the fresh, pure, sweet expression and the lovely oval face of the young farm girls that one can see when traveling in the Veneto countryside. It was as though we had always known her. She transcended the material of which she was made to become a bearer of patience and love. I am unequal to the task of describing how it felt to abandon our home to others and leave Venice, but it may be inferred from reading these pages.

At home in Venice with our Madonna

The movers had come and gone; our apartment was empty except for our suitcases and a folding chair. We had booked seats on the afternoon express to Milan, we had reservations at a hotel, and an appointment the following morning for the closing at the office of the purchasers' *notaio*. A *notaio* in Italy is a special kind of lawyer who examines, certifies, and personally guarantees the validity of legal documents, such as those for the purchase of real estate. It is an exceptionally lucrative profession, because the *notaio* receives a handsome percentage of the value of all transactions that he handles. In every Italian municipality, there are only a few openings for a *notaio*, which are filled through rigorous oral and written examinations, preferably reinforced by influential recommendations.

We had just finished packing our bags and were preparing to go to lunch when our telephone, which had not yet been disconnected, rang. It was the purchaser of our apartment.

"There is a discrepancy in the documents establishing your title to the property," she said. "Your identity papers show that you were born on April fifteenth, 1924, but in the certificate of title, your date of birth is given as April twenty-fourth, 1924. Our *notaio* says this raises a doubt that you are the same person who purchased the apartment from Mrs. Kaley, and unless you can conclusively dissipate that doubt, he cannot execute the sale."

"But there are so many proofs that I am that person, the books I have written, the people who know me!"

"According to our *notaio*, there is no absolute proof that there aren't two persons, one born on the fifteenth, the other, the one to whom Mrs. Kaley sold her apartment, on the twenty-fourth."

"So how can I prove I am the owner of the apartment that used to be Mrs. Kaley's?"

"He would be satisfied if you can get a sworn statement from Mrs. Kaley that you are that person."

"That is impossible. No one has had any contact with Flora Kaley in years. Very likely, she is not even alive, but if she is, she could be anywhere in the world."

"Our *notaio* is an excellent man, but he can be impossibly legalistic. Let me work on it. Where can I find you?"

"I don't know, because there is nothing left in this apartment. As soon as I know where we shall be staying I'll call you."

We went to the Fiaschetteria Toscana, where they were expecting us for lunch, but we were no longer hungry. Mariuccia, the restaurant's owner, whom we brought abreast of developments, urgently called the legal people she knew, the most prominent in Venice, all of whom said the *notaio* in Milan was letting a technicality sway him, but that he was within his rights to do so. I couldn't believe the situation we were in: We had an empty apartment that was no longer clearly ours yet was not anybody else's, and no place to lie down. When all the customers had left, out of desperation, I stretched out on one of the Fiaschetteria's banquettes, where I promptly fell asleep.

Victor called Natale to inform him of our predicament and to ask if he could put us up. The Cipriani was closed for the winter, but one of the buildings in the complex was open. It was the Palazzo Vendramin, a fifteenth-century palazzo that had been transformed into luxury suites. One of them was available, and Natale sent the launch over to collect us and our luggage. We had dinner there, with enough wine for Victor and enough Jack Daniel's for me to desensitize us. We went up to our room, hoping for at least one night's oblivion. We were in bed, on the point of attaining that oblivion, when the telephone rang. It was our purchaser. She had found another *notaio* who assured her he could overlook the discrepancy in birth dates and would be available in the morning to execute the closing. To get to Milan in time, we would have to catch a very early train from Venice the following morning. Our papers had gone back into the apartment's safe. Victor slid out of bed, got dressed, and went to retrieve them, returning to our apartment for his last time.

After the closing, we went to say good-bye to my hometown, to Cesenatico. My mother had died at 101 three years earlier, and I had sold our adjoining flats. Cesenatico no longer had anything of mine, except for my oldest and dearest memories. We boarded our plane in Milan, decanting our lives once more, pouring them one final time out of Italy and into America.

In Appreciation

To put my life on paper is the kind of exposure that I didn't think I would ever agree to. Had anyone else asked me but Bill Shinker, Gotham's publisher, I would not have accepted. I came to know Bill thirteen or fourteen years ago. He was then the publisher of HarperCollins and I had just ended my seventeen-year relationship with Knopf. The teaching and traveling that my husband and I were doing left us only a little bit of private time, and I was reluctant to use it for the writing of another cookbook. Then Bill wrote me a marvelous letter. He had been using my cookbooks with pleasure and profit, he said, and assured me that if I agreed to write a book for HarperCollins, I would have full control over it. It was the first time I'd received such a letter, or a letter of any kind, from a publisher, and it moved me. Although Bill left HarperCollins before *Marcella Cucina* was published, that book is witness to the birth of a friendship. Sometime later, he enrolled in one of my courses in Venice. When I taught at the French Culinary Institute in New York, he signed up for those classes as well. He was both the first and the last person from any of the book publishers and magazines I wrote for to have had sufficient interest in my work to take my courses.

It is said sometimes that it is difficult to form a genuine, tarnish-proof friendship late in life. My feelings, and those of my husband, for Bill contradict that. I regret that I had only one life to lay down on paper for him.

I didn't know Erin Moore before I accepted Bill's invitation to write my memoirs. That she became my editor has been one of the most fortunate events of my publishing career. Her editing arm is all muscle, but her touch is gossamer. She has nudged, squeezed, sliced, and pressed, with firmness equal to her gentleness, and if the shape of this book is agreeable, considerable credit goes to her sculpting.

It's not a saint, exactly. It's Marcella Hazan.

Index

Note: Page numbers in *italics* refer to illustrations